D1264053

UNCLE JOE CANNON
ARCHFOE OF INSURGENCY

Uncle Joe Cannon
Archfoe of Insurgency

A History of the Rise and Fall of Cannonism

by

William Rea Gwinn

BOOKMAN ASSOCIATES

Printed in the United States of America

PREFACE

This study has been undertaken in an attempt to explain the basis of Uncle Joe Cannon's power as the Speaker of the House of Representatives and the repercussions of his system in the subsequent history of the Speakership. It does not purport to be a full scale biography. The Insurgent-inspired fight over the rules of the House, which brought Cannon's eight years as Speaker to a close, was by far the most notable part of his forty-six year career in Congress under eleven administrations. But the chief events of Insurgency did not occur until Cannon was a "grand old man" in his seventies. Therefore, this study, based mainly upon manuscript materials and contemporary newspaper and periodical accounts, is concerned principally with the personality and public doings of Speaker Cannon during the administrations of Theodore Roosevelt and William Howard Taft. The imperatives of historical perspective made necessary the inclusion of material on Cannon's early career, on the Speakership of Thomas B. Reed, and on the history of the Speaker's office before and after Cannon.

When this study on Cannon as the "Archfoe of Insurgency" was begun, there were already available a number of important published works on the Roosevelt and Taft years. Five were of special significance: Henry F. Pringle's able, critical biographies of Roosevelt and Taft; Mark Sullivan's readable and informative *Our Times;* Kenneth W. Hechler's exhaustive study on *Insurgency;* and George Mowry's scholarly *Theodore Roosevelt and the Progressive Movement.* There were also biographies and memoirs of varying quality on such prominent political figures as

George W. Norris, James E. Watson, Champ Clark, William Allen White, Robert M. LaFollette, Nelson W. Aldrich, John Sharp Williams, Thomas B. Reed, William Peters Hepburn, and especially there was L. W. Busbey's *Uncle Joe Cannon.*

Busbey, a onetime Chicago newspaper reporter, served Speaker Cannon faithfully for many years as a combination secretary and Boswell. His work, written in the form of an autobiography, is for the most part good humored reminiscence. Busbey's own introductory character sketch places Uncle Joe under a friendly but nevertheless revealing spotlight. However, in serving the Speaker's interest, Busbey indulged of necessity in Cannonical apologetics.

To be fair toward the Insurgents and Cannon alike, and, at the same time, to provide a study which would illuminate American political history from a conservative point of view, has been the writer's aim. To that aim may these pages contribute!

The writer is indebted to the former Illinois state historian, Jay Monaghan, and to Margaret C. Flint of the Illinois State Historical Library and to C. Percy Powell and the staff of the Manuscripts Division of the Library of Congress for aid in procuring relevant manuscript material. He is especially grateful to the Reverend Thomas T. McAvoy, C.S.C., head of the history department in the University of Notre Dame, for perceptive criticism and encouragement and to two members of the department, the Reverend William McNamara C.S.C., for inspiration in things historical, and Dr. Aaron I. Abell for his uncommonly patient direction of this study.

TABLE OF CONTENTS

CHAPTER ONE

A Pioneer American in Congress

> "I am one of the great army of mediocrity which constitutes the majority. I have made little effort to separate myself from that majority, and it has not been difficult for me to keep in sympathy with the average citizen, for I have always belonged to that class, if it is a class. All my experiences have been as an average man."
>
> Joseph G. Cannon in the foreword to L. W. Busbey's *Uncle Joe Cannon*

As long as the United States Congress meets, deliberates, and records its actions for posterity, reference will be made to the career of the gentleman from Danville, Illinois, Joseph G. Cannon, who was Speaker of the House of Representatives from 1903 to 1911. In his day, Speaker Cannon, standing forth in all of his bewhiskered and rustic elegance for his interpretation of Republican party principles, conducted the legislative business of the House in a vigorous fashion that has never been matched.

In 1951 a new work on Cannon was published, Blair Bolles' *Tyrant from Illinois, Uncle Joe Cannon's Experiment with Personal Power.* Basing his writing solidly on manuscript sources, Bolles ventured to present a novel thesis:

> The role of Cannon was to quicken the pace and broaden the scope of the process of enlarging the government's powers by forcing upon the American voters the issue of the nature of American govern-

ment as relentlessly as the southern secessionists had forced upon them the issue of the nature of the American union. . . .[1]

Cannon was the emery wheel against which Americans sharpened their understanding of their own political problems. The educative process was slow, however, because like every epic event the struggle developed gradually. Cannon's abilities gave him strength enough to stave off the reformers at the outset of the conflict. He supported his dictatorship by shrewd use of his wit, ingenuity, and temperament. He was determined, sagacious, and confident that right was with him . . .

When Cannon's heroics failed him, his idea crashed. In overturning the Speaker, the public invited America to begin the creation of the modern welfare state, which horrified him. Cannon's fall opened the way for bigger government, for Wilson and New Freedom, leading in time to the New Deal and Fair Deal of Franklin Roosevelt and Harry Truman. The fall also planted the seed for the puzzling confusion that besets us in the question whether by empowering the state to save us, we are putting the state in a position eventually to swallow us. In other words, Uncle Joe's experiment in heroism ushered the United States politically and intellectually into the twentieth century.[2]

Such views are, of course, debatable.[3] Certainly Joe Cannon did not see himself as the catalytic agent of reform. He believed that the United States of America was one "hell of a success" and that he and his like-minded colleagues in the Republican party were thwarting the evil designs of those who wanted to tamper with it. Perhaps Blair Bolles gives Cannon too much credit for the sub-

---

1. Blair Bolles, *Tyrant from Illinois*, 225.
2. *Ibid.*, 39.
3. Frederick Lewis Allen, *The Big Change*, 106, asserts that "there are few things deader today, (1952) than the enthusiasms and angers which were engendered by . . . the struggle to deprive Speaker Joe Cannon of his arbitrary authority over the House of Representatives."

sequent trend toward welfare statism. Undoubtedly the reformers, by making of Cannonism a symbol and of Cannon a devil, were better able to dramatize the major issues of William Howard Taft's era. Since then, however, a host of factors has combined to alter radically the political climate of America toward more and more centralization. Among these may be listed: the continuing, accelerated growth of industrialism; a great depression at a time when there were no longer western frontiers awaiting conquest; world wars calling for unprecedented national effort; and, a decline of faith in the principles of federalism, fostered by intellectuals and politicians, and accepted by people yearning for security. Also, partisans of the New and Fair Deals can argue that Cannon's little reign as a "Czar" in Congress was doomed to failure from the very beginning.

It can fairly be stated that Cannon and the ism named for him (which implied all things undemocratic and tyrannical) have had a continuing and direct influence since 1910 upon the House of Representatives, its Speaker, and its rules of procedure. This study stresses that aspect of Cannon's career. The words of George Brinton McClellan, a Democratic Congressman from New York shortly after the turn of the century, may well serve as a theme. In 1911, McClellan wrote concerning the House of Representatives: "The majority always has had its will and always will have its will. No man nor set of men, no Speaker nor Committee on Rules has ever succeeded in thwarting it." On Cannon, he added: ". . . a gallant fearless old fighter . . . He will leave behind him a record of an honest and brave man who, believing in party government and charged with great power, used that power to work his party's will, who strove unceasingly with resource and ability and courage to do what he deemed to be his duty."[4]

---

4. George Brinton McClellan, "Leadership in the House of Representatives," *Scribner's* XLIX (May, 1911), 597, 599.

II

By 1910, the most important year of his long career in national politics, Uncle Joe Cannon had achieved a position of eminence in the Republic. He was serving his fourth term as Speaker of the House of Representatives. Few of the House members could help liking him personally. He was a rather lovable old prairie politician who said what he meant, kept his word, stole nothing. Of homely visage with a suggestion of Lincoln about him, Cannon was also a shrewd, opinionated, earthy, and profane old man, who was fond of spitting tobacco juice and quoting scripture or census reports to make his arguments clear. Although some Congressmen were hardly delighted with his tight control over the procedings of the House, journalists and cartoonists took delight in depicting Uncle Joe in action.

The most discerning descriptions of Cannon's character were penned by George Fitch in an article with cartoons by John T. McCutcheon for the *American Magazine* and by Mark Sullivan for *Collier's*. Sullivan later rewrote his appraisal for *Our Times* and for his autobiographical work, *The Education of an American*.

Fitch presented a keen portrait:

> Joseph Gurney Cannon is a self made man of prairie design and Washington finish. He is a Quaker by birth, a farmer by nature, a lawyer by profession, and a statesmen by an average majority of 15,000 . . . a man-of-the-world and a son-of-the-sod millionaire . . . He is one of the finest agricultural products of the Illinois prairie and by thoughtful contact with the world had learned to be old-fashioned in an up-to-date manner, for which he is now universally admired by the common people for his quiet elegance, and by the financially swollen class for his boisterous simplicity . . . a plain rugged, well-groomed, hard-spoken soft-voiced, flinty hearted gentle mannered friend of the trusts and of the people. . . . Mr. Can-

> non is a man of simple tastes. ... His amusements are few. He loves to raise the tariff in the afternoon and raise the ante in the evening in a pleasant little semi-occasional game between friends. . . . Democrats in Cannon's district insist that (his entrance into Congress) was the other crime of '73.[5]

In physical appearance, Cannon's Uncle Joeness stood out for all to see. Medium-sized, with his smooth, pink face outlined by a chin beard, he seemed much younger than his seventy years. His homespun grammar and quaint manner were a match for his plain dress, his tilted felt hat, his ever present cigar. His clothes were expensive, but old-fashioned and non-descript. Apparently they had no influence over him and were thankful to be worn at all. In fact, there was no better thermometer than Cannon's clothing. At eighty degrees his coat came off; at eighty-five his suspenders drooped at half mast; at ninety his collar, necktie, and cuffs were likely to disappear.[6]

His beard was a pleasant thing to look upon; it lent a rock-ribbed dignity to his face which could not be disturbed by a hat worn at a rakish angle or a collar worn on a nearby table. His mouth was really a double barreled phenomenon. A small loop on one side held his formidable cigar; from the larger loop on the other were ejected stories, reminiscences, and general conversation. In repose his expression was stern and eminently proper. But when Cannon smiled, friendliness and the brotherhood of man stood across his whole face.[7]

Mark Sullivan's view, somewhat less picturesque and certainly less favorable, was tinged with stronger political acid. Sullivan thought that Cannon had become

> the most sophisticated man in American public life, the most familiar with every subterranean chan-

---

5. George Fitch, "A Survey and Diagnosis of Uncle Joe," *American Magazine* LXV (December, 1907), 185-190.
6. *Ibid.,* 185-88.
7. *Ibid.,* 189-90.

nel of politics, the most cunning in its devious ways, the most artful in the tricks of the craft, the most adroit in picking his secretive path through the intricate field where politics overlaps business. He told bucolic stories, . . . In one and the same story or adage he would combine the religiosity of the pulpit with the profanity and Rabelaisian raciness of the horse sheds behind the meeting house. . . . His pose of untutored countryman, of a quaint character, a primitive personality, a vulgarian, he preserved no more for any personal advantage of himself than as a deliberate contribution to his function of keeping the United States a going concern. . . . His role of commonness, of Lincolnian simplicity, was useful to keep the faith which the public must have in the occupant of high place.[8]

Lithe, poised, and confident in the Speaker's Chair, Cannon neatly exerted his will on almost four hundred men, most of whom said Sullivan, yearned to defy him. His hard-shelled resistance to innovation was partly due to his native temperament, and partly a detail in his job of keeping the country on an even keel. Half of the proposals for change were harmful and the rest useless in Uncle Joe's estimation. It could be said of him that "if he had attended the caucus on creation he would have been loyal to chaos."[9]

Even a critical observer like Mark Sullivan was willing to admit that Cannon was honest. He said that Uncle Joe's espousal of the interests of the great corporations had not a touch of corruption. Actually, he was not subservient to them but was the stronger partner. By no means did he grant all that the corporations wanted. He found them occupying a powerful position; he was willing to preserve it not because he favored corporations, but just because it was the *status quo*. Universally called a standpatter, he was

8. Mark Sullivan, *Our Times,* IV, 374-6.
9. *Ibid.,* IV, 376-7.

really a "stand-stiller." This trait, said Sullivan, served the purposes of the corporations. It was not that he gave them new privileges, for what corporations asked for that was new, he resisted as sternly as he resisted proposals for change from other sources. He could and did defy the National Association of Manufacturers as readily as the American Federation of Labor. His service to the corporations consisted in his acting as a stone wall against change, and thereby helping the corporations to protect the advantages they had gained since the Civil War and the Fourteenth Amendment.[10]

Cannon was habitually vulgar in speech. His private conversation made his public utterances in the House sound like

> The chatter of pink tea. Cannon's vulgarity was of the spirit; it was innate; it was of the essence of him. It was at once the unconscious and the deliberate expression of his personality. . . . In his speeches he did not faintly approach statesmanship; he did not pretend to; he used the locutions and adopted the postures of a stump speaker before a frontier audience. . . . No one ever heard of Cannon reading a book. His diversion was poker, in which he had a special vocabulary that became the language of Washington poker players.

Along with his natural vulgarity went unenlightenment. He could not understand, for example, the outraged cry that went up when, as a solution to provide individual offices for senators and representatives, he suggested that the offices be constructed by superimposing on the ends of the Capitol building two skyscrapers. But it was not his vulgarity and not his architectural tastes that made him an undesirable Speaker in the eyes of those who became "progressive." Their real objection to him was

10. Mark Sullivan, *The Education of an American*, 244-6.

that he used his power as Speaker in a way to preserve the privileges of corporations and to safeguard them against reform. [11]

Undeniably, Cannon's forensic ability had helped him to attain the Speakership. He was at his best in the House before a severely critical audience, buttressing his arguments with fact and humor and advancing them skillfully and logically against his Democratic foes. On the stump, because of his very human attributes, he could invariably win a hearing on controversial issues. His ability to gauge the thinking and feeling of his listeners helped him to direct his "pitch" to suit his audience. Of course, his most common tactic was to extol the GOP as the custodian of virtue, prosperity, and progress, while assigning "poverty, panic, and despair" to the Democrats. Highly informal language, plain and unadorned, was the trademark of Uncle Joe's oratorical work. And despite his penchant to rambling discourse, it can be recorded that he regularly held his audiences.[12] Perhaps his antics helped him. While speaking, he was constantly in motion. Speaker Reed once interrupted him, calling out, "Joe, are you making this speech on mileage?" Champ Clark once referred to him as "The Dancing Dervish of Danville."[13] In the more dignified position of Speaker his exercise was confined to the wielding of a left-handed gavel, a task for which he displayed native talent.

Indeed, his talent for the Speaker's office roused Republican Insurgents and muckraking journalists to oppose his methods which they termed "Cannonism." For them Uncle Joe was a national scoundrel. They held him personally responsible for the iniquitous deeds of President Theodore Roosevelt's "malefactors of great wealth." They assured each other and the nation-at-large that the Speaker

11. *Ibid.*, 246-8.

12. William Dennis Lucas, "A Study of the Speaking and Debating of Joseph Gurney Cannon." *Summaries of Doctoral Dissertations, Northwestern University*, XVI, 117-9.

13. *Congressional Record*, 64-1, 7525, 7528.

was personally responsible for the slow progress of reform. They demanded that his power be curbed by a revision of the House Rules.

For several decades prior to the fight over "Cannonism" political discontent had been brewing, the Populist movement of the 1890's being especially notable. Farmers, workers, and consumers had become more and more antagonistic to the corporations and other interests which they considered specially privileged, interests which Uncle Joe Cannon staunchly represented in Congress. The farmers complained about oppressive and discriminatory railroad rates, the workers about the judicial injunction against strikes, and consumers generally about high prices which they ascribed to an excessively high tariff. These interested groups, adopting the position of agrarian radicalism of the nineteenth century and believing that the corporations could not be checked by the states, concluded that national regulation was the only positive remedy. At the same time, in order to insure that the national government became more responsible and representative, the "progressives" as they were called, sponsored a host of reforms aimed at making constitutional government more democratic.

Although the progressive movement was of midwestern origin,[14] and some of its most faithful protagonists came from the Old Northwest and the Middle Border, Joe Cannon never became associated with the apostles of change. Republican Congresses of the era, and especially the House when Uncle Joe was Speaker, turned a deaf ear to the increasingly strident demands of the progressives, most of whom were trying to work within the Grand Old Party. As head of the party machine in the House, Cannon appointed all committees and was chairman of the Rules Committee which had in its power the direction of legislative traffic. More often than not in the heyday of his

---

14. Russel B. Nye, *Midwestern Progressive Politics, a historical study of its origins and development*, 1870-1950, 195-204.

power, Speaker Cannon insisted upon unity in the party for his proposals to "stand-pat." The increasing opposition to him, coincident with other strife, in the GOP between progressives and conservatives, cracked the party at the seams and wrecked it in 1912.

The revolt against Cannon exploded in the House chamber on St. Patrick's Day, 1910. The Republican progressives, who were dubbed Insurgents and led by Nebraska's George W. Norris, joined the Democrats to launch a long-planned attack against the Speaker and his power. Seizing a parliamentary opening which Cannon unwittingly had provided, Norris introduced a resolution to reform the House rules of procedure. After two days and a night of turbulence, the House passed Norris's resolution removing the Speaker from the Rules Committee and making its members elective by the House. Dramatically, Cannon delivered from the chair an artfully prepared apology for his conduct of the Speakership and abruptly offered to resign. This threw the opportunist coalition opposing him into consternation. Most Insurgents, who had always declared they had no personal animus against the Speaker, returned to the Regular Republican fold; they sustained him in his office but claimed a substantial victory because of the change in the rules. Those March days were the culmination of Insurgency in the House. However, the Regulars' retention of control in the GOP, the sweeping Democratic victories in the 1910 elections, and subsequent developments in the operational machinery of the House, left the reality of the Insurgent victory in doubt. The seventy-four year old Speaker, who so carefully embodied the pioneer tradition, tried hard to show that he had lost no powers for which he really cared.

III

Joseph Gurney Cannon, born in the hill country of North Carolina at New Garden, Guilford County, on May 7, 1836, was of pioneer stock. His parents, Dr. Horace

Franklin Cannon and Gulielma Hollingsworth Cannon, were Quakers, his mother proudly tracing her descent from George Fox. His father, of Scotch-Irish descent, was the founder of a Quaker school in North Carolina, Guilford College.[15] "Quaker and Huguenot, God-fearing and man-loving people, hunted from the haunts of Christian civilization, non-conformists in religion and non-combatants in war – these were my ancestors," reads the version in Busbey.[16]

During the era of Jacksonian Democracy into which young Joseph was born, the slavery question was becoming a subject for serious political differences. Peaceful-minded and sincere Quakers like the Cannons detested the South's peculiar institution, and others of their brethren were of like mind. In 1840 while the future politician was a small child, his family joined a group of their co-religionists in going west by wagon. The Quaker migration from the Carolinas in the 1830's and 1840's was not an ordinary one inspired by adventure or economic gain. In about ten years, eighteen thousand Quakers left a beautiful country where they had prospered to move to the Old Northwest where hardships were assured. Through Ohio and Indiana, the North Carolina party followed the National Road, then the great emigrant highway to the west as well as a meeting place for travelers from New England and New York and the South. They passed through Richmond, Indiana, first Quaker settlement in the west, and moved on to the Wabash country. There they stopped in the timbered lands along the river and made their frontier settlements. The Cannons located on an 80 acre tract in Parke County, Indiana, near Bloomingdale and began to chop out a farm.[17]

---

15. William MacDonald, "Joseph Gurney Cannon," *Dictionary of American Biography,* III, 476, Unless otherwise noted the basic factual details of Cannon's early life were derived from this source or from the article on Cannon in the *National Cyclopedia of American Biography,* XXII, 4-5.
16. L. W. Busbey, *Uncle Joe Cannon,* 3.
17. *Ibid.,* 8-9, 19-21, 27.

The family was tragically disrupted in 1851 by the death of Horace Cannon. A practicing "country doctor," he was drowned on the way to a patient while trying to cross a creek swollen by spring rains.[18] Although the community was willing to help the family, self-help was deemed best in keeping with Quaker and frontier inclinations to self-reliance. Fourteen year old Joe became a clerk in a country store. With the savings of five years work, $500, he began the study of law. He spent six months in the metropolis of the west at the Cincinnati Law School and one year in the office of John P. Usher of Terre Haute. Usher became a staunch Republican and was eventually rewarded with the post of Secretary of the Interior in Lincoln's cabinet. On top of a meager education gained in country schools Joe Cannon's legal training was hardly exhaustive. But apparently it was sufficient for the legal profession of the Old Northwest in the 1850's. In Cannon's case, also, more study was made impossible by lack of finances. His Cincinnati experience was valuable in broadening his horizons. He came into closer contact with the political agitation growing out of the slavery issue. He had the opportunity of hearing the lectures of the famous Unitarian preacher, Moncure D. Conway, and of seeing Edwin Booth on the stage. He wanted more than ever to become a successful lawyer.[19]

The remaining parallels to the Lincoln story are too obvious to mention. Joe Cannon, the fledgling lawyer, continued to move west, settling upon Shelbyville, Illinois, in 1858 as a likely place to hang out his shingle. Either the need there for legal advice was slight, or the slim, wiry Cannon did not appear old enough to be able to dispense it; in any event, Cannon was never overwhelmed by a parade of clients. Collecting what remained of his worldly wealth after a year of waiting . Cannon departed for the booming city of Chicago. He had money enough to

18. *Ibid.*, 63.
19. *Ibid.*, 70-75.

get only as far as Mattoon where he had to change trains. Nevertheless, he boarded the Chicago train there. As told in reminiscence: "I got on the train and the conductor asked me for ticket. I had none. So he kicked me off the train at Tuscola, Illinois, and that's where I stayed."[20]

To be exact, Cannon stayed at Tuscola until 1876 and founded his career in that city before finally settling with his business-minded brother in Danville. While living in Tuscola, Joe took his mother's advice and married, though not to a Quaker as she had hoped — nor did he procure a cow and some bees and take up farming as she had wished. The girl of his choice was Mary P. Reed, a schoolteacher of Methodist persuasion from Canfield, Ohio. Thereafter his religious attachment was to the Methodists although he remained friendly to the Quakers. The marriage took place in January, 1862, and until her death in 1899, Mary proved in every way to be a helpmate.[21]

Shortly before his marriage, Cannon had been elected state's attorney for the 27th judicial district comprising Douglas and Coles counties. This was a quick success for a resident of only two years and even more remarkable when it is considered that he defeated Ward Hill Lamon, who was enough of a political personage to be made Marshal of the District of Columbia by President Lincoln.[22] Cannon held office as a Republican from 1861 through the Civil War until 1868. Referring to this part of his career many years later, he said: "While there was much main strength and awkwardness in what I accomplished, I did occasionally win a verdict."[23] The fact that he had not served in the Union army was held against Cannon as late as 1917.

20. "Taps for Uncle Joe, Old Fashioned American," *Literary Digest* XCI (December 4, 1926), 36.

21. Two daughters, Helen and Mabel, were born to the Cannons. After her mother's death, Helen became her father's hostess and graced Washington functions in that role. Mabel married Ernest X. LeSeure who eventually managed the family's financial interests.

22. North Overton Messenger, "The Speaker Prospective of the Next House," *Independent* LV (February 5, 1903), 308.

23. *Congressional Record,* 56-1, 2334.

At that time his secretary, L. W. Busbey, presented a third hand version of why he had not served to Cannon's son-in-law. Busbey wrote that "Mr. Cannon was drafted to stay at home and protect the soldiers from the operations of the Copperheads of that day." Busbey indicated that Governor Richard Yates would have given Cannon a commission in the army, but that the governor was more interested in keeping Lincoln's state loyal and so could not spare the young state's attorney for actual military service.[24]

Cannon related many years later that while he had been state's attorney he had quietly disposed of a charge of theft which had been lodged, he believed for political purposes, against the President's stepmother, Sarah Bush Lincoln.[25] According to Jay Monaghan, a Lincoln scholar and once the state historian of Illinois, the existence of such an action must rest on Cannon's statement alone, made over fifty years after it was reputed to have taken place. Of course there would have been no written record of discussions said to have been held in the greatest secrecy.

As a practicing politician on the national scene, Cannon played his Lincoln associations for all they were worth. Eventually journalists and public alike took what he said for granted. After all, however sophisticated he really became, it seemed apparent from his artless manners, the cut of his loose fitting clothes, and his ability to make a stump speech full of Biblical references and sturdy pioneerisms, that he was truly an old-fashioned, rural American in the beloved log cabin tradition of Abe Lincoln. Cannon referred to himself as an acquaintance of Lincoln's, their relationship being based on the briefest of meetings. He always delighted in recalling that he had been in the audience during the Lincoln-Douglas debate at Charleston, Illinois, in 1858. He was also willing to give his version of Lincoln's remark to the Republican state

24. L. W. Busbey to E. X. LeSeure, April 29, 1917, Cannon Papers.
25. Busbey, *op. cit.*, 108-112.

convention in 1860 at Decatur where Honest Abe, the presidential aspirant, had said that he was too much of a candidate to go to the national convention in Chicago's Wigwam and hardly enough of a one to stay away. When Cannon became a thorough-going partisan for Republican principles, he found it advantageous to identfy his own traits with the Lincoln tradition, also.[26] L. W. Busbey, Cannon's faithful Boswell and secretary, was entirely aware of the predilection. In his restrained way Busbey says: "Mr. Cannon never considered himself a Lincoln; but I think it is not at all improbable that he may have thought to himself, as men will in the privacy of their own communing, that, given the opportunity he might leave this impress upon the country."[27]

In a limited sense Cannon certainly was justified in publicizing his identification with the great American hero.[28] Their many homely similarities were easily recognizable, and it was not Uncle Joe's fault that no one was interested in cataloguing their differences point by point. It is amusing, nevertheless, to see to what lengths some enterprising journalists went in order to establish the identification. Two examples will suffice. In an otherwise sensible article, A. R. Kanaga wrote in the *New York Times*: "In 1859 Joe Cannon was looked on in Illinois as a far bigger man intellectually than Abraham Lincoln. I will not discuss this question of intellect, but one thing is worthy of mention and that is this. Lincoln's greatest prototype is Cannon."[29] Henry L. Stoddard made the identification in still another way. Describing Cannon when an old man – the last of the old guard – in attendance at the 1920 GOP convention, he hinted that Uncle Joe was the only one present who had supported

26. February 12, 1910 Speach at Pittsburgh, Cannon Papers.
27. Busbey, *op. cit.*, xxiv.
28. J. Adam Bede, "Speaker and Leader," *Leslie's Monthly Magazine* (1904), 248, Cannon Papers.
29. A. R. Kanaga in the *New York Times*, September 16, 1906.

Lincoln in the 1860 convention.[30] This is another error, for in C. A. Church's history of the party in Illinois there is a list of the Illinois delegates who attended. Cannon's name is among the missing. He did speak for Lincoln during the campaign of 1860.[31] To Cannon's credit was his refusal in later years to lend his prestige to the Lincoln memorial of doubtful authenticity that was constructed at Hodgenville, Kentucky, under the sponsorship of *Collier's*.[32] He refrained from using his famed "autocratic power" in behalf of a federal appropriation *Collier's* wanted for its memorial. He gave his support to the plan to build the Lincoln memorial in Washington, D.C.,[33] although he protested against putting the building where it now stands, on the grounds that it would surely collapse of loneliness and ague-fever.

Joe Cannon kept his zeal for politics after the Civil War had ended. The wide circle of acquaintances he had made as state's attorney, his brother William's nerve, and their joint savings of $10,000 were considered sufficient assets with which to open a bank. When Joe was elected to Congress in 1872, after a losing effort in 1870, William opened the Vermilion County Bank (later the Second National Bank) in Danville. The bank prospered under William Cannon's tutelage — Joe paid little attention to his interest in it except during such periods as his "vacation" from Congress in 1890 — and eventually the Cannons acquired the majority stock of the Danville Gas Company, the Danville Electric Light Company, the Danville Street Railway, besides owning considerable farm land.[34] Of course, Congressman Joe's prestige and sociable nature helped to attract business for their interests, but their continued prosperity was due to a combination of shrewd-

30. Henry L. Stoddard, *It Costs to be President*, 72.
31. Charles A. Church, *History of the Republican Party in Illinois*, 1854-1912, 75, 80.
32. Dixon Wecter, *The Hero in America*, 222.
33. Cannon to Isaac N. Phillips, March 14, 1910, Cannon Papers.
34. A. R. Kanaga in the *New York Times*, September 16, 1906.

ness, honest dealing, and above all, to William's thrift and business sagacity.[35] At the time of his death Joe Cannon's estate had an estimated value of $500,000.[36] At no time as Congressman had his salary exceeded $5000 a year.

Joining his brother in Danville in 1876, Joe Cannon and family established residence at 418 North Vermilion Street. Their house was "a rambling brick residence, marked by a cupola, mansard roof, and other ornamental features of Victorian architecture."[37] This was Cannon's home for the rest of his life.

IV

In the Congressional election of 1872, Joe Cannon polled 11,244 votes to 10,603 for James H. Pickrell, his Democratic opponent in the 14th Illinois district. Thus began his public career in national politics which continued to 1923 save for involuntary "vacations" caused by defeats in 1890 and 1912, both of which were very poor years for Republicans generally. His first election by a rather narrow margin was an indication of the heated campaign fought in Illinois in 1872. That was the year of the Liberal Republicans who wanted to purge the party of "Grantism." Many of the Liberal leaders were respected political figures from Illinois, among them, U.S. Supreme Court Justice David Davis, Senator Lyman Trumbull, Governor John M. Palmer, and the Chicago editor, Joseph Medill. But Illinois remained "Regular," helping to re-elect Ulysses S. Grant by giving him a majority of sixty thousand and sweeping other Republican candidates into office. Cannon had been nominated in the first place by the "Regulars" because of disagreement between two former Congressmen, Jesse Moore and H. P. Brownell concerning the nomination. In later years Cannon declared: "I

---

35. Will Payne, "A Plutocrat in Homespun," *Saturday Evening Post,* (July 28, 1906), 10-12.
36. *New York Times,* January 16, 1927.
37. John Drury, *Old Illinois Houses,* 82.

have never flattered myself that my first nomination and election to the House was either the result of foreordination or good political strategy. . . . I guess I was a political accident."[38]

From four different districts and against an ever changing assortment of opponents, Democratic and otherwise, Cannon was able to win twenty-three campaigns for Congress. Sometimes the total vote of his opponents was greater than his, but usually he managed a clear-cut majority — particularly after the redistricting prior to the elections of 1894 and 1902. Many reasons can be advanced for Cannon's success at the polls. His districts were always strongly rural in character. After the Civil War, in fact, east-central Illinois was a prosperous cattle kingdom, and its inhabitants were likely to follow the Republican lead of the new agrarian aristocrats who were also leaders in the Grange reform.[39] Joe Cannon, who took pride in being called a "hayseed," ably represented their views in Congress. Then, too, the fact that the Republican party represented itself as the heir of the martyred Lincoln, the true upholder of the national faith, proved an aid to its candidates even when war feeling had subsided. The influential G.A.R. in the Danville district became grateful to the party for federal pensions and to Congressman Cannon for the appearance of a soldier's home in the vicinity in 1898. Besides, Illinois politics of the 70's and 80's was characterized by a blind adherence to party platforms. In that day of the party man, independent voting was regarded with great suspicion. In no other period of the history of the state was the professional politician so bold or his position so secure.[40]

Indeed, Cannon's allegiance to the Republican party cannot be underestimated as a factor in his success at the

38. L. W. Busbey, *op. cit.*, 117-127.

39. Paul W. Gates, "Cattle Kings in the Prairies," *Mississippi Valley Historical Review* XXXV (December, 1948), 379-412.

40. Ernest L. Bogart and Charles Manfred Thompson, *The Industrial State*, 1870-1893, 142.

polls. According to Russel B. Nye, the historian of midwestern progressivism:

> The Republicans had fought and won a war and consolidated a victory; theirs was the party of Lincoln, Grant, and Sherman, a party of loyalty, military allegiance, and a colorful past. How could a farmer, or a workman, or a veteran disown the party that had saved the nation.[41]

The Democratic party had little influence in midwestern politics because the old pre-war coalition of northern and southern farmers had been disrupted. As Nye points out, from 1865 to 1932 the Democrats elected only a scattering of governors, state legislatures, and congressmen. In the midwest, as Brand Whitlock put it with some exaggeration, Republicanism was "a fundamental and self-evident thing like life, liberty, and the pursuit of happiness, or the flag or the federal judiciary.[42] Thomas Jefferson had once written, "If I could not go to heaven but with a party, I would not go there at all."[43] Cannon never expressed sentiments even remotely similar.

But the reasons for Cannon's popularity were deeper than mere partisanship and temporary benefits for his constituents. Without a doubt he represented the majority feeling of his district with almost unerring accuracy on important public questions. Although he was a man of humble beginnings who had made good, Uncle Joe always remained a homely and incomparable friendly character. What cared the voters of his district if muckrakers from the metropolitan centers levelled charges at their representative for not being progressive enough. As he had risen to a place of authority in the House some of the

41. Russel B. Nye, *Midwestern Progressive Politics, A Historical Study of its Origins and Development,* 1870-1950, 44-45.
42. *Ibid.*
43. Thomas Jefferson to Francis Hopkinson, March 13, 1789 in Adrienne Koch and William Peden, ed., *The Life and Selected Writings of Thomas Jefferson,* 460.

luster of his position had come to be shared by his constituents. They were proud of the fame as well as benefits he had bestowed upon them.[44] They were inclined to react favorably to the charge that through Uncle Joe's power the Danville district was really running the national House of Representatives. Out of pure cussedness, which may not have seemed so pure to outsiders, they repeatedly returned the man who represented them so completely to the scene of his labors in the House.

His fame as the originator of barnyard witticisms, poker techniques, and as "the incarnation of reaction in the Republican party"[45] continue to prosper. He was called the "Iron Duke of American Politics," and it was said that had he attended the caucus on Creation he would have remained loyal to Chaos,[46] but his brand of optimistic conservatism was peculiarly American and almost invariably attractive to his electorate. His personal integrity and studied unconventionality of manner did not lose him any votes.

Cannon's record of longevity was unusual for reasons set down so eloquently by James Bryce. "So far from its being a reason for re-electing a man that he has been a member already," Bryce wrote in *The American Commonwealth,* "it is a reason for passing him by and giving somebody else a turn. . . . Ability, tact, and industry make their way in the long run in Congress, as they do everywhere else. But in Congress there is, for most men, no long run. Only very strong local influence, or some remarkable party service rendered," he continued, "will enable a member to keep his seat through two or three Congresses. Nowhere therefore does the zeal of a young politician sooner wax cold than in the House of Representatives."[47]

---

44. Hubert Bruce Fuller, *The Speakers of the House,* 255.
45. William Allen White, *Masks in a Pageant,* 155.
46. Fuller, *op. cit.,* 252.
47. James Bryce, *The American Commonwealth,* I, 196, 200.

When Cannon journeyed to Washington for the first time in 1873, General Grant had begun his second term in the White House; the painful reconstruction process was going its sordid way, and the country's business interests were in the saddle as never before. As Representative Job E. Stevenson of Ohio, a Democrat, saw it: "The House of Representatives was like an auction room where more valuable considerations were disposed of under the Speaker's hammer than in any other place on earth."[48] James G. Blaine of Maine, who was to become the GOP's "plumed knight" and perennial presidential hopeful, sat in the Speaker's chair as the 43rd Congress began. He was serving his third and last term in that capacity. From Speaker Blaine, Cannon received an appointment to the Committee on Post Offices and Post Roads which he had requested. It was as the champion of post office reform that he first attracted the attention of his fellow members.

The new member from Illinois, acting as the chairman of a subcommittee to revise the postal laws, brought forward and saw passed a law establishing the pound rate of paying postage on second class mail. The postage on newspapers previously had been paid by the subscriber and collected by the postmaster making the delivery. Under Cannon's legislation the postage had to be paid at a pound rate at the office of publication.[49] Of course this was a boon to his constituents and eventually publishers also found the new method more convenient.

In order to defend his measure and another which would have allowed all public documents including seeds to go through the mails free under signature of a member of Congress, Cannon was obliged to make his maiden address on the floor. In doing so he demonstrated a rough and ready style that was accentuated by the windmill ac-

48. Matthew Josephson, *The Politicos,* 118.

49. "Taps for Uncle Joe, Old Fashioned American," *Literary Digest* XCI (December 4, 1926), 40. The prepaid second class postage law passed, June 6, 1874, by a vote of 110-73, *Congressional Record,* 43-1, 4659-64.

tion of his arms. He adopted the pose of a Granger in debate, said that his intelligent and patriotic farmers, the real producers of the nation, were very anxious to receive public documents. William Walter Phelps of New Jersey interrupted to note that "The gentleman from Illinois must have oats in his pocket." Cannon was prompt with a reply:

> I understand the gentleman. Yes, I have oats in my pocket and hay-seed in my hair, (great laughter.) and the western people generally are affected in the same way; and we expect that the seed, being good, will yield a good crop, I trust tenfold; and the sooner legislation is had, not only as proposed by this bill, but in all other respects as the people desire and equity and justice shall dictate, the better it will be in the long run for all people in this country, whatever may be their calling or wherever they may reside.[50]

Reviewing the incident a few days later, Representative Phelps told a House which evidently enjoyed his wit; "That hay-seed glowed around his head like the halo of the martyrs and when he spoke of the oats in his throat, it was with such a force and such eloquence that I knew he felt them."[51]

This exchange drew publicity for the self-styled hayseed in the eastern newspapers. Cannon recalled:

> I did not court publicity and did not appreciate it in the beginning. It was thrust upon me, but I soon learned that an introduction with a laugh is better than no introduction or a mere mention as "also spoke." I became the butt of the House as the Hayseed Member from the Wild and Woolly West and held that title for many years.[52]

50. *Congressional Record,* 43-1, 1609.
51. *Ibid.,* 43-1, 1753.
52. L. W. Busbey, *Uncle Joe Cannon,* 131.

In later years his opponents could testify that he was a very wise and hard-boiled hay-seed.

For decades Cannon remained inordinately proud of the passage of his minor post office bill, and invariably during election campaigns he listed it as an example of his progressive record in the House, perhaps, because there was so little else to take personal credit for. Uncle Joe generally approved or disapproved of legislation according to his party's policy. After fifty years in Congress he left behind no specific measure bearing his name.

In reminiscing following Theodore Roosevelt's administration and the Insurgent bitterness, Uncle Joe found his good old days to be the Congresses of the 70's, 80's, and 90's. This was true for him, he said, because the men of that era were always vigorous partisans. No one thought of criticizing Speaker Blaine for being a partisan and for trying to aid his Republican party in its legislative efforts. Latter day reformers who expected a Speaker "to be nothing more than a Sunday School teacher, to pat all the good little boys on the head and turn the other cheek when the bad boys use him as a target for their bean shooters" received the acid scorn of Uncle Joe, one of the most partisan Speakers of them all. Cannon found Blaine to be a Speaker after his own heart, for that gentleman also considered the Republican majority in the House responsible for legislation and looked upon himself as the special representative of that majority. The members, of course, were strenuous partisans, too. As the majority and minority fought out their contests watchful of each other they gave the voters real, representative government that could not be had if the people were under the spell of hero worship and ready to give all their allegiance to one man.[53] It is conceivable that as far as Cannon was concerned the "one man" might have been a powerful executive of the Roosevelt or Wilson type.

53. *Ibid.,* 138-140.

From the outset in Congress, Cannon was a forthright partisan. On the surface he might appear to be the thoroughly individualistic hay-seed from Illinois, but beneath his rustic exterior Joe Cannon was dedicated to what were called Republican principles. The statement in Rutherford B. Hayes' Inaugural Address, March 5, 1877, "He serves his party best who serves his country best," was simply reversed in Uncle Joe's mind. His actions foreshadowed the stubborn convictions and the standpattism that were to become celebrated after the turn of the century. On currency matters, for example, he was an inflationist before 1896. When the party committed itself to gold at that time he too became a "gold bug." As a youngster in the House, he had voted in 1875 against the resumption of specie payment. In 1877 he voted for the Bland-Allison Act which was supposed to rectify, at least partially, the so-called Crime of '73 which had demonetized silver. He had some distinguished Republican company in the House, William Kelley of Pennsylvania and J. Warren Keifer and William McKinley of Ohio among others. President Hayes was not a member of the pro-silverite group nor was the Secretary of the Treasury, John Sherman.[54] But Senator James G. Blaine was a convinced bi-metallist. In the Senate on February 7, 1878, with copious quotations from Alexander Hamilton, Blaine argued that establishing gold as the sole unit of value must have a ruinous effect on all forms of property except those investments yielding a fixed return in money. He thought foreign demands for the payment of U.S. government bonds in gold were in "ill grace."[55] The bi-metallist forces with which Cannon sided won out, securing the passage, over a presidential veto, of the Bland-Allison Act for the limited coinage of silver. Since the act was not administered by the Treasury Department to the liking of the silver men, the arguments continued.

---

54. Marion Mills Miller, *Great Debates in American History,* XIV, 53-58.
55. *Ibid.,* 112-113.

Republican national platforms repeatedly endorsed bi-metallism. The 1884 plaform urged the calling of an international conference on bi-metallism to fix the relative values of gold and silver for all time. Four years later the GOP, still favoring bi-metallism, charged the Democrats with desiring a gold standard. When it became clear that the Bland-Allison Act had neither halted the decline of the price of silver nor cheapened the value of the circulating dollar, the silver interests were placated once again by the passage of the Sherman Silver Purchase Act of 1890. By this measure the Treasury was required to buy practically the entire annual output of American silver mines. Joe Cannon voted for it; three years later when a Democratic President, Grover Cleveland, urged and secured the repeal of the Sherman Silver Act with some Republican help, Cannon maintained his previous position.

With partisan malice Uncle Joe levelled invective at the President. Cleveland, he said, "for eight long years in office and out of office (had) followed the silver currency of the country with as great ferocity as Herod followed the infant Savior when he commanded that all children under two years of age should be put to death in order to make sure of the destruction of the Infant King."[56] Significant for Cannon's general attitude toward politics was his remark, "I will not help change existing law unless you put something better in its place." He would not vote for free silver until the ratio between gold and silver was settled by international agreement. But silver would always be one of the money metals of the world, and repeal of the Sherman Silver Act, a Republican law which had been "beneficent in its operation," would not strengthen the government's credit. Instead, the repeal would encourage a contracting currency in an ever increasing population. Besides, who could tell whether the "Democracy" that dared to tamper with the country's currency would

56. James A. Barnes, *John G. Carlisle, Financial Statesman*, 269.

not strike down the last vestige of protection of American industries and labor and place upon the books a revenue tariff. That is "the feast to which we are invited by our Democratic friends. For one I will go hungry before I dine at such a table; for that matter I would go hungry if I dined at such a table."[57]

Uncle Joe's devotion to party discipline was very well expressed during the discussion of the so-called Force Bill in 1890, the bill that proposed to erect in the South a system of federal election controls reminiscent of the Reconstruction period. The bill was hotly contested for three days in the Republican caucus. Cannon led the attack on it, but the caucus adopted the bill as a party measure by a majority on one vote. Loyally accepting the verdict, Cannon brought from the Rules Committee an order for its immediate consideration. Other Republicans rallied round and gave the Force Bill almost unanimous support when it passed the House.[58] The entire project was abandoned when the Senate failed to concur and the Republicans lost the subsequent Congressional elections.

From the record may be gleaned many other illustrations of Cannon's party constancy and resistance to change before he became Speaker in 1903. For example, in 1882, he spoke against civil service reform in much the spirit that some Jacksonian leaders had expressed in contending "to the victors, belong the spoils." He gave every appearance of being a candid believer in the spoils system. Before his colleagues in the House he ridiculed the idea of civil service examinations by telling the story of a woman who aspired to a post in the Treasury but could not answer the question of how far distant the sun was from the earth. She only knew that it was near enough to afford sufficient light for her to count notes in the Treasury Department more efficiently than anyone else. In answer to a question, he announced his complete agree-

57. Marion Mills Miller, *op. cit.*, XIV, 351-353.
58. Samuel W. McCall, *The Life of Thomas Brackett Reed*, 175-176.

ment with the proposition that deserving soldiers who had bared their breasts to the leaden storms would not have a chance in examinations against fresh, college-bred youngsters.[59] Nevertheless, Cannon joined with the Republican majority in voting for the Pendleton Civil Service Act in 1883.[60] The *Nation* commented that the Democrats would some day wish that all the opposition to the bill had not come from their party.[61] Shameless partisan that he was, Uncle Joe took the floor during Cleveland's administration to defend the civil service system against imagined presidential attacks. Admitting that he once had had grave doubts about the Liberal Republican notion of civil service reform, he was, however, glad to adopt it as a measure of wisdom when his Democratic opponents at long last had the patronage plums at their disposal.[62]

When the subject of the tariff was raised, Joe Cannon was always an unabashed protectionist. He attacked the Cleveland Administration's Mills Bill for tariff revision with his customary vigor. Roger Q. Mills of Texas introduced the original bill in response to the President's annual message of December 6, 1887. Cleveland had devoted his entire message to the subject of tariff reduction. He argued that the government was building up a surplus that might soon bring distress to the business community. Calling the existing tariff laws "vicious, inequitable, and illogical," he demanded revision at once. On July 21, 1888, the Mills Bill passed the House, 162-140, but the session closed before the Senate took action. The Republican victory in the 1888 election killed the bill for good.[63] During the discussion of the bill in the House, Cannon scornfully rejected the Democratic argument that tariff revision was the best means of combatting trusts at home. Expressing confidence that trusts could be dealt with by

---

59. *Congressional Record,* 47-1, 5804.
60. *Congressional Record,* 47-2, 867.
61. *Nation,* XXXVI (January 11, 1883), 22.
62. *Congressional Record,* 49-1, 5430-34.
63. Marion Mills Miller, *op. cit.,* XIV, 222-6. 255, 260.

other legislation, he told the House that trusts of foreign growth were beyond the power of Congress "except as we reach them by development of home industries." A protective tariff was not the only element in America's marvelous development, but protection, he declared, was the "quickening principle" underlying American progress and prosperity. "Ours is the greatest agricultural and the greatest manufacturing country on earth. Listen Democrats; over nine-tenths of all these products find a market within our own borders." The country could not afford to decide in favor of the Democrats who proposed "to reverse the engine" and pursue an opposite policy, the Sage of Danville concluded.[64]

The Sherman Anti-Trust Act of 1890 found Cannon joining his Republican colleagues to insure its passage. The act branded as illegal "every contract, combination in the form of a trust or otherwise, or conspiracy in restraint of trade or commerce among the several states, or with foreign nations." Fines up to $5000 and imprisonment not to exceed one year, or both, were designated as criminal penalties under the law. Moreover, any person injured by means that the act declared unlawful might recover triple damages in a civil suit. When the history

---

64. *Congressional Record,* 50-1, 3934-38. The tariff—to the despair of many reformers—was the most persistent issue bteween the two major parties from the time of Grover Cleveland to Woodrow Wilson. The issue was primarily a local one, but party divergence on it was also clearly evident. While Joe Cannon held positions of influence in the GOP majority, three tariff bills were enacted—McKinley (1890), Dingley (1897), and Payne-Aldrich (1909). Except in a few details, each of these measures raised the existing level of rates. Joe Cannon's speech on the Mills Bill reflected the Republican conviction that the essentials of Henry Clay's American system should be good public policy at the end of the century as they seemed to have been in the 1820's and 30's. Republicans argued, in general, that American manufacturers and farmers had a huge, lucrative market at home, that they deserved to be protected from cheap foreign competition by a high level tariff. To tamper with the protective policy was to court a possible depression which would upset "the full dinner pail." The Democrats, in general, were close to Adam Smith and true to a long party tradition by insisting for a low tariff "for revenue only." They claimed that high tariffs, more than any other factor, were responsible for the growth of large trusts and for the unjust effect of raising the cost of tariff protected goods to the ultimate consumer.

of Sherman Act enforcement is taken into consideration, Cannon's reasons for favoring the act become all the more interesting. He called it "a measure of great value, conservatively drawn." He was not at all fearful of how the courts might construe it. "If we do our duty," he said, "it is reasonable to believe that that coordinate branch of government will do its duty."[65] Incidentally, Cannon had also supported Senator Shelby M. Cullom's Interstate Commerce Act of 1887, which established a five man Interstate Commerce Commission, branded rebates, pools, and rate discriminations of railroads illegal, and empowered the Commission to investigate and rule on complaints subject to judicial review. Again, Cannon argued that the Cullom measure was wise and conservative.[66] He could hardly have been unmindful of the strength that the Granger tradition still commanded in his district.

The tariff act of October 1, 1890, named after the chairman of the House Ways and Means Committee, William McKinley of Ohio, gave son-of-the-sod Cannon a chance to display his down-to-earth good nature and show what a faithful protectionist he was.

Among other things, the act raised the duties on woolen and cotton goods, iron and steel manufactures, and on a number of agricultural products such as eggs, butter, wheat, barley, and potatoes. These latter items were included primarily for their psychological effect upon the farmers. Raw sugar, from which the Treasury had realized $55,975,610 in the year previous, was included on the free list. Republican protectionist principles were in no way violated, however. The Havemeyer interests, which had a virtual monoply on sugar refining in the United States, could now purchase their raw material at a low rate, while a tariff of one-half cent per pound still guarded their refined sugar against foreign competition. The McKinley Act even took care of the American producers of

65. *Ibid.*, 51-1, 4098-99.
66. *Ibid.*, 49-1, 4335.

raw sugar and the Treasury surplus which had annoyed Grover Cleveland by authorizing a bounty payment of two cents per pound on all raw sugar produced in the United States.

With none of this did Joe Cannon quarrel. When he arose in the House on May 20, 1890, it was to move that the existing duties upon works of art be maintained — the McKinley Bill had placed them on the free list. Cannon objected: "I believe, Mr. Chairman, that the law had better stand as it is touching these productions. They are luxuries. They go to the few, and the policy of the Republican party . . . requires that they shall be upon the dutiable list."[67] McKinley opposed an amendment Cannon offered to the effect. He said that a survey taken by artists had brought 1435 replies, 1345 of which petitioned Congress to remove the duty on works of art. McKinley read their statement into the *Record* to the effect that "proud of our country," we "ask no protection, deeming it worse than useless. All we ask is that there should be a free field and no favor, and the prize adjudged to the best."[68]

The gentleman from Massachusetts, Henry Cabot Lodge, reinforced McKinley's plea.[69] Cannon remained adamant:

> The gentleman from Ohio says the artists in this country are not demanding protection. I do not vote for this bill as a matter of protection for the artist. I vote for it in harmony with the platform of my own party, recognizing that these works of art are luxuries and therefore, in the language of the platform, the men who buy them in this country to the extent of a round million of dollars every year can afford to pay 30 per cent *ad valorem* upon them. . . . Another thing; over on the other side, in Italy, the sculptor who does the mechanical work and carves out the slab

67. *Ibid.*, 51-1, 5061.
68. *Ibid.*, 51-1, 5063.
69. *Ibid.*, 51-1, 5063-4.

> of marble works cheap. It is not done by the artist who conceives the sculpture himself; and therefore I can readily understand how parties of great wealth in this country, who are able to buy these works of art when they do come over, and how people of this country who desire to avail themselves of that kind of labor on the other side, can go to the marble quarries there and make this statuary out of cheap marble, utilizing the cheap labor for that purpose.[70]

A Kentucky Democrat, William Breckinridge, interjected appropriately that he favored putting works of art on the free list as McKinley's bill provided. He feared that the French, when they found the United States excluding their art which they loved next to glory, would retaliate and hurt American feelings in their most sensitive part by excluding the midwestern hog from French markets![71]

Cannon's amendment was defeated by a non-partisan vote of 54 ayes to 77 nays. The tariff bill passed the House by a strict partisan vote on May 21, 1890, 164 to 142. The Senate passed it on September 10, 40 to 29. President Benjamin Harrison signed the final version on October 1, 1890, just in time to make the tariff law the chief campaign issue in the congressional elections.[72] The *New York Sun* of October 17, 1890, correctly predicted that the McKinley tariff might "prove a more effectual argument against the Republicans than all the statistics and eloquence of the tariff spouters." Noting that the cost of living undoubtedly had advanced, the Sun surmised that "a small pinch of the pocketbook makes a great howl."[73]

Joe Cannon was one Republican Congressman who found that out. He went down to defeat, his long career in Congress being interrupted for the first time. Joseph Medill's *Chicago Tribune* was sure it knew why; he had

70. *Ibid.*, 51-1, 5064.
71. *Ibid.*, 51-1, 5064.
72. Miller, *op. cit.*, XII, 285.
73. Candace Stone, *Dana and the Sun*, 297.

voted for an unnecessary increase of duties in the McKinley tariff and against the reciprocity measures of James G. Blaine. "He is a valuable man and will be reelected if he follows THE TRIBUNE advice instead of that of the East." The paper went on to say that the only way Cannon and other Republicans could retrieve their defeat would be to repeal the McKinley Bill, particularly the duties on woolens, linens, glass, and tinplate.[74] Cannon felt his defeat keenly. While dining in Chicago after the election with two other losers, William McKinley and Benjamin Butterworth, he could not conceal his disappointment when his companions claimed that they did not regret the result. "Oh, hell! boys," he blurted out, "tell that to the marines. There's no use for us to lie to one another! It hurts and it hurts damned bad!" [75] No wonder, then, that he did not enjoy having his Republicanism challenged by the *Chicago Tribune.* In a published interview he attributed his defeat to the *Tribune.* What the party needed, he declared, was a cheap Republican paper that would reach the masses of the people. "The *Tribune,*" he declared, "does us more harm in four years than it does good."[76]

Of comparatively minor importance in Uncle Joe's downfall was his so-called "foul-mouthed speech" which the *New York Sun* widely publicized. During his canvass for re-election in the 15th district of Illinois, the *Sun* printed a picture showing only the lower part of Cannon's face. A scathing caption went with the picture:

> Let the picture of the dirty mouth of Joseph G. Cannon be reproduced in the columns of the local press. Then every constituent whom Cannon's mouth has insulted and humiliated will have a chance to scan its foul outlines.[77]

---

74. Philip Kinley, *The Chicago Tribune: Its First Hundred Years,* III, 170.
75. Champ Clark, *My Quarter Century of American Politics,* I, 223.
76. Kinsley, *op. cit.,* III, 186.
77. Stone, *op. cit.,* 134.

Cannon made the speech on August 27, 1890, in criticism of a fellow member, William Gibbs McAdoo, a New Jersey Democrat. He used coarse wit to suggest that McAdoo's voting record on the Mills tariff bill had been inconsistent. McAdoo denied the suggestion. Declaring that he would not "indulge in blackguardism" with Cannon, he demanded an apology. Uncle Joe declared that his figures of speech could be found "everywhere in polite literature" and even refused the pleas of fellow Republicans that his remarks be stricken from the record.[78]

For Cannon politics was the politician's domain, not a proper refuge for reformers of any sort. In a government of, by, and for the people, it was the politician's job to carry out the popular will as he saw it; he needed no ideological middle men to tell him what to do. He would have agreed wholeheartedly with a statement on the subject by Thomas B. Reed, the original "Czar" in the Speaker's chair. In a letter to Sereno E. Payne in 1902 Reed defined reform as "an indefinable something is to be done, in a way nobody knows how, at a time nobody knows when, that will accomplish nobody knows what." In this sense college professors, labor leaders, prohibitionists, pure food advocates, conservationists, and occasionally even business interests were reformers Cannon believed, and he steadfastly steered clear of their ideas. Probably without knowing it, Cannon was a disciple of one noted college professor, Yale's William Graham Sumner. In setting forth his highly individualistic sociology, Sumner declared: "You need not think it necessary to have Washington exercise a political providence over the country. God has done that a good deal better by the laws of political economy."[79] Cannon would have said 'Amen' to that, although he always remained a hardened sinner on one subject, the protective tariff.

78. *Congressional Record,* 51-1, 9234-8.

79. Sumner quoted in Frederick Lewis Allen, *The Big Change: America Transforms Itself,* 1900-1950, 68.

Illustrative of his habit was Cannon's usual stand on conservation matters – though around election time he sometimes claimed to have started the whole conservation movement in Congress. Busbey's biography contains a revealing passage on Cannon's general attitude toward conservation. A few miles from Danville a valuable piece of walnut timber had been preserved for many years before finally being sold for half a million dollars to be cut and sent to market. To Cannon it appeared that the land ought to have been cleared long before for lucrative farming operations. "The man who saved that section of walnut timber," he said, "merely buried his talent and his heirs have dug it up and put it on the market."[80] Obviously Cannon was not a man who cared whether western woodmen spared their pine forests.

The Republican administration of Benjamin Harrison passed the Forest Reserve Act of 1891 which permitted the President to set aside reserves in the far west. On February 22, 1897, under this law, President Cleveland, who was going out of office in ten days, issued a proclamation creating thirteen new reserves comprising 21,000,000 acres, more than doubling the existing reserves. A conflict broke out on the 28th. Senator Clarence Clark of Wyoming offered an amendment to the Sunday Civil Appropriation Bill to nullify the Presidential proclamation and restore the new reserves to the public domain. Western Senators being favorable, the amendment was passed the day it was offered. In the House, John Lacey of Iowa, who was always a friend of conservation, introduced a substitute to placate the westerners. Lacey's measure authorized the selling of timber from the reserves, the exclusion of agricultural lands from the reserves, and their free use for mining. Joe Cannon was for the Lacey amendment though he told Gifford Pinchot quite frankly that it was not because he gave "a damn" about conserva-

80. Busbey, *op. cit.*, 26.

tion but because he wanted to save the appropriation bill. Although angered by "a senate of nits and lice," he was hopeful that the Lacey amendment would mollify the western senators and get the appropriation through intact. His hope was not fulfilled. The Lacey amendment passed the House, but a Senate-House conference committee did not include it in the final bill. Cleveland vetoed Uncle Joe's pet appropriation bill in order to keep the reserves safe from Senator Clark's amendment.[81]

The Lacey Bill of 1902 proposed to transfer complete control of the reserves to the Department of Agriculture. Although a Bureau of Forestry had been set up in the Department of Agriculture, all of the forest reserves were in charge of the General Land Office in the Department of Interior, while the Geological Survey was responsible for the mapping and description of the timber. "So the national forests had no foresters, and the Government foresters no forests."[82] In his first message to Congress in December, 1901, President Theodore Roosevelt attacked this division of power, stating that "the present diffusion is bad from every standpoint. It prevents that effective co-operation between the Government and the men who utilize the resources of the reserves, without which the interests of both must suffer." He recommended that the scientific bureaus generally should be put under the Department of Agriculture.[83] That was what the Lacey Bill, approved by chief forester Pinchot, proposed to do.

Some western men, notably Republicans Frank Mondell of Wyoming and Wesley Jones of Washington and Democrats John C. Bell and John Shafroth of Colorado, were bitterly opposed to the transfer.[84] But the opposition that

---

81. Gifford Pinchot, *Breaking New Ground,* 107-13. An act of June 4, 1897, contained the Lacey concessions and at the same time provided increased appropriations for the reserves. It postponed the effective date of Cleveland's proclamation to March 1, 1898—John Ise, *The United States Forest Policy,* 141.
82. Harold Jacobs Howland, *Theodore Roosevelt and His Times,* 137.
83. James D. Richardson, *Messages and Papers of the Presidents,* X, 432.
84. John Ise, *op. cit.,* 156.

counted most came from Joe Cannon, then chairman of the Appropriations Committee and heir apparent to the Speakership. Cannon and the chief forester did not admire each others' talents. Pinchot wrote in his autobiography, "From my point of view Uncle Joe was usually wrong."[85] On the matter of the transfer of the forest reserves to the Department of Agriculture Uncle Joe apparently cared little for the opinions of either the President or Pinchot. As Pinchot put it: "Cannon closed the debate with a vitriolic standpat denunciation of scientific men, foresters, reformers, and in general of those who, by the use of their heads would make progress in the world."[86] His oratory was decisive in killing the proposed reform for a few years.

The *Record* provides an indication of how effective Cannon's ridicule was. "College professors, wise men, and so on" who "could not make a faint imitation of a hoe handle" would benefit from the transfer of jurisdiction for the reserves. But so would a number of scientific pretenders "industrious to fasten upon the public teat." He did not want to transfer public timber lands from the General Land Office which had had an honorable record since 1789. It was important to know whether "some bug with an unpronounceable name is bred in the leaves of a certain tree, and what will cure it." But Cannon suggested that Chief Forester Pinchot could do that kind of scientific work just as well in the Land Office of the Interior Department. In no sense was Roosevelt's recommendation connected with Republican party policy. The issue was one of encouraging extravagance. In a closing gibe at the scientists, he joked that some day they might "develop fish that will climb trees and live on dry land." "The public service," he concluded, did not demand the transfer bill, "and the best thing to do with it is cut its head off right back of its ears and strike out the enacting

85. Gifford Pinchot, *op. cit.*, 158.
86. *Ibid.*, 200.

clause."[87] The House did just that by a majority of a single vote, 37 to 36, showing a moderate interest in the reserves to say the least. The final vote on the Lacey Bill was 73 for, 100 against, 19 present, and 159 not voting at all.[88] Party divisions in the vote were anything but clear, but Pinchot seems justified in saying "Many Republicans and other Eastern Representatives voted against the Lacey Bill not because they were against it, but because Joe Cannon was."[89]

The Newlands Reclamation Act of 1902, the principles of which had been promoted by two reformers, George Maxwell and F. H. Newell, before being adopted by President Roosevelt,[90] was another conservation measure that Joe Cannon opposed[91] but this time without success. The Newlands proposal that the federal government construct irrigation works in the arid states enjoyed too much support from both parties and the various sections of the country to be defeated by even so influential a Congressman as Cannon.

Roosevelt sent an earnest plea to Cannon not to oppose the Newlands measure. He said that he respected the Cannon attitude toward stopping expense, but from his acquaintance with the far west, the President said he believed "it would be a genuine and rankling injustice for the Republican party to kill this measure. I believe in it with all my heart from every standpoint."[92] During a debate on an omnibus appropriation bill in February, 1901, Nevada's Francis G. Newlands took the opportunity to chide Republicans and Democrats alike for doing nothing about their platform promises of 1900 on reclamation. The Democrats had favored "an intelligent system

---

87. *Congressional Record,* 57-1, 6568-9.
88. *Ibid.,* 57-1, 6573.
89. Pinchot, *op. cit.,* 201, A transfer bill finally passed on January 17, 1905, without a discernible murmur from either party, *Congressional Record,* 58-3, 964.
90. James D. Richardson, *op. cit.,* X, 434-6.
91. John F. Ganoe, "Origin of a National Reclamation Policy," *Mississippi Valley Historical Review* XVIII, (June, 1931), 34-52.
92. Theodore Roosevelt to Joseph G. Cannon, June 13, 1902, Roosevelt Papers.

of improving the arid lands of the West, storing the waters for the purposes of irrigation, and the holding of such lands for actual settlers." The Republicans had said: "In further pursuance of the constant policy of the Republican party to provide free homes on the public domain, we recommend adequate national legislation to reclaim the arid lands of the United States, preserving the control of the distribution of water for irrigation to the respective States and Territories."[93]

Cannon replied in his characteristic off-hand style. He declared that Nevada with its 40,000 people would make "a respectable county in the State of California," whereupon Newlands interjected that if Cannon's policies were followed, Nevada would remain a State of 40,000 people. Uncle Joe, thinking himself a better democrat than the gentleman from Nevada, then began a lecture on pioneering.

> I believe in local self-government, I stand ready with proper guards, to donate every acre of the arid lands to the respective states. . . . I do not believe that any other policy ought to be pursued, or can be successfully pursued, without making the population of the 13 arid and semi-arid States dependent upon the United States and without robbing them of good citizenship; because, when you give something for nothing, and upon a large scale let the few benefit by the taxation of the many for schemes of this kind, you necessarily break down the good manhood of the people who ought to depend upon their own industry and intelligence to work out their own salvation.

Under Newlands' questioning, Uncle Joe said that such was his interpretation of the Republican platform. Reiterating his firm opposition to a grant from the Federal Treasury to pay for irrigation projects, he said, in conclusion: "It would breed maladministration; it would be a

---

93. *Congressional Record,* 56-2, 2660.

great draft upon the Treasury; it would breed great scandals in the public service and destroy the manhood of the very constituents that the gentleman represents."[94] For once he was in agreement with William Peters Hepburn, the Iowa Republican, who, with his own contented rural constituents in mind, told the House that the reclamation bill was "the most insolent and impudent attempt at larceny" that he had ever seen. The western representatives, he said, were asking the federal government "to give away an empire" in order to make their own private property more valuable. Reclamation projects might well be postponed, he believed, until more land was needed.[95]

It is interesting to note, as Pinchot does, that Cannon, in spite of his pronounced antipathy for reformers and their forest reserves, was willing and able to use the reserves for his personal political advantage. According to Pinchot:

> Political appointees, many of whom had never seen a western forest, were sent thousands of miles from all over the Union to handle Western Forest Reserves. . . . Influential members of the House and Senate shared the loot. Joe Cannon of Illinois had a man named Buntain an invalid, incapable and ineffective. He was given charge of Reserves in Arizona and New Mexico. Buntain was in the last stages of consumption. Another of Uncle Joe Cannon's men was a one-lunger with one leg. When Buntain resigned another of Uncle Joe's men took his place. This man made the Forest Reserve a sort of private benevolence, recommending the appointment of many consumptives who had gone to Santa Fe for their health.[96]

Thus, considerate of his electorate, blunt but friendly, regularly stubborn was Uncle Joe Cannon. Politicking

94. *Ibid.*, 56-2, 2665-6.
95. *Ibid.*, 57-1, 6742.
96. Pinchot, *op. cit.*, 163.

was his game, in fact his life's work, and on the Republican team of the 80's and 90s' he played important positions. His faithful assumption of the robes of party regularity plus his ever homely manner endeared him to his fellows who were acting in Congress as the heirs of Abraham Lincoln. Membership in the Rules Committee and on the Appropriations Committee (where he finally became renowned as "the Cerberus of the Money-box"), and eventually, the possession of the Speakership were the means that men who knew him best used to show their trust in him. Higher honors were not theirs to bestow, and Cannon's narrow partisanship made it impossible for him to capture the nation's most exalted office. For the self-appointed average man of the people, however an active career in Congress for fifty years served as a better than average substitute.

CHAPTER TWO

Czar Reed's Henchman

"In Thomas B. Reed there was combined the greatest intellect with the greatest courage, the keenest appreciation of humor and the greatest command of sarcasm I ever knew. . . . Single-handed he carried through a revolution . . . that was accepted by his partisans and made their own by his opponents."

Joseph G. Cannon in L. W. Busbey's *Uncle Joe Cannon,* 164-5.

"I have never heard my distinguished friend from Maine take the floor upon any subject but that I did not feel sometimes regretful that I could not crystallize an idea, if I had one, as he does, roll it up with my hand into proper shape and hurl it at the head of my opponent."

Joseph G. Cannon in William A. Robinson's *Thomas B. Reed, Parliamentarian,* 262.

Before the turn of the century Joe Cannon's fame in Congress derived from two things; his association with Speaker Reed and the new "dictatorial" rules and his chairmanship of the important House Appropriations Committee. The adoption of the Cannon-designed "Reed rules" by the 51st Congress in 1890 marked the real beginning of his rise to the Speakership. Until then his eight-term career as a Congressman had been rather undistinguished. Certainly it had not brought him power and prestige, and twice the Illinois legislature had turned him down as a candidate for the U. S. Senate. The fight over the rules of the House brought him national recognition besides enhancing his standing among his colleagues. The refusal of the Springfield legislators to send him to the Senate made certain that if he remained on the national political scene it would be as a Congressman.[1]

The "Reed rules" strengthened the power of the majority in the House of Representatives. In so doing they augmented the powers of the Speaker which had already become formidable in the century following the adoption of the Constitution.

The Constitution, article I, section 2, simply says: "The House of Representatives shall choose their Speaker." In fact, during the Conventon, the founding fathers had wasted little time over the question of the Speakership and its powers.[2] Even such a thorough commentary as the *Federalist* ignored the office entirely. Indeed, when the First Congress convened in 1789, the first Speaker of the House, Frederick A. Muhlenberg of Pennsylvania, tried to be an impartial moderator and presided over the meetings in a calm, deliberate manner. The prestige of the office then lay in its honor rather than in its power.[3] But the Speakers of the colonial assemblies had not been do-nothing figureheads or non-political moderators, and it is reasonable to assume that the founding fathers, acting upon colonial experience, expected the Speaker to be a strong political leader.[4]

In the First Congress the House selected its committees by ballot, but as the system was found cumbersome, that

---

1. Blair Bolles, *Tyrant from Illinois*, 33.
2. Chang-wei Chiu, *The Speaker of the House of Representatives Since* 1896, 20-1.
3. Hubert Bruce Fuller, *The Speakers of the House*, Preface, 22-5.
4. M. P. Follett, *The Speaker of the House of Representatives*, 12-20, 25-6; also, Robert Luce, *Legislative Procedure*, 465-6.

power was soon vested in the Speaker.[5] "This was the first factor in the evolutionary development of the power of the Speaker."[6] For two decades the power lay dormant until Henry Clay became Speaker. As the first Speaker to realize the potentialities of the office, Clay did not hesitate to use his position to carry out partisan policies, first of all, the war with England in 1812. He constructed the committees to suit his purposes, was not bashful about ruling the House from the chair or addressing it from the floor, and he never neglected to vote. Clay even managed on occasion to subdue the spirited eccentric, John Randolph of Roanoke. He frequently manipulated the rules to his party's advantage.[7] Elected six times he presided four full terms and portions of two others. As the boldest of the Speakers, Clay added more power to the Speakership than anyone who followed him in the office. Yet the cries of "Czar" and "Despot" made against less autocratic Speakers in a later age were never hurled at the charming and masterful Henry Clay.[8]

Despite the forceful example provided by Clay, the power and influence of the Speaker on legislation was not completely established before the Civil War. From 1829 to 1837 during Andrew Jackson's tenure in the White House, Speakers Andrew Stevenson and James K. Polk assisted in bending the House to the Executive's will.[9] When Jacksonian Democracy faltered and fell, the persistent issue of slavery (exemplified by the gag resolutions and the fight of John Quincy Adams against them) bedeviled the House, and encouraged the selection of weak Speakers. Partly for this reason the era has been called one of "unadorned mediocrity." So keen was the feeling between North and South over slavery and associated issues, and so evenly balanced were their forces in the House,

5. *Annals of Congress,* 1-2, 1056.
6. Fuller, *op. cit.,* 25.
7. *Ibid.,* 39-42.
8. *Ibid.,* 57-8.
9. *Ibid.,* 71-2.

that it became impossible to elect any member as Speaker who was the exponent of definite views.[10] The prolonged debates and innumerable ballots necessary on several occasions for the choice of a Speaker is almost incredible. The conflicts suggest, however, that the Speakership was held in high esteem by the House membership.[11]

Some progress was made during the two decades preceeding the Civil War to strenghthen the rules for the benefit of the House management. The "hour rule" for the control of debate was first put into effect in 1841 by a Whig majority.[12] At the same time an instrument that was particularly effective in the hands of the more determined Speakers was invented – the Rules Committee. The committee was given the right to report at all times, and Speaker John White of Kentucky ruled that a simple majority vote sufficed for its reports to be adopted by the House. In 1858, the House, feeling that the experience of Speaker James Orr of South Carolina would strengthen the Rules Committee, designated him as a member of it. This appointment cemented an alliance between the Speaker and the Rules Committee and set a lasting precedent. Every Speaker from Orr to Cannon was made a member of it.[13] The Rules Committee began to be a genuine instrument for directing the business of the House in 1883 when John G. Carlisle became Speaker.[14]

After the Civil War, with the possible exception of J. Warren Keifer, the Speakers were all "men of commanding power." Every Speaker conserved and magnified the political and personal influence of the office.[15] Speaker Samuel J. Randall, a Democrat from Pennsylvania, showed his mettle when he forced the completion of the 1876 electoral count despite some attempts at filibustering by

10. *Ibid.*, 82.
11. *Ibid.*, "Turmoil and Contested Elections," 82-119.
12. George Rothwell Brown, *The Leadership of Congress*, 90.
13. Kenneth W. Hechler, *Insurgency*, 27.
14. Robert Luce, *op. cit.*, 479.
15. Fuller, *op. cit.*, 280.

fellow Democrats. Under his guidance the rules were completely revised, 144 sections being condensed to 45. No mention was made of such questionable tactics as the attachment of "riders" to appropriation bills or the "disappearing quorum," but the result was a more orderly scheme of precedure. Speaker Randall had fought for the new code from the floor, but his most substantial contribution to the Speaker's powers was made when he defined the Speaker's right of recognition.[16] He announced firmly on February 28, 1881, "There is no power in the House itself to appeal from a recognition of the Chair. The right of recognition is just as absolute in the Chair as the judgment of the Supreme Court of the United States is absolute as to the interpretation of the law."[17] Soon after, Carlisle also declared that the power of recognition should be used "in accordance with the Speaker's individual judgment."[18] It was Carlisle who began the practice whereby members were required to seek the Speaker's prior consent in order to address the House.[19]

Thus, by 1890, through the development of the Speaker's powers to appoint committees, his membership on the Rules Committee, and his right of recognition, the Speakership had risen to a prominence in national affairs challenging even the Presidency. But the closely divided party composition of the House at that time made things difficult for the party in power. It was then that Speaker Thomas B. Reed, ably assisted by Joe Cannon, became the chief architect of further refiniments in the office.[20]

---

16. Albert V. House, "The Contribution of Samuel J. Randall to the Rules of the National House of Representatives," *American Political Science Review* XXIX (October, 1933), 838-9.
17. Asher C. Hinds, *Precedents of the House of Representatives* II, 1425. A few years later Speaker Reed said there could be no appeal on a question of recognition and added, "That is very well known." *Ibid.*, II, 1427.
18. M. P. Follett, *op. cit.*, 262.
19. George Brinton McClellan, "Leadership in the House of Representatives," *Scribner's* XLIX (May, 1911), 596.
20. James Bryce, *The American Commonwealth* I, 153, was favorably impressed with the House of Representatives of this time: "This huge gray hall, filled with perpetual clamour, this multitude of keen and eager faces, this ceaseless

II

By a close margin the Republicans in 1888 gained control of the White House and Capitol Hill. Joe Cannon, William McKinley, and Reed contended for the Speakership in the party caucus. Reed won out, and the two losers accepted consolation prizes calling for service as majority members of the Rules Committee, (Cannon had been a minority member of the committee with Reed from 1883 to 1889). From that vantage point Cannon could watch the masterful and unique manner in which Speaker Reed presided over the House. Uncle Joe, however, was an active participant in his management, not merely an innocent bystander.

The new Speaker was a man of undoubted integrity on the national political scene of the 80's and 90's. He best typified the ideal of an American Speaker. Well grounded in parliamentary law but also an avowed partisan and an able debater, Reed was truly *Primus inter pares* as the presiding officer of the House.[21] But it could be said that he sat "in his chair with his feet on the neck of the Republican party."[22] As William Allen White described him:

> Reed was from Maine, a huge six-foot gelatinous walrus of a man, who brought into a dull and sordid day in our politics a keen mind, a twinkling eye, an iron will, a sense of humor so gorgeous that he scorned his own power certainly, but before that despised the weakness of his adversaries. He had a modern scholar's erudition. Wise saws and modern instances were always at Reed's command. He was idol of the House, but he was also tainted with a certain mugwumpian

coming and going of many feet, this irreverent public watching from the galleries and forcing its way to the floor, all speak to the beholder's mind of the mighty democracy . . . whose affairs are here debated. If the men are not great, the interests and the issues are vast and fateful. Here, as so often in America, one thinks rather of the future than of the present. Of what tremendous struggles may not this hall become the theater in ages yet far distant, when the parliaments of Europe have shrunk into insignificance."

21. Chang-wei Chiu, *op. cit.*, 288.
22. M. P. Follett, *op. cit.*, 117.

independence. He stood foursquare – stronger than McKinley ever stood – for the gold standard but to Reed the tariff was not sacrosanct. He had his moments of doubt about the spoils system and loathed its acolytes. Party regularity was a conventional garment with Reed, but not a high priest's robe.[23]

Democrat Champ Clark, who became Speaker in 1911, found the so-called Reed rules to his advantage in that office, and was sure that time had vindicated Reed's famous quorum count in the 51st Congress. In addition Clark observed that Reed deserved well of history for demonstrating to the country that the House could carry on its business in an orderly manner.[24]

Invariably attractive to the Maine electorate, Reed was never defeated for public office between 1868 and 1899. He was the master of the short, impromptu speech. Quick at repartee, his style was eminently suited to conditions in the House which militated against long-winded oratory. He delivered only three long set speeches in his career – against the Mills tariff of 1888 and the Wilson tariff of 1894 and for the repeal of the Sherman Silver Purchase Act in 1893.[25] With the possible exception of James G. Blaine, the Republicans of Reed's day generally approved of Reed's methods. Joe Cannon certainly did.

The uncommon gentleman from Maine who received their approbation first arrived in Congress in 1877. Although he supported federal election laws aimed at securing the Negro's right to vote in the South, Reed was never renowned as a waver of the bloody shirt. First on the Rules Committee in January, 1882, he introduced at that time amendments to the House rules to enable a majority to get prompt consideration for business regardless of its place on the calendars. But the Republi-

23. William Allen White, *Masks in a Pageant,* 217-8.
24. Champ Clark, *My Quarter Century of American Politics,* II, 257-8.
25. Kirt Earl Montgomery, "The Speaking of Thomas B. Reed," *Summaries of Doctoral Dissertations, Northwestern University,* XVI, 130-132.

cans were comparatively impotent, the Democrats indifferent, and Reed's proposal got nowhere. Party leadership, however, was his for the asking after he delivered a speech in 1888 against the Mills Bill for tariff reduction. In the opinion of his Republican colleagues, he verbally annihilated the opposition. Reed's chance to revise the Rules finally came when the Republicans made him Speaker of the 51st Congress in 1889. The GOP had only a slight majority; routine absences and silent Democrats could stifle the administration program in the House.[26] On December 16, 1889, shortly after Congress opened, Reed announced that he expected to look out for the interests of the Republican party from the chair and that the Democrats would have to take care of themselves.[27] He was as good as his word.

Throughout the 80's the ability of the majority to run the House had been diminishing. One individual could delay the House indefinitely. Two of the most effective means were the disappearing quorum and dilatory motions. To overcome the disappearing quorum some state legislatures had adopted the expedient of counting members who did not vote.[28] Such a procedure had been suggested in the Congress by John Randolph Tucker and Joseph Keifer.[29] Of course, any attempt to count a quorum was certain to start a heated debate. The campaign of 1888 had been hard fought and the Democrats were determined not to let the Republican majority enjoy its narrow victory in peace. They resolved to take the fullest advantage of the rules which gave to them the real command over legislation.[30] But the speaker's audacity stopped them cold.

---

26. William A. Robinson, "Thomas B. Reed," *Dictionary of American Biography* XV, 457.
27. James A. Barnes, *John G. Carlisle, Financial Statesman,* 168.
28. *Ibid.*, 166-7. The technique of the disappearing quorum found members remaining silent, although actually present for the purpose of blocking legislative action displeasing to them.
29. Champ Clark, *op. Cit.,* 257.
30. Busbey, *op. cit.,* 171-2.

At the beginning of the Congress, Speaker Reed requested the Committee on Elections to dispose of the question of disputed seats as soon as possible. He carefully matured his plans; confident that the Republicans would support him, he waited for the Democrats to present him with an opportunity. On the day the quorum battle opened he gave no advance notice of his course of action. "Neither Republican nor Democrat," Cannon wrote in later years, "knew that Reed was ready to stage the revolution. He sent no word either to McKinley or me. He had previously told us to be constantly in readiness for he did not know when the time for action would come, but on that eventful morning we went into the House and sat at our desks with no premonition that before the day was over history would be written."[31] The *Washington Post* of January 6, 1890, had predicted that new House rules were going to be designed for Reed to count a quorum. The newspaper added that "even Mr. Cannon" was opposed to such an innovation.[32] In fact, Reed had long planned the quorum count. If the House failed to sustain him, he had determined to resign the Speakership, retire from the House, and enter into law practice with Elihu Root.[33]

The date was January 29, 1890. Republican John Dalzell of Pennsylvania proposed to take up one of nine disputed election contests, the contest of Smith *versus* Jackson from West Virginia. Charles Crisp, Democrat from Georgia, objected and demanded a roll call. At that point Reed went into action — the vote was 161 to 2, less than a quorum, and Crisp who had demanded the roll call did not answer. It took several hours, but the Speaker finally established that practically the entire membership was present.[34] "Not once during the 2 weeks

---

31. *Ibid.*, 171-5, 175-6.
32. William A. Robinson, *op. cit.*, 203.
33. Samuel W. McCall, *The Life of Thomas Brackett Reed*, 166-7.
34. Busbey, *op cit.*, 176-8.

siege did he change his opinions or yield to the denunciatory epithets by replying in kind."[35]

By way of reply to the Democrats who had demanded a roll call and then refused to vote, Speaker Reed, with magnificent serenity, simply announced: "The Chair directs the Clerk to record the following names of members present and refusing to vote." He then proceeded to make his count.[36] One of the Democrats who was present but had not voted appealed the decision of the Chair. The appeal was tabled by the House. The next morning the battle was renewed. Again Reed counted a quorum, this time to secure approval of the journal. He refused to entertain an appeal on the ground that the House had already settled that question.[37]

From that point on the House chamber was bedlam; the silent Democrats suddenly found their voices. They exhausted their vocabularies of vituperation on the Chair. Tyrant, czar, despot, were among the milder epithets heaped upon Reed. Occasionally the protest of an individual member was heard above the din. Representative McCreary of Kentucky shouted: "I deny the right of the Speaker to count me as present." Replied the calm and confident Speaker: "The Chair simply stated the fact that the gentleman from Kentucky appears to be present; does he deny it?" Verbal protests apparently being useless, Democratic members dodged under their desks, scrambled for the doors.

> In the mad rush for the exits, members lost all sense of official dignity and some of them incurred physical injuries. Upon the order of the Chair, the doors were bolted and with each test of the quorum count the defiant minority spent their anger in madly raving about the chamber, — pictures of furious inef-

35. Kirt Earl Montgomery, *loc. cit.*, XVI, 133.
36. James A. Barnes, *op. cit.*, 168.
37. Hubert Bruce Fuller, *op. cit.*, 219-20.

ficiency. On one occasion Kilgore of Texas kicked open a door and effected his escape from the chamber.[38]

When the initial excitement had subsided, more reasonable discussions took place. Joe Cannon said that at one time he would have called Reed's procedure illegal.

> but after a careful and honest examination of the Constitution itself, and of the discussions which were had at the time it was made and at the time of its adoption, and construing it in the light of sound reason and parliamentary usage, I must confess that I find myself standing today upon the Constitution and saying that if I am present in this House of Representatives . . . I count, under the Constitution, one towards making a quorum, whether I vote or refuse to vote.[39]

Uncle Joe bluntly defended majority rights:

> I say that a majority under the Constitution is entitled to legislate and that, if a contrary practice has grown up, such practice is unrepublican, undemocratic, against sound public policy, and contrary to the Constitution.[40]

When a Democrat twitted him about his refusal to vote upon occasion in the past, Cannon was ready with an answer:

> The gentleman knows that in this popular body, the House of Representatives, members from time to time do, and perhaps always will do, under a supposed partisan necessity, that which is in their power to do, and then, having done it, the desire to be sustained

38. *Ibid.*, 220-1.
39. Barnes, *op. cit.*, 169.
40. *Congressional Record*, 51-1, 957.

> makes them claim a construction of the Constitution to justify that which nothing in sound sense or good morals can justify else.[41]

John G. Carlisle, the Kentucky Democrat who had preceded Reed in the Chair, presented a constitutional argument against the position of the entrenched majority. In Carlisle's view the makers of the Constitution expressly intended that a quorum be present to conduct business. And the record of the House was "the only conclusive evidence of the facts;" the names set down at Reed's direction were not a proper record, simply evidence of his will. As Speaker he had no authority to make the journal. If he had such a right, then one man could pass a bill or pass a measure over the veto of the President. Said Carlisle: "I am not here to deal in epithets, but it is evident to everyone that if this ruling stands it will work a complete revolution in the methods of transacting business in this House." Less than a majority of all the members could pass laws binding upon the entire country, for the Journal would no longer be the conclusive evidence of whether there was a quorum present and participating in the business of the House.[42]

In the days which followed, Reed continued to preside with calm good humor; the clerk continued to call the roll and include the voiceless in his totals; Democrats continue to make denunciatory speeches, and lost their voices only when a vote was taken. The Speaker was permanently enrolled in American political history as "Czar" Reed by the press of the country which followed the lead of the *New York Times* writer, Julius Chambers.[43]

A week after the fracas began, the House Rules Committee, in order to make the Reed procedure established

41. William A. Robinson, *op. cit.*, 212.
42. Barnes, *op. cit.*, 169-70.
43. Marion Mills Miller, *Great Debates in American History,* IX, 343.

custom, presented a new code to the House. On February 6th Joe Cannon submitted the Committee's majority report to the House. Four days later it came up for debate.[44]

The report specifically provided a new rule that "No dilatory motion shall be entertained by the Speaker." Uncle Joe explained the majority view to the House:

> Now, motions made in this House if used to forward legislation or for legitimate purposes are perfectly proper; but the moment motions proper in themselves, framed to assist the House in shaping legislation, are not used for the purpose of consideration, but by a minority of one or more to hold the majority at bay and say that legislation shall not be had, that moment they are perverted from the legitimate use for which they are made, they become dilatory, and would fall within the clause of this general rule.
>
> There is no legislative body on this earth so jealous of its privileges and power as the House of Representatives. The Speaker is a member as you and I are. We made him, and a majority of the House can unmake him at any time, because it is the privilege of the House, and not of the Speaker. So no Speaker would dare to refuse to entertain a motion until it becomes patent to all that it is a dilatory motion, and then he ought to refuse to entertain it.
>
> You have come to the point where you must lodge this power with the Speaker subject to the revision of the House or the Speaker and a majority of four-fifths of the House must abdicate power, one and all, and let a minority of one or of a handful of members run the House and the country.
>
> Gentlemen say this is 'tyrannical.' I deny it. But if it be tyrannical, then the 'tyranny' is exercised by the Speaker sustained by the majority of the House; and on the other hand the tyrannical minority that has controlled heretofore fails to control now. If I must

44. *Ibid.*

choose between the 'tyranny' of a constitutional majority, responsible to the people, or the 'tyranny' of an irresponsibility of one, I will stand by the Constitution and our form of government, and so act as to let the majority rule.[45]

The proposed code also legalized Speaker Reed's quorum counting activities, setting the quorum for the Committee of the Whole at 100. Cannon presented the official defense for his party on that matter also:

> Now, gentlemen, we have counted a quorum in this House and entered their names on the Journal when they were present, through the Speaker, and the action of the Speaker has been ratified time and time again by the House; and in placing this rule in the code we do it as a matter of convenience so that the clerk may perform that duty under the eye of the Speaker and hand the names when the vote is handed to the Speaker. If you gentlemen on that side want to go to the country on the principle contained in this rule, we are ready to go and let the people choose between. But as sure as we remain here and remain in a majority during this Congress, after due consideration and debate, a majority of the House of Representatives in the Fifty-first Congress will perform the function that the Constitution and the people made it their duty to perform.

If the country ceased to be ruled by a majority, Uncle Joe warned that it would become "a mere aristocracy."[46]

The *Nation* of February 6, 1890, maintained in an editorial that Speaker Reed was doing "enormous harm" to free institutions. The paper said that the Democrats were entitled to "every sort of opposition short of violence," and that not even a George Washington ought

45. *Ibid.*, IX, 345-6.
46. *Ibid.*, IX, 348-9.

to have the power wielded by Reed.[47] The Democrats in the House were just as zealous in attacking the Reed rules. Their oratory on the subject was long, loud, partisan, and occasionally wide of the mark.

Roger Q. Mills of Texas recalled acts of the majorities during the Reconstruction as he argued that the revised code was "a new departure in parliamentary law." Mills agreed that the majority was supreme – but only within narrow limits. "Pass the rules as you have reported them, tear down the barriers, and enthrone arbitrary power." He chided the Republicans: "You have the majority. Keep them in the House and attend to your own business, and do not put any part of it on our shoulders. You know that you can have a majority when it is absolutely necessary, why can you not have it all the time?"[48] William Holman of Indiana angrily predicted: "Permit me to say to you gentlemen who are framing this despotic code of rules that manacle the minority that the next House of Representatives will wipe out these arbitrary rules you are grafting upon an honored code approved by the experience and wisdom of a century, with the same spirit that animated our fathers when they struck the Alien and Sedition laws from the statute-books of the United States."[49]

Amos J. Cummings of New York went back to January 5, 1642, to find a precedent against quorum counting. On that day Charles I had appeared at the door of the English House of Commons with an armed force – the Commons having failed to respond to requests for the arrest of five of its members the day before – and he had angrily asked Speaker Lenthal where they were. The Speaker had resolutely replied: "May it please Your Majesty, I have neither eyes to see nor tongue to speak in this place but as the House is pleased to command

47. William A. Robinson, *op. cit.*, 232.
48. Marion Mills Miller, *op. cit.*, IX, 351-2, 356, 364.
49. *Ibid.*, IX, 372.

me, whose servant I am here." The King, then, had used his own eyes and said, "I see the birds are flown," before making his exit. Representative Cummings drew a moral for his colleagues from this incident: "From that day down to the opening session of this Congress no person occupying the Speaker's chair in either the House of Commons or the House of Representatives has ever presumed to use his eyes except as directed in advance by the House."[50]

An Iowa Republican, David B. Henderson, (Speaker from 1899 to 1903) waxed sarcastic about the election methods in the Southern states which he said enthroned minorities. He stated flatly: "I shall relax no effort that will make it impossible for the minority to throttle the expressed wishes of the majority in this country. The Constitution is my warrant, and I shall fight for the rules reported to this House."[51] His fellow Republicans apparently felt the same way, for on February 14, 1890, the Reed Rules were adopted by a strictly partisan vote of 161 to 144, 23 not voting.[52]

The argument over the rules was also waged outside the halls of Congress in the pages of the *Century* and the *North American Review.* Speaker Reed presented his case in these periodicals with his usual candor. Above all, his was a forceful plea for the kind of majority rule that Joe Cannon was to find so congenial when he was in power. The Czar wrote:

> Our government is founded on the doctrine that if 100 think one way and 101 think the other, the 101 are right. It is the old doctrine that the majority must govern. Indeed, you have no choice. If the majority do not govern, the minority will; and if the tyranny of the majority is hard, the tyranny of the

---

50. *Ibid.,* IX, 384.
51. *Ibid.,* IX, 392.
52. *Ibid.,* IX, 398. Among those voting for the Reed Rules was Robert M. La-Follette of Wisconsin.

minority is simply unendurable. The rules, then, ought to be so arranged as to facilitate the action of the majority. This proposition is so simple that it is a wonder that there should be any discussion about it, and yet recently in the House there was much said in debate about the 'rights of the minority,' and that the rules of the House, instead of being merely business regulations, a mere systematization of labor, were a charter of privileges for those whose arguments were to weak to convince the House.

This indicates confusion of thought. . . . Under the Constitution and within its scope whatever a majority does is right. Regulations and rules, then, are not made to protect those who are wrong, but to facilitate the proceedings of those whose action when it takes place becomes the law of the land. Of course such rules ought to provide for debate and for due and careful consideration. But after debate and after due and careful consideration there ought to be no hindrance to action except those checks and balances which our Constitution wisely provides.

... if he (the Speaker) did unjustifiably exercise that power reposed in him as the organ of the House, an appeal to the House would easily rectify the abuse. The danger in a free country is not that power will be exercised too freely, but that it will be exercised too sparingly; for it so happens that the noise made by a small but loud minority in the wrong is too often mistaken for the voice of the people and the voice of God.[53]

Disdainful of the Democratic arguments against his methods, Reed dubbed their attacks "simply rhetoric." Shifting to sarcasm he said: "Our fathers knew nothing of this modern system of metaphysics whereby a man could be present and absent at the same moment; could be visible to demand his yeas and nays, and invisible when they were called." He ventured a prediction:

---

53. Thomas B. Reed, "The Rules of the House of Representatives," *Century* XXXVII (March, 1889), 794-5.

> When the passions of the hour have subsided, when filibustering has been forgotten, and men have returned to the notion that public office implies public duties, the scene described but faintly in the *Congressional Record* of January 30 will be read with amazement, even by some of those who participated as actors. The very fact that a great constitutional question was met on a great occasion by mere explosions of turgid rhetoric and rank disorder will seem almost incomprehensible on any basis, and quite so on the part of men so eminent as to be chosen among thirty thousand of their fellows for high political office.[54]

Immediately, however, the effect of the Reed Rules was lost by the Republican defeat in the election of 1890. John G. Carlisle considered the result to be a vindication of the Democrat's stand against Reed's "outrages upon the right of representation." He thought the rules change was the last straw which showed that the public's patience with the Republicans had been completely exhausted.[55] Of course, other elements entered into the Republican defeat, notably the McKinley tariff.

As Cannon recalled it, the Democrats were returned with "a thumping majority." They ignored the Reed rules and adopted the old ones. But the Republicans were "such hardened sinners" that they filibustered without shame under the leadership of Thomas B. Reed. "If the Democrats really liked that sort of thing we were quite willing," he said, "to give them all they wanted." In the succeeding Congress, following Cleveland's second election to the presidency in 1892, the Democrats were still in power but with a reduced majority. "They made a wry face and swallowed the Reed Rules, and I suppose no man in our political history ever had a greater triumph," wrote Uncle Joe. "The rules which the Democrats de-

54. Thomas B. Reed, "The Limitations of the Speakership," *North American Review* CL (March, 1890), 382, 384.

55. John G. Carlisle, "The Recent Election," *North American Review* CLI (December, 1890), 642, 648.

nounced as infamous and so bitterly fought were now Democratic rules in good standing. The vindication of Reed had come at the hands of his political opponents."[56] Indeed, the Democratic humiliation was great, but Reed did not rub salt in their wounds; he congratulated the House upon a wise action. Cannon was not so magnanimous. He taunted Speaker Charles Crisp for surrendering his principles to mere expediency and for "holding goods that he obtained under false pretenses." The opinion of the *Nation* reflected the changing attitude toward the Reed Rules. Although the Godkin paper had been critical of the original quorum count, its issue of April 26, 1894, cheered the action of the Democrats and declared representative government to be safe.[57]

Theodore Roosevelt, a rising young Republican identified with solid citizenship and clean government, added his voice to those praising the re-adoption of the Reed rules by the House. Roosevelt congratulated the Democrats for finally sustaining the man they had once called a "Czar." He also made some significant remarks about the character of the Speaker's office. The tendency to turn to English precedent in this matter was, he said, "an instance of a curious colonialism of spirit" surviving in America's educated class. The American Speaker was not meant to be a mere moderator in the English sense, but a vigorous party leader responsible for legislation, who held the nation's most important office except for the office of the Presidency."[58] Certainly Roosevelt

---

56. Busbey, *op. cit.,* 183-4.
57. Quoted in William A. Robinson, *op. cit.,* 303.
58. Theodore Roosevelt, "Thomas Bracket Reed and the Fifty-First Congress," *Forum* XX (December, 1895), 413, 418. The rules episode has been presented at some length because of its implications for the Speakership and for Joe Cannon. For a most interesting debate in the *North American Review,* see the following articles: John G. Carlisle, "The Limitations of the Speakership." CL (March, 1890), 390-99; X. M. C. "Speaker Reed's Error," CLI (July, 1890), 90-111—a very critical article probably written by James G. Blaine; Thomas B. Reed, "Reforms Needed in the House," CL (May, 1890), 537-546 and "A Reply to X. M. C.," CLI (August, 1890), 228-36; Judex, "The Speaker and His Critics," CLI (August, 1890), 237-50—a Democratic defense of Reed; and, James

as President could never afford to under-estimate the position and power of the Speaker when Joe Cannon was in that office from 1903 to 1909. American colonial experiences and over a century's practice under the Constitution definitely had augmented the resources of the Speakership so that by T. R.'s time the holder of the office could insist that his desires on legislation be considered in the White House.

A unique political creature was the Speaker – responsible to no state or section of the country, with his authority free of Constitutional or statute limitations. As one writer phrased it: "The Speaker is the slave of the majority – and its absolute master." Nine times out of ten he had to yield when in disagreement with his party. For whenever a majority of the House was "sufficiently determined to pass a measure," it could do so sooner or later notwithstanding what the Speaker wanted. His powers, derived from a majority, were held only at its will. But the Speaker had a pretty tight rein over legislation. He directed general policy on appropriation bills, leaving the details to the committees; his views were given great weight on all the important public bills; pension bills were out of his domain, but other private bills were passed invariably by unanimous consent, and hence fell within his sphere of influence.[59]

To the able historian of the House of Representatives, M. P. Follett, the prestige and power of the Speaker seemed both inevitable and desirable as long as the American congressional system survived. Writing in 1896, she declared that power and responsibility were rightly united in the office of Speaker and that on the whole the Speaker's increased power had been used conservatively. The caliber of the Speakers had improved as the powers

---

Bryce, "A Word as to the Speakership," CLI (October, 1890), 385-98, favorable to the Reed rule as "common sense."

59. Ewing Cockrell, "The Place and the Man: The Speaker of the House of Representatives," *Arena* XXII (December, 1899), 653, 660-2.

of the office had grown, and she thought this an answer to Woodrow Wilson's objection, in his *Congressional Government,* that the United States possessed an insufficient number of prizes for leadership calculated to stimulate talented men to enter the public service. Miss Follet argued that "it would be absurd to retard our development by a too strict adherence to an ideal of democracy impossible for a great nation." In reality Congress was not competent to legislate wisely on the pattern of a New England town meeting.[60] Whatever one's view on the desirability of a strong Speaker, Miss Follett concluded that the trend had to be recognized – "the whole history of the House of Representatives, from an institutional point of view, has been the history of the concentration of legislative power in the hands of the Speaker of the House."[61]

James Bryce clearly recognized the trend. "In quiet times," he wrote, "the power of the President is not great. ... He has less influence on legislation, – that is to say his individual volition makes less difference to the course legislation takes, than the Speaker of the House of Representatives."[62]

C. Perry Patterson, a more recent champion of responsible government for the United States on the English model, found the period from 1869 to 1911 closest to his ideal, because the Speakers of those days were powerful and so closely identified with their party's record that they could go before the country every two years as responsible leaders. In fact Patterson rather gloomily contends that the nation may have lost its last chance to escape purely executive government by the President through his dominance of Congress and control of the bureaucracy and the courts.[63]

---

60. Follett, *op. cit.,* 308-14.
61. *Ibid.,* 330.
62. James Bryce, *The American Commonwealth* I, 65.
63. C. Perry Patterson, *Presidential Government in the United States,* 105-8.

A lofty statement of principles for the new Speakership was promulgated by "Czar" Reed:

> The Speaker of the House holds an office of dignity and honor, of vast power and influence. The extent of that power and influence cannot be described even by one who has been honored by its possession. All this dignity, honor, power, and influence were created not to adorn or glorify any individual but to uphold, support, and maintain the well-being of the people of the United States.
>
> That that office should be respected and esteemed concerns every Member of the House not only as a Member, but as a citizen of the United States.
>
> No factional or party malice ought ever to strive to diminish its standing or lessen its esteem in the eyes of the Members or of the world. No disappointments or defeats ought ever to be permitted to show themselves to the injury of that high place. Whoever, at any time, whether for purposes of censure or rebuke or any other motive, attempts to lower the prestige of that office, by just so much lowers the prestige of the House itself, whose servant and exponent the Speaker is. No attack whether open or covert, can be made upon that office without leaving to the future a legacy of disorder and of bad government.
>
> This is not because the Speaker is himself a sacred creation. It is because he is the embodiment of the House, its power and dignity.
>
> If efforts of that kind have been made in the past, if at any time in the heat of passion or in the flush of resentment over unexpected defeat or overthrow, action has been taken which has been thus inimical to the public good and to the public order, let us leave to those who so acted the honor or the shame, and in no way give their example the flattery of imitation. . . . [64]

---

64. Chang-wei Chiu, *op. cit.*, 291-2.

This was the inheritance and the credo bequeathed by history and Tom Reed to Uncle Joe Cannon.

III

Before reaching his destination as the ruler of the House of Representatives, however, Joe Cannon received some seasoning on the Appropriations Committee. As chairman of that body during four Congresses (Fifty-first, fifth, sixth, and seventh), he was known as "the Watchdog of the Treasury" by admirers and detractors alike. The more classically minded preferred the term, "Cerberus of the Money-box."[65] As such he uttered a profound truth: "You think my business is to make appropriations, but it is not. It is to prevent their being made."[66] In that capacity, however it be described, Cannon's "unconquerable Uncle-Joeness"[67] was still evident as he fumigated new schemes with cigar smoke. But his usual common friendliness was not extended to those government servants who appeared before his committee seeking more funds. Cannon knew how to say "No" and mean it.

Frederick H. Gillett, Republican Speaker in the 1920's, recalled that Cannon had really been in his element while serving as chairman of the Appropriations Committee. In committee, dauntless and resourceful, he had defended the Treasury against all comers, fearlessly, tenaciously, judiciously, with a success never equalled. Then, in the thick of the fray on the floor of the House, he had the task of getting his committee's measures passed.

> No one knew better than he how to appeal to both the judgment and the prejudices of the House. His quick and fertile mind not only grasped and developed all the intrinsic force of the argument but also took advantage of the foibles and self-interest of his audi-

65. "Speaker Cannon: A Character Sketch," *Review of Reviews* XXVIII (December, 1903), 674.
66. "Groping for a Budget," *Nation* XCVII (July 3, 1913), 4.
67. Charles Willis Thompson, *Party Leaders of the Time,* 174.

ence. He did not simply argue the merits of the proposition but he fought strenously to make his side prevail. He made speeches, not to circulate in his district or to win applause, but to win votes, and if he could not succeed the cause was hopeless.

The adversary who anticipated an easy victory just because he had the popular side had little appreciation of the persistence, the knowledge and the resourcefulness of Mr. Cannon. He was, of course, sometimes beaten, but he often won where another would not have dared to fight.[68]

Toward the end of his career Uncle Joe wrote his considered opinion of the men who had come before his Appropriations Committee to seek money:

I have found executives – members of the cabinet, bureau chiefs, and subordinate officials, including commissioners – very human in wanting what they want when they want it and without regard to the demands of other departments. They are specialists and each devotes attention to his one specialty as though it were the universe. There are many very bright and clever men among them, and they are all energetic in their own fields of endeavor, but Congress has to look at the whole government together. Their enthusiasm is commendable, but not conclusive. They are also like other people, imitative, and when one conceives the idea for a new government function the others jump in and want the same function with the result too often of half a dozen rival functions in as many different departments.[69]

During the 90's Theodore Roosevelt, while acting as a Civil Service Commissioner and later as Assistant Secretary of the Navy, encountered Cannon's stern opposition more than once. In the 51st Congress the young

68. *Congressional Record,* 64-1, 7525.
69. Joseph Gurney Cannon, "The National Budget," *Harper's* CXXXIX, (October, 1919), 624.

New Yorker feared that the entire appropriation for the Civil Service Commission was in danger of being cut off. He was so vexed that he urged those in favor of the merit system to attack Cannon publicly since he was believed to be the center of opposition.[70] As Busbey saw it, Roosevelt firmly believed in

> a permanent secretariat and a life tenure for the minor employees of the Government. To Cannon all those things were foolish. It was more in consonance with his principles to reward the man who worked than the man whose only claim was superior knowledge. Mr. Cannon believed the harvest of victory was to be garnered in the federal offices; the soft and comparatively well paid life of a government employee he thought demoralizing to a young man; life tenure would create an aristocratic and privileged class which was naturally contrary to the beliefs of a Jeffersonian political philosopher.[71]

Roosevelt, frequently careless of details in money matters, wanted more clerks and more funds for the Civil Service Commission, or more ships for the Navy which was never large enough for him. It is not strange that he became a little annoyed when his requests were not granted at once by the House Appropriations Committee. Chairman Cannon, used to listening to pleas for more money and still more money, felt that it was his duty to draw the purse strings tight. His eye was always on the government's balance sheet. As the more deliberate and experienced politician, he was naturally antagonized by the younger man's breezy and impetuous manner. Neither could picture the time when one was to be President, the other Speaker – both wielding enormous influence within their respective spheres. [72]

---

70. Henry Cabot Lodge, *Selections from the Correspondence of Theodore Roosevelt and Henry Cabot Lodge,* II, 107.
71. Busbey, *op. cit.,* xxxi-xxxii.
72. *Ibid.,* xxxii-xxxiii.

Hard to fool, on to the tricks of legislative "horse-traders" and "log-rollers," Cannon played his part without moralizing or preaching. Although claiming to be ready to do his part for the needs of an expanding nation, he customarily "smoked-out" those who had found new ways to spend government money and then refused to be budged. "The man who did not have sense enough to quit usually found it necessary to wait only about sixty seconds for the explosion of a volcanic vocabulary which surprised and overwhelmed him." For Uncle Joe always "stood like a rock against waste and extravagance, and foolish schemes."[73]

Yet this bugbear of bureau chiefs could be moved. He could be dealt with easiest by returning candor for candor, a method found successful by a Superintendent of the Coast and Geodetic Survey who used to present plain statements of his wants devoid of extreme claims. On one occasion a Commissioner of Fisheries went before Cannon's committee to explain his estimates only to have them riddled by the Chairman, as usual. The next morning a newspaper attack on the administrative methods of the Commission was published. The worried Commissioner, unused to such treatment, sought out Cannon to ask about his requested appropriation, Uncle Joe reassured him the committee based its actions on its own judgments not on newspaper attacks. Smiling, he added: "I've got to such a point that if I go through a week without being caricatured or lampooned, I really miss it. I feel as if I must suddenly have lost my grip, or done something I ought to be ashamed of."[74]

While Cannon was chairman of the Appropriations Committee, Professor Samuel P. Langley of the Smithsonian Institution asked for $10,000 to experiment with a flying machine. The "Watchdog" almost jumped out

73. "Speaker Cannon: A Character Sketch," *Review of Reviews* XXVIII (December, 1903), 674.

74. Francis E. Lenpp, "The New Speaker," *Outlook* LXXV (November 21, 1903), 685-7.

of his chair when he heard the request, but in the end, he was won over and got the appropriation through the House. When Langley's machine fell into the Potomac, Cannon was heaped with ridicule. Actually, the nose-dive of the Langley machine into the Potomac aroused more public merriment than serious interest. Typical was the *Chicago Tribune's* comment, just a week before the flight of the Wright brothers, that there was little possibility of men flying until they became angels. Since Uncle Joe's espousal of such a progressive undertaking had failed to work out, he returned quickly to his old ways.[75]

Cannon did not confine his campaign for economy to the relatively cloistered confines of the committee room. His feelings on the subject were so intense that he was accustomed to launch extemporaneous forays on the House floor against what he believed to be wanton extravagance. He had an opening when a proposition was placed before the House to have the government pay the losses of the Buffalo Pan-American Exposition of 1901. Uncle Joe was opposed to the measure and was especially exasperated by the certainty that the House would override him. Shaking his fist at Buffalo's Republican Congressman, D. S. Alexander, he voiced his grievance: "Yes, make the government a partner in your expositions. Then the next step will be to make the United States pay the losses of county fairs; and after that, I suppose, we'll become the backers of a Wild Bill West Show."[76]

But Cannon's most spectacular act on the Appropriations Committee did not further his economy crusade. It prepared the United States for involvement in the Spanish-American War of 1898.

Speaker Reed, a disappointed Presidential aspirant in

---

75. "Taps for Uncle Joe, Old Fashioned American," *Literary Digest* XCI (December 4, 1926), 38; *Chicago Tribune*, December 10, 1903.
76. Charles Willis Thompson, *Party Leaders of the Time*, 178-9.

1896, had scant respect for the McKinley administration though he had started the President on his political rise in the House of Representatives, and as leader of the House in the 55th Congress was expected to fight for McKinley's measures. Reed was bitterly opposed to the annexation of Hawaii and to American intervention in the Cuban war on the ground that both actions were contrary to traditional practice as well as impracticable. In fact he resigned from the House itself in disgust on September 4, 1899, because of his convictions.[77]

Reed's antipathy toward imperialism had been evidenced time after time. On one occasion, during a lull in the late afternoon business, the leader of the minority had tried to present a resolution recognizing Cuban belligerency. Reed ignored him. Meanwhile, Nelson Dingley of Maine was at his desk oblivious of what was going on. Without further ado, the Speaker announced: "The gentleman from Maine moves that the House do now adjourn. Do I hear second? The motion is seconded. The question is now on the motion to adjourn. All in favor will say 'aye.' Those opposed, 'no.' The 'ayes' have it. The — House — stands — adjourned." Dingley had not uttered a sound, there had not been a second, and members of the House who were on the floor had been so unconscious of the proceedings that few had voted on the motion. "Still the House stood adjourned by the unauthorized but deliberate conduct of the man who had been elected merely to give voice to its will."[78]

As an object lesson in "Czarism," Reed's action can hardly be improved upon. The McKinley administration could not be blamed if it steered clear of the Speaker in making its war preparations.

The destruction of the Maine on February 15, 1898, precipitated matters; the President realized that the coun-

---

77. William A. Robinson, "Thomas B. Reed," *Dictionary of American Biography* XV, 458.

78. Hubert Bruce Fuller, *op. cit.,* 234-5.

try was woefully unprepared for an eventual war and could not get ready without an emergency appropriation. On Sunday evening, March 6, 1898, William McKinley, who, Uncle Joe thought, kept his ear so close to the ground that it frequently got filled with grasshoppers, sent for the Appropriations chairman to ask his advice on the best way of securing extraordinary funds. Cannon suggested that the President send a special message to Congress recommending an appropriation of $50,000,000; with the help of Senate Appropriations chairman, William B. Allison, he thought the bill could be passed in a week. McKinley liked the idea of the appropriation but hesitated about the message. Consequently, Cannon agreed to take responsibility for getting the appropriation through.[79]

Uncle Joe rose in the House on March 8, 1898, to announce that his committee had agreed on a $50,000,000 emergency deficiency bill for national defense. The money to be appropriated was to last out the year and cover the time when Congress would not be in session. As funds were in the Treasury to meet the appropriation, no new taxes were necessary. The government could do no less, he said, to protect "the national honor, justice, and the right."[80] The burst of oratory which followed was unusually splendid for the House. Northern Republicans and Southern Democrats alike exulted that the bitterness of the 60's was past, that the nation united was hoping for peace but ready for anything.[81] The vote of 313 to 0, 44 abstaining, gauged their enthusiasm for the appropriation.[82]

But the enthusiasm on the floor was not equalled in the

---

79. Busbey, *op. cit.*, 186-190.
80. *Congressional Record*, 55-2, 2603.
81. *Ibid.*, 55-2, 2603-20.
82. *Ibid.*, 55-2, 2620-1. According to C. S. Olcott, *William McKinley*, II, 13, American Minister to Spain, S. L. Woodford reported from Madrid that the Spanish government was "simply stunned" by this evidence of confidence in the McKinley administration.

Speaker's Chair. Reed asked Joe why he had done it. Cannon recalled that he had replied:

> Because it was necessary. I suppose I should have consulted you but you had left the Appropriation Committee to my direction, and after considering the the whole situation I felt that this was the only way to get ready for the war that is sure to come. We can't prevent it. If I had consulted you and you did not approve I would have introduced the bill anyway without your approval, and that would have given you cause for feeling that I had not been sincere in seeking your advice.

All that Reed could say was that perhaps Cannon was right; the two men never discussed the matter again.[83]

After the war, the fact that Reed was entirely out of sympathy with the Republican party in its treatment of the former Spanish colonial possessions caused him to resign. Scornfully he denounced the acquisition of the Philippines. "The Senate is arranging to pay two dollars apiece for the little brown bellies, but in the end they will cost us many thousands each," was one of the barbed observations.[84]

Joe Cannon, on the other hand, told the world that the war and the imperial acquisitions following it had been salutary events. In a speech, "Our Newly Acquired Possessions," made at Philadelphia, he rejoiced that "in material prosperity we stand in this glorious year 1900 not only the peer but the superior of any other nation on earth." The Spanish war had been "irrepressible," and "for better or for worse, for weal or for woe" new possessions had been acquired. Despite the arguments of many "Small Americans" the acquisitions had not been a mistake. Nor did the Constitution prohibit the assumption of the burden. It provided "full power" to do "all things that are neces-

83. Busbey, *op. cit.*, 191-2.

84. Hubert Bruce Fuller, *op. cit.*, 236.

sary in the acquisition of new territory for the well being of the Republic and for the salvation of such people as come under our control."[85]

In a statement made in the House on February 27, 1900, he sounded very much like another well known patrioteer, Senator Albert J. Beveridge of Indiana. He said:

> I believe in our civilization, in our blood, and in what comes to us by heredity; in our literature, in our capacity to govern ourselves and to help better the condition of those that are necessarily brought in contact with us. I believe in the progress of the Anglo-American-German-French-Irish-Scotch combination.[86]

Such jingoistic expression gave evidence that Uncle Joe was still in tune with his party and that his ear was close to the ground. With Reed in retirement, the Sage of Danville, as an inveterate supporter of tried and true Republican principles, seemed certain at last of becoming Speaker of the House.

---

85. 1900 Speech at Philadelphia, Cannon Papers.
86. *Congressional Record,* 56-1, 2337.

CHAPTER THREE

Speaker Cannon and President Roosevelt

"A President without both houses of congress back of him doesn't amount to much more than a cat without claws in that place that burneth with fire and brimstone."

Joseph G. Cannon, quoted in the *Chicago Tribune,* November 13, 1926.

If there had ever been any doubt that Joe Cannon would eventually become Speaker, it had been dispelled long before his final selection for the office by the Republican caucus on November 7, 1903. David B. Henderson of Iowa, Reed's immediate successor as Speaker, had retired from the contest. His fellow Iowan, William Peters Hepburn, who might have been a serious contender, had declined to try for the office. He had declared to friends that Iowa should not have two Speakers in a row, that his stand on rules reform made him unacceptable to the Old Guard, and that Cannon had the votes necessary for success.[1] Indeed, Colonel Pete would have presented a strange spectacle in the Speaker's chair; he really deserved the title of being the Republican party's first insurgent. Since 1893 he had been battling ineffectually for rules revision, and against the joint dominion of the Speaker and the Rules Committee.[2]

---

1. Chang-wei Chiu, *The Speaker of the House of Representatives Since* 1896, 294-5.
2. John Ely Briggs, *William Peters Hepburn,* 309.

Cannon did not reach the most exalted station in the House by reason of the discovery of any overwhelming genius. He reached it by long experience, close study, and persistent effort. In March 1903, during the final days of the 57th Congress, he clinched the Speakership by directing a telling blast at the Senate and all of its works that roused both sides of the House to cheer him. The lame duck session was in its closing hours. But South Carolina's redoubtable Senator, "Pitchfork" Ben Tillman, took advantage of the Senate's rule for unlimited debate to hold up the Sundry Civil Appropriations Bill, the catch-all measure dear to the hearts of every member of Congress. As Tillman explained it in his usual inelegant fashion, he simply wanted "a generous appropriation for South Carolina appetites, a nice dish of pork." The House was furious, and Cannon played to its temper as he launched his remarks with his customary arm-waving.[3]

Uncle Joe called upon the House to assert itself and end what he referred to as the "legislative blackmail" of the Senate. He protested "in sorrow and humiliation" that the Senate would have to change its methods of doing business or the House backed by the people would compel it to change "else, this body, close to the people, shall become . . . a mere bender of the pregnant hinges of the knee to submit to what any one member of another body (the Senate) may demand of this body as the price of legislation."[4] That night Cannon was a made man, and the Republican bigwigs in the Senate had a rival whom they had to convert into an ally—on his own terms.[5]

Such a staunch defense of the rights of the House could hardly go unrewarded, particularly when powerful interests outside Congress were also on Cannon's side. One of those was J. P. Morgan and Company's legislative rep-

---

3. Nathaniel W. Stephenson, *Nelson W. Aldrich,* 213-215. See also Busbey, *Uncle Joe Cannon,* 338-41.
4. *Congressional Record,* 57-2, 3058-9.
5. Nathaniel W. Stephenson, *op. cit.,* 215.

resentative, George Perkins, who assured Cannon of hearty support in "broadening" his "great career of public usefulness."[6]

The Roosevelt administration, apparently as early as November, 1902, had conceded Cannon's election as Speaker; at that time William H. Moody, the Secretary of the Navy, forwarded congratulations to Cannon upon the "reasonable certainty" that he would be chosen Speaker when the newly elected 58th Congress met. Moody also forwarded the news that the Cabinet and the President himself were with Uncle Joe on the tariff and understood that nothing could be done unless there was "a very general consent in Congress."[7]

President Roosevelt was also directly solicitous of the opinions of the onetime Treasury watchdog who was the prospective Speaker. In August 1903, the Big Four of the Senate held a special session at Oyster Bay.[8] T. R. wrote at once to Cannon concerning their deliberations:

> Last night Aldrich, Spooner, Allison, and Platt came out here to discuss the proposed financial legislation. They have no definite plan, of course, as they wish to find out what your views are before even formulating their own and as they also wish to sound out certain colleagues and to find out, probably through you, what your lieutenants in the House feel about this financial matter. I earnestly hope we can get some legislation not of a radical or revolutionary sort which will provide a certain amount of elasticity, that is, will provide not merely for expansion in time of stringency, but for contraction when the stringency is over. . . . Now what are your views on the subject? We are all decided that of course we would not make up our minds in any way until we found out what your judgment was.[9]

---

6. George Perkins to Charles G. Dawes, November 20, 1902, Cannon Papers.
7. William H. Moody to Joseph G. Cannon, November 21, 1902, Cannon Papers.
8. Nathaniel W. Stephenson, *op. cit.*, 224. The Four were: Nelson W. Aldrich of Rhode Island, William B. Allison of Iowa, Orville H. Platt of Connecticut, and John C. Spooner of Wisconsin.
9. Theodore Roosevelt to Joseph G. Cannon, August 13, 1903, Roosevelt Papers,

This statement indicated a shift of power in the GOP. Had Henderson still been Speaker, the Four might have sent him a mandate instead of an invitation for advice. Uncle Joe Cannon with the House behind him was another matter. Senator Allison was sent to Chicago to meet Cannon, and they had an amicable exchange of views.[10]

The prospective Speaker, however, was not reticent about reporting his views directly to the President. He said that he saw no reason to attempt financial legislation on the eve of a presidential election. (The proposal in question was the Aldrich Bill which would have authorized the limited use of customs receipts and of securities other than the government's as a basis for the issue of currency.) "Nothing short of inflation, pure and simple," Cannon wrote, "would satisfy . . . those who are talking the most about financial legislation. . . . In my judgment, any or all legislation along the lines indicated would lead to much debate and if enacted, such legislation could not demonstrate its wisdom before the National election in 1904, and would be subject to attack according to the imagination and necessities of the enemy." Cannon did agree that the necessity of acting upon Cuban reciprocity justified the calling of an extraordinary session on November 9, but he declared, "It is good policy to have as little general legislation as possible in the approaching session, and to make the appropriations and get out of Washington before the Presidential Convention."[11] The President replied that he agreed with Cannon as to the inadvisability of an extra session for financial matters, "unless there is some great change in the situation I shall treat this opinion of yours as conclusive."[12]

---

10. Nathaniel W. Stephenson, *op. cit.*, 225-6.
11. Joseph G. Cannon to Theodore Roosevelt, August 24, 1903, Roosevelt Papers.
12. Theodore Roosevelt to Joseph G. Cannon, August 24 and 26, 1903, Roosevelt Papers. Most of the gentlemen of the Fourth Estate, finding Cannon a colorful subject for their prose, predicted that the country would consider itself fortunate in having secured such a deserving, veteran politician for the Speaker's chair.

As Uncle Joe had suggested, then, the special session opened on November 9 to deal solely with Cuban reciprocity. The Roosevelt-Cannon working relationship was off to a good start. The two men remained officially congenial until near the end of Roosevelt's tenure in office.

II

The chief hope of reformers in 1903 was the man in the White House, the energetic young gentleman from New York, Theodore Roosevelt. As the skilled cartoon-journalist John T. McCutcheon has written:

> Whoever delves through the files of the first decade of the twentieth century will come to an inevitable conclusion. The most important news of that time was Mr. Theodore Roosevelt, President, politician, statesman, sociologist, reformer, defender of the faithful, exposer of shams, protagonist, antagonist, hunter, diplomat, apostle of peace, wielder of the Big Stick, and founder — but not a charter member of the Ananias Club. A historian might be puzzled to decide whether Mr. Roosevelt was an imperialist or a socialist, a Democrat or Republican.[13]

Although he was something of a political accident, the President lost no time in ingratiating himself with the nation's voters. During his seven and one-half years in office, by alternately prodding and placating his Republi-

---

But the *New York Times*, July 7, 1903, reserved its praise, stating that Cannon as Speaker, "blinded by prejudice," could practically run the Rules Committee and in the immediate future could stop any attempts to make the country's currency system more elastic.

13. John T. McCutcheon, *Drawn from Memory*, 242.

can majorities,[14] and by capturing sizeable blocks of Democratic support for most of his major proposals, the first Roosevelt was able to turn in a creditable record by the time he left public life in Washington in 1909 for his African safari. Never the least of his worries was the crusty old Speaker of the House who rarely fretted about the possible consequences of defying the Grand Old Party's titular leader. Among other things Uncle Joe's obvious distaste for Roosevelt's espousal of conservation had been made clear during the debate on the Newlands Reclamation Act. It was usually the President who had to watch his step in dealing with the Speaker.

The English political analyst, Harold J. Laski, has pointed out quite properly that under the American system the President is never really the master of Congress; he can argue, bully, and cajole, but the solons on Capitol Hill are beyond his will. "Even if his party has a majority in both houses, he has to win the good will of his party in Congress; he cannot exact it."[15] In fact the "instinctive and inherent tendency" of Congress is "antipresidential." It may give the President spasmodic support, but never feels so really comfortable as when it affirms its own reason for existence by finding a cause for difference.[16] The traditional Republican view of the matter was drawn for Benjamin Harrison by Ohio's John Sher-

---

14. *Historical Statistics of the United States,* 1789-1945, 293. The party affiliations in Congress under both Roosevelt and Taft:

Congress		*Democrats*	*Republicans*	*Others*
57 (1901-03)	House	151	197	9
	Senate	31	55	4
58 (1903-05)	House	178	208	
	Senate	33	57	
59 (1905-07)	House	136	250	
	Senate	33	57	
60 (1907-09)	House	164	222	
	Senate	31	61	
61 (1909-11)	House	172	219	
	Senate	32	61	
62 (1911-13)	House	228	161	
	Senate	41	51	

15. Harold J. Laski, *The American Presidency, An Interpretation,* 13.
16. *Ibid.,* 123.

man. "The president," he wrote, "should have no policy distinct from that of his party, and this is better represented in Congress than in the executive."[17] Yet the President and the members of his party in Congress always had a common interest in getting something done with a view to gaining future victories at the polls.[18]

To Theodore Roosevelt was presented the monumental task of pressing for just those objectives that could be fought for and won. The reins of leadership in both houses were in the hands of conservative Republicans and they remained there through both of his terms. Of these leaders Roosevelt later wrote: "These men still from force of habit applauded what Lincoln had done in the way of radical dealing with the abuses of his day; but they did not apply the spirit in which Lincoln worked to the abuses of their own day."[19] Roosevelt's "great verbal audacity" was accompanied, however, by a relative caution in action.[20] As Henry F. Pringle puts it in his excellent biography of T. R.; "Until he led his hosts at Armageddon in 1912 and battled for the Lord, no banners proclaiming radicalism marked the onward march of Theodore Roosevelt. He stood close to the center and bared his teeth at the conservatives on the right and the liberals of the extreme left."[21] Henry Adams, never much of an admirer of Roosevelt's would have concurred. "I find him exceedingly conservative." Adams wrote to a friend in 1906, "but he scares the timid wayfarer into fits."[22]

Roosevelt manifested a ready understanding of the value of exerting his leadership through the Speaker of the House. No sooner had Joe Cannon been elected Speaker than the White House door was opened to him. Probably better organized and with a higher *esprit de*

17. *Ibid.*, 127.
18. *Ibid.*, 159.
19. Theodore Roosevelt, *An Autobiography*, 351.
20. Harold J. Laski, *op. cit.*, 93.
21. Henry F. Pringle, *Theodore Roosevelt*, 208.
22. Worthington Chauncey Ford ed., *Letters of Henry Adams*, 1858-1918, II, 469.

corps than at any other time in its history, the House was proud of its place in the federal system and wary of encroachment on its power. Since Roosevelt could not possibly confer personally with each Republican member to determine the party's sentiments, he recognized the Speaker as the head of the majority and consulted with him.[23] And as C. Perry Patterson has pointed out: "a large amount of the credit for his control over the Congress as a whole and over the House in particular belongs to Uncle Joe Cannon."[24] T. R., then, became one of the underwriters and the chief beneficiary of the system called "Cannonism."

Roosevelt's appreciation of the Speaker's role in legislation was so great that he was even willing to inaugurate a special Speaker's dinner (the custom has been continued) to conciliate a willful Joe Cannon. In February 1905, Roosevelt had planned a formal dinner for the Supreme Court, all of the justices being invited as his special guests. Although extended an invitation, Cannon bluntly declined to grace the banquet table with his presence. He thought that he had been invited in his official capacity as Speaker of the House and argued with his host that he deserved to be seated next in line to the Chief Justice and the Vice President, over the other Justices who were honored guests. Uncle Joe wrote to the President that even if "a wooden Indian" were Speaker of the House, he would deserve that courtesy. So Roosevelt, in order to soothe Cannon's feelings, decided to place on his social program a Speaker's dinner and invite no one of higher rank than the Speaker.[25] When President Taft extended the custom during the time of the insurgent tide, objections were made that he was too friendly toward Uncle Joe, and that by inviting the Speaker to dinner,

---

23. Wilfred E. Binkley, *President and Congress,* 195-6; also L. W. Busbey, *Uncle Joe Cannon,* 216-9.
24. C. Perry Patterson, *Presidential Government in the United States,* 134.
25. Joseph G. Cannon to Theodore Roosevelt, and Roosevelt to Cannon, February 2, 1905, Roosevelt Papers; also Ike Hoover, 42 *Years of the White House,* 292.

he was associating himself in the public mind with the unholy system called "Cannonism."

In 1919, a writer friendly to Theodore Roosevelt, noting that his most significant work related to domestic affairs went on to refer to him as "The Young David of the New Ideals" who had gone forth to battle with the "Goliath of Conservativism. He had been waiting twenty years for this opportunity."[26] Roosevelt himself did much to publicize his radical attitude for posterity in his *Autobiography*. He wrote that under his leadership "the Republican party became once more progressive and indeed the fairly radical progressive party of the nation."[27]

From the vantage point of 1943, Gerald W. Johnson, a solid admirer of Woodrow Wilson, opined that Roosevelt was really "a true conservative, the greatest the twentieth century has as yet produced."[28] It was plain enough to Johnson that Roosevelt's surface uproar was really helping to insure the domestic tranquillity by persuading the people that their government as it stood was powerful enough to protect their interests, and so need not be altered or abolished. The very term "conservation" which has become associated with his name suggested conservatism, particularly since Gifford Pinchot and his associates in that program were "the warmest advocates of a restoration of the old moralities including common honesty."[29]

Prominent men at opposite wings of the Republican party certainly disagreed with the picture of their President as even a mild type of American radical. Elihu Root proudly told the Union League Club of New York on February 3, 1904, that Roosevelt was a man the business classes could trust. "I say to you," Root declared, "that he has been the greatest conservative force for the protection of property and our institutions."[30] The party's

---

26. William Roscoe Thayer, *Theodore Roosevelt*, 1919.
27. Theodore Roosevelt, *An Autobiography*, 352.
28. Gerald W. Johnson, *American Heroes and Hero Worship*, 243.
29. *Ibid.*, 237-8.
30. Matthew Josephson, *The President Makers*, 1896-1919, 159.

leading radical, Robert M. LaFollette, wrote in retrospect that Roosevelt's public utterances were "highly colored with rhetorical radicalism." LaFollette, never content with half-loaf measures himself, thought that the President had sought mistakenly to win approval from both radicals and conservatives. "This cannonading, first in one direction, and then in another," he wrote, "filled the air with noise and smoke which confused and obscured the line of action. But when the cloud of battle drifted by and quiet was restored, it was always a matter of surprise that so little had been accomplished."[31]

To be sure, if Roosevelt is pictured as a conservative in the American tradition Uncle Joe Cannon may seem to be left somewhere in the Pleistocene period. Whatever Roosevelt's political outlook is understood to have been, no one could fail to observe that the President was a man of extraordinary energy with a wide range of interests. Walter Hines Page characterized T.R. as "a stimulating breeze which was blowing over the National Government."[32] John Morley observed that he was "an interesting combination of St. Vitus and St. Paul."[33] To Henry Adams, "Roosevelt, more than any other man living within the range of notoriety, showed the singular primitive quality that belongs to ultimate matter—the quality that medieval theology assigned to God—he was pure act."[34] "Theodore is never sober, only he is drunk with himself and not with rum."[35] Cecil Spring Rice, a close British friend of Roosevelt's was a bit more sympathetic. "If you took an impetuous small boy on to a beach strewn with a great many exciting pebbles," he told a *London Times* correspondent, "you would not expect him to remain in-

---

31. Robert M. LaFollette, *Autobiography,* 478-9.
32. George Fort Milton, *The Use of Presidential Power,* 173.
33. Harry Thurston Peck, *Twenty Years of the Republic,* 1885-1905, 669.
34. Henry Adams, *The Education of Henry Adams,* 417.
35. Worthington Chauncey Ford ed., *op. cit.,* II, 374-5.

terested for long in one pebble. You must always remember that the President is about six."[36]

Indeed, nothing seemed too large or too small to escape his enthusiasm, whether it was a crusade for simplified spelling, the "strenuous life," or serious political action. "It was only when Theodore Roosevelt came to power," wrote a recent observer, "that the philosophy of the executive dominant in legislation became reality. During his seven years in office, Roosevelt invested the presidency with a dramatic and aggressive spirit."[37] The spirit became manifest in such executive triumphs as the brisk settlement of the 1902 coal strike, the swift action with regard to Panama, the forthright application of the Sherman Act to the Northern Securities Company and other trusts.[38]

The assumption by the President of responsibility for molding a legislative program and of subsequently striving to induce Congress to adopt it, constituted a profound change in the working of the American political system.[39] But even though Roosevelt's "big stick" methods might be considered revolutionary, his aims generally remained suitable for adoption by his conservative Republican cohorts in Congress.

As a believer in direct action, Roosevelt saw himself in a Jacksonian role as a steward of the people. In his *Autobiography* he set down his conception of a strenuous presidency:

> My view was that every executive officer, and above all every executive officer in high position, was a steward of the people bound actively and affirmatively to do all he could for the people, and not to content himself with the negative merit of keeping his talents undamaged in a napkin. I declined to adopt the

36. Stephen Gwynn ed., *The Letters and Friendships of Cecil Spring Rice*, I, 437.
37. Lawrence Chamberlain, *The President, Congress and Legislation*, 13.
38. Harold Jacobs Howland, *Theodore Roosevelt and His Times*, 91-2, 115.
39. William F. Willoughby, *Principles of Legislative Organization and Administration*, 68-9.

> view that what was imperatively necessary for the Nation could not be done by the President unless he could find some specific authorization. . . . I did not usurp power, but I did greatly broaden the use of executive power. In other words, I acted for the common well-being of all our people, whenever and in whatever manner was necessary unless prevented by direct constitutional or legislative prohibition.[40]

His stewardship theory was not acceptable to William Howard Taft's judicial mind. Taft wrote in 1916: "The true view of the executive functions is, as I conceive it, that the President can exercise no power which cannot be fairly and reasonably traced to some specific grant of power justly implied and included within such grant as proper and necessary."[41]

These views of Roosevelt and Taft on the Presidency have important implications for the study of "Cannonism" and Insurgency. In the course of time, those Republicans in Congress who became Insurgents associated themselves with the Rooseveltian attitude and berated Taft for a legalistic attitude which they said gave aid and comfort to the regular forces on Uncle Joe's side.

III

At the turn of the century, Finley Peter Dunne amused the nation with the rambling philosophizing of Mr. Dooley on Archey Road. Popular magazines filled their pages with short stories and other entertainment features, but a few were primarily engaged in unearthing all sorts of evils. Such journalistic investigators as Ida Tarbell, David Graham Phillips, Lincoln Steffens, Charles Edward Russell, and Upton Sinclair aroused the country's indignation with their articles.[42] President Roosevelt labeled their work "muck-

40. Theodore Roosevelt, *op. cit.*, 357.
41. William Howard Taft, *Our Chief Magistrate and His Powers*, 139-40.
42. See C. C. Regier, *The Era of the Muckrakers*, for details.

raking" and the name stuck. The occasion for Roosevelt's attack was an article by David Graham Phillips, "The Treason of the Senate," in the *Cosmopolitan* for March, 1906. Roosevelt made it first in the privacy of the Gridiron Club on March 17, 1906 at a dinner given by Joe Cannon.[43] The "Muckrakers" were really nothing but refined Populists voicing middle class discontents. Their complaints were insistent but softly modulated compared to the ranting of Mary Ellen Lease, who had admonished the Kansas farmers of the 90's to raise "less corn and more hell." What became known as the progressive movement, that vast jumble of measures aimed at extending political democracy, curbing excessive corporative power, and aiding labor unions, was stirred up by their agitation. Theodore Roosevelt, who had been impressed by the dire predictions of Brooks Adams regarding the decay of American civilization,[44] and was imbued with his own desire to make the United States a predominant world power, did take heed of the journalistic cries for reform. In his own inimitable fashion he wanted to eliminate the weaknesses apparent in America's way of life. He told James Ford Rhodes that it was his job to stand midway between the rich and the poor to prevent the excesses, that had destroyed the Grecian, Roman, and Italian republics.[45]

Both the Old Guard, representing financiers and industrialists, and Roosevelt wanted the same thing—the preservation of the status quo. "Their paths diverged," asserts Pringle, "because the Old Guard had no apprehensions and no fears; in smug complacency it was satisfied merely to let things drift. The President, so often torn by anxiety for the future, was led to radicalism by his desire to perpetuate the existing order. Specifically, he was led to adopt the program of William Jennings Bryan and the Demo-

43. *Washington Star,* March 18, 1906.
44. Matthew Josephson, *The President Makers,* 1896-1919, 24-8.
45. James Ford Rhodes, *History of the United States from the Compromise of* 1850, IX, 395.

cratic Party." Of course, Roosevelt never acknowledged this debt to Bryan. In fact, he was curiously intolerant toward him. "He was to follow, more or less consistently, the policy of recoiling in horror from the radical ideas of the Democrats, then adopting them with slight modifications, and finally condemning, as obstructionists, those who opposed his adaptations or called them dangerous."[46]

In the Roosevelt-Cannon relationship the issues of conservation, railroad regulation, pure food and meat inspection, tariffs, trusts, and labor legislation as they appeared on the national political scene, in varying degrees, were the issues used by the Insurgents in their case against Cannon. Hence, these issues have greater importance, in effect, than the essential agreement between the President and the Speaker on the Panama Canal question, a matter without insurgent repercussions in which Cannon was in complete harmony with the idea of a canal across the Isthmus despite the expense involved.[47] He also was one of the first men in Congress to suggest the feasibility of the Panama route, providing that a satisfactory agreement could be negotiated with Columbia. And on that point he provoked the House to laughter by saying: "Now, if greed and desire for great profit are Anglo-Saxon traits, then our Latin friends . . . are a long way upon a high road to civilization."[48]

Frequently, informal conferences proved to be a reasonably effective way for the President and the Speaker to bridge the gap made by the separation of powers. Cannon is the authority for the statement that they often disagreed.

> Roosevelt had the outlook of the executive and the ambition to do things; I had the more confined outlook of the legislator who had to consider ways of

46. Henry F. Pringle, *Theodore Roosevelt,* 368-9.
47. *Congressional Record,* 57-1, 481.
48. *Ibid.,* 57-1, 545.

> meeting the expenditures of new departures and expansions in Government. . . . I think Mr. Roosevelt talked over with me virtually every serious recommendation to Congress before he made it, and requested me to sound out the leaders in the House, for he did not want to recommend legislation simply to write messages. He wanted results and he wanted to know how to secure results with the least friction. He was a good sportsman and accepted what he could get so long as the legislation conformed even in part to his recommendations.[49]

When they disagreed, wrote the journalist Arthur Wallace Dunn, Cannon did not always strike his colors to the impetuous President, and Roosevelt knew that Cannon could not be crowded into a corner without making a fight. On one occasion an intimate of the President earnestly suggested that he must "lay down on Uncle Joe." The President retorted that it would be "a good deal like laying down on a hedgehog."[50] J. Hampton Moore, a GOP congressman from Pennsylvania, recalled that Cannon sometimes had difficulty in keeping his temper in check, that once he told a delighted group of congressional bystanders: "That fellow at the other end of the Avenue wants everything from the birth of Christ to the death of the devil."[51]

For the record, Uncle Joe was as loyal as he could be. John Wesley Gaines, a Tennessee Democrat who liked to get his name in the *Record,* once deplored the news that President Roosevelt had disposed of a treasured piece of White House furniture—a sideboard presented to Mrs. Rutherford B. Hayes by the W.C.T.U. as a tribute to her temperance convictions. Gaines pointed out with horror that the sideboard had been sold to a saloonkeeper, who operated a popular thirst-quenching stand called Han-

49. L. W. Busbey, *op. cit.,* 217, 219.
50. Arthur Wallace Dunn, *From Harrison to Harding,* II, 86-7.
51. J. Hampton Moore, *Roosevelt and the Old Guard,* 219.

cock's at 1234 Pennsylvania Avenue. Uncle Joe squelched Mr. Gaines with a little humor by saying, "tradition tells us that on rainy days Dolly Madison used to hang the White House washing on an old-fashioned clothesline in the East Room of the Executive Mansion. My God, . . . where is that clothesline?" In the view of James E. Watson of Indiana, House whip under Uncle Joe who liked to tell that story, Roosevelt and Cannon were friendly only in a partisan sense, but he said, "they sustained each other heartily in that regard, because they were both Republicans, and both party men, and they knew that it was necessary to stand together or they would not stand at all."[52]

Relations between President Roosevelt and Speaker Cannon during 1904 were most cordial. There was nothing out of the ordinary in that, for, as keen party men, both desired to win the November presidential sweepstakes from the Democrats, who, in their view, were not fit to conduct the nation's affairs. Uncle Joe took Illinois factional disputes to Roosevelt, and the President gave him both sympathy and advice.[53] Perhaps their sincerity was tempered with mental reservations. Cannon, for instance, could hardly be expected to forget his disapproval of the methods Roosevelt used in getting the law creating the Department of Commerce and Labor passed in 1903. To Uncle Joe, the use of the "Rockefeller telegrams" to influence the House and the Senate at that time, always remained a typical example of Rooseveltian mendacity.[54]

---

52. James E. Watson, *As I Knew Them,* 56-7.
53. Theodore Roosevelt to Joseph G. Cannon, May 27, 1904; Joseph G. Cannon to William R. Loeb, June 24, 1904, Roosevelt Papers.
54. Busbey, *op. cit.,* 216-23; Henry F. Pringle, *Theodore Roosevelt,* 340-2, takes the view that T.R. was substantially though not technically truthful. The attitude of business toward the proposed department was hostile, for its Bureau of Corporations was to be given power to investigate the operation and conduct of corporations engaged in interstate commerce. Roosevelt told the press that six influential Senators had received telegrams from John D. Rockefeller urging that no anti-trust legislation be enacted. The President's statement, which made it seem that Standard Oil interests were brazenly attempting to influence legislation, created such a storm that Congress acted swiftly and passed the law

It may be added that Cannon had had grave doubts about the wisdom of Roosevelt's action to end the coal strike of 1902.[55] For his part, the President must have recalled their clashes of personality while he was serving as Civil Service Commissioner and Cannon was chairman of the House Appropriations Commitee. There always remained differences of outlook between the President, born to wealth, well educated and widely traveled—the embodiment of the gentleman in politics, and Joe Cannon, self made, narrow, and vulgar—the embodiment of rural Illinois in Washington.

The Republican national convention of 1904 met on June 21 in Chicago. Definitely a humdrum affair, its entire program had been carefully prearranged by administration forces. "Dominating the Republican convention in 1904," George Mowry has written, "Roosevelt selected Elihu Root and Joseph Cannon as its presiding officers and his friend Henry Cabot Lodge as chairman of the Committee on Resolutions. It would have been difficult to find three more reverent archbishops of high conservatism in the entire Republican apostolic succession. . . . The platform was completely innocent of anything savoring of progressive action. Conservatives everywhere rejoiced—they had misjudged Roosevelt."[56] William Allen White recalled that "The only burst of pure felicity came from the convention to greet Joe Cannon, who stood in Washington, even in Roosevelt's first term, as the type of old fashioned "honest politician; whom the President's enemies openly worshiped as their political god."[57] The

---

establishing the Department of Commerce and Labor. It was never proved that any Senators had ever received telegrams from Rockefeller. (Cannon insisted that the telegrams originated in the brain of the President). The Hearst press, however, published a telegram from John D. Archbold of Standard Oil to Senator Matt Quay of Pennsylvania which protested against "vexatious interference with the industrial life of the country." Hence, Pringle takes the view that T.R. was substantially, if not technically, truthful.

55. Watson, *op. cit.,* 63-4.

56. George E. Mowry, *Theodore Roosevelt and the Progressive Movement,* 22.

57. William Allen White, *Masks in a Pageant,* 312. William Jennings Bryan, *The Commoner Condensed,* IV, 237, presents a similar view.

platform was brief, and, significantly, it said nothing about tariff revision or reciprocity. Evidently the GOP was standing pat with Roosevelt.[58] The President wrote to Cannon, indicating that he was pleased with the efficient manner in which the convention had finished its job.[59]

The Democratic convention met at St. Louis on July 6, 1904. The delegates had an exciting time before finally selecting a safe and sane New York judge, Alton B. Parker, as their Presidential nominee. On one issue the party of the outs could agree, namely, that Theodore Roosevelt should be defeated. John Sharp Williams of Mississippi, the party's scholarly minority leader in the House, voiced this sentiment when he declared that Roosevelt's administration was "a continuing experiment, too theatrical for the business interests of the country, without sufficient time between the acts to allow the people a good breathing spell." Williams feared that "on some strenuous occasion" he was going to embarrass the country greatly in a grave matter of state.[60]

The Republican *New York Sun* worried about the election as much as any conservative Democrat. The paper charged that Roosevelt was on the side of "men who are every day seeking to overthow the Constitution, and who entertain for it nothing but derision and hatred."[61] The President reassured Cannon that the *Sun* was angry with him because he had received in the White House "every decent delegation of labor men just as I have received every decent capitalist." He noted that "populist papers" attacked him for inviting heads of large corporations to the White House and indicated that he would disregard all such complaints.[62] His confidence was undiminished, for he told Uncle Joe: "As far as I can see the outlook

58. J. H. Latane, *America as a World Power,* 1897-1907, 228-9.
59. Theodore Roosevelt to Joseph G. Cannon, June 24, 1904, Roosevelt Papers.
60. Henry Litchfield West, "American Politics," *Forum* XXXVI (July, 1904), 5.
61. *New York Sun,* July 30, 1904.
62. Theodore Roosevelt to Joseph G. Cannon, August 3, 1904, Roosevelt Papers.

is favorable, but I suppose there is no man less competent to judge than the candidate himself."[63]

In keeping with tradition, Roosevelt waited until September 12, 1904, before formally notifying Joe Cannon, chairman of the convention's nominating committee, that he was willing to be the party's candidate for President. He added a few political remarks. The Democrats, he said, were improvisers who always doubted how firmly they should assert their beliefs in anything. "The party now in control of the Government is troubled by no such difficulties. We do not have to guess at our own convictions, and then correct the guess if it seems unpopular." With reference to the Democratic soft pedal on Bryanism, T. R. added: "A party which with facile ease changes all of its convictions before election cannot be trusted to adhere with tenacity to any principle after the election. A party fit to govern must have convictions."[64] The *Nation* thought that the cocksure Rough-Rider at the head of the Republican troop was the dangerous improviser. "The one part of the Constitution which President Roosevelt takes seriously," it editorialized, "is the 'general welfare' clause. He regards himself as the judge of that welfare, rushes ahead and does what he thinks best, and then tells you that any Constitutional objection to his course is a 'false construction' by which he will not be bound."[65]

Cannon traveled the rails in a private car from September 15 until election time on behalf of the Congressional campaign. He visited fifteen states from Nebraska to Rhode Island making sixty speeches. Most of Uncle Joe's stump speeches, were, of course, devoted to his favorite topic, the tariff. At Eldridge, Iowa, on October 1, he dismissed Republican Governor Albert B. Cummins' so-called "Iowa Idea" for revision. "We don't pay much attention to that over in Illinois where I live, and really,

63. Theodore Roosevelt to Joseph G. Cannon, August 29, 1904, Roosevelt Papers.
64. Theodore Roosevelt to Joseph G. Cannon, September 12, 1904, Roosevelt Papers.
65. "Re-Enter the Rough Rider," *Nation* LXXIX (September 15, 1904), 210.

you don't seem to be paying much attention to it here in Iowa." At New Brunswick, New Jersey, on October 25, he argued that for forty years under a protective tariff the country had prospered and that 92% of America's markets had been developed at home. Believers in free trade, he said, held their ideas because of "prejudice or crankiness." Their plans showed "splendid mental construction," but were worthless since it was impractical to bring all nations under one government.[66]

Despite the oratory of Cannon and others the country exhibited only languid interest in the progress of the campaign. There was no anxiety about the outcome as in 1896. The voters, realizing that no matter which party won, the country would not be wrecked, manifested only a polite interest in the campaigners. The parties differed on few points. Both were pledged to the gold standard, professed that they abhorred trusts, affirmed their belief in honest and economical government.[67] But the result was a personal triumph for Theodore Roosevelt. He received an unprecedented popular plurality of more than 2,500,000 votes over Judge Parker; the electoral count was 336 to 140. The GOP kept its healthy majority in the Senate and gained 42 seats in the House.[68] Roosevelt wrote to Kermit: "I am stunned by the overwhelming victory we have won. I had no conception that such a thing was possible. . . . This was the day of greatest triumph I have ever had or ever could have, and I was very proud and happy."[69] To Cannon, the newly elected President sent "Hearty thanks. No one did a greater work during this campaign and during the preceding two years than you did toward bringing about our success."[70]

---

66. Campaign Tour of Hon. Joseph G. Cannon and Party, September 15 to November 3, 1904, compiled by H. F. Dodge, Cannon Papers.
67. Henry Litchfield West, "American Politics," *Forum* XXXVI (October, 1904) 165.
68. *Historical Statistics of the United States*, 289, 293.
69. John Morton Blum, *The Republican Roosevelt*, 70.
70. Theodore Roosevelt to Joseph G. Cannon, November 9, 1904, Roosevelt Papers. George W. Norris, who was to lead the House Insurgents in 1910, also con-

Roosevelt, faced with the necessity of sending his annual message to the lame duck session of the 58th Congress, began to sound out House leaders on the possibility of tariff revision. He wrote to James A. Tawney of Minnesota, one of Uncle Joe's henchmen: "It seems to me that our party ought to revise the tariff now, but of course I do not want to say anything about it unless the leaders of the House approve, because I realize thoroughly that the matter is primarily one for you all in the House."[71] To Cannon, the President sent a "rough draft" of what he might say on the tariff. He assured the Speaker that he wanted the "essence" of the beneficial protective system to remain; but he hoped the Congress could provide "for reciprocity by a maximum and minimum scale to be applied in the discretion of the Executive." Perhaps the Senate Finance Committee and the House Committee on Ways and Means could be made a joint commission to take up the tariff question and report to a special session of Congress. In any event, the President concluded, "I send the above merely for the sake of having something which can be worked out after you have consulted the men fresh from the people in the various sections of the country."[72]

Cannon received the letter at Danville just before leaving for Washington. He called on the President shortly after his arrival, and they had "a very frank discussion." Uncle Joe advised against any opening of the tariff question especially since the President admitted that the business of the country was most satisfactory. There was no tariff recommendation in Roosevelt's message when it was delivered to Congress.[73]

gratulated Cannon for a "splendid victory." Confidence in Uncle Joe had "made many votes for the Republican ticket all over the country," and, Norris added, had helped increase his own plurality from 181 votes to almost six thousand. George W. Norris to Joseph G. Cannon, November 14, 1904, Norris Papers.

71. Theodore Roosevelt to James A. Tawney, November 10, 1904, Roosevelt Papers.
72. Theodore Roosevelt to Joseph G. Cannon, November 30, 1904, Roosevelt Papers.
73. L. W. Busbey, *op. cit.,* 207-8. Cannon thus had more success in Washington than in Illinois where the state GOP convention (seventy-nine ballots in twenty-

In the first week of 1905, a conference of conservative leaders, including Senators Aldrich, Hale, Allison, and Spooner, and Speaker Cannon met at the White House. President Roosevelt told them he wanted a great navy, would not oppose the majority views of both Houses on the tariff, and that he would continue to urge interstate commerce legislation.[74] The *Nation* commented: "Those whose strength is in sitting still are in control. . . . It is said there are to be further conferences, but the more they confer, the more things will remained unchanged."[75]

Having acknowledged the Speaker as the head of the Republican majority in the House, Roosevelt was careful to keep his good will. T. R. wrote to Cannon early in 1905:

> Stop in here as soon as you can. I care very little for what the newspapers get in the way of passing sensationalism; but I do not want the people of the country to get the idea that there will be any split or clash between you and me on the tariff or anything else. I have deeply appreciated your willingness to go on with the building up of the navy — it not being so important that we shall go so fast as that we shall keep going. As you know, I shall be entirely content to have less than I want so long as we get something real.[76]

Despite Cannon's determined attitude, T. R. apparently wanted to pressure the Speaker into agreeing on tariff revision. In the middle of February 1905, Uncle Joe was invited to the White House along with other party leaders. Included in the group were Senators Aldrich of Rhode Island, Allison of Iowa, Hale of Maine, Platt of Connec-

---

two days) over which he presided nominated Charles S. Deneen for governor. Cannon had favored Frank O. Lowden and was somewhat chagrined to have delegates from his own Congressional district vote for Deneen. Wendt, Lloyd and Herman Kogan, *Big Bill of Chicago,* 54-65.

74. Nathaniel W. Stephenson, *Nelson W. Aldrich,* 257.

75. "The Programme," *Nation* LXXX (January 12, 1905), 24.

76. Theodore Roosevelt to Joseph G. Cannon, January 13, 1905, Roosevelt Papers.

ticut, Cullom of Illinois, Penrose of Pennsylvania, and Representatives Payne of New York, Dalzell of Pennsylvania, Grosvenor of Ohio, Tawney of Minnesota, and Dolliver of Iowa. The President explained to the select company that many people had urged him to say something about tariff revision in his inaugural address. He added that his own inclination was to indicate that he would recommend to Congress that it take up the question of revision when it first met in the following December.

He then asked for the views of the legislators. Senator Aldrich briefly commended the President's proposal. Two other members of "The Four," Hale and Allison concurred, though without enthusiasm. So did Payne, Tawney, and Grosvenor. O. H. Platt was the first to register vigorous disapproval, and Cannon joined him. When Uncle Joe had finished, T.R. grinned, and according to Cannon, said: "It is evidently the consensus of opinion that the tariff should not be revised until after the next presidential election." That ended the tariff conference.[77] Roosevelt continued to worry about the tariff, especially at election time. But as long as he was in the White House, the Democrats could cry that the tariff was the mother of trusts without gaining any appreciable result.

The lame duck session of the 58th Congress did give the President the two battleships he had wanted, and the House also passed an interstate commerce measure, the Esch-Townsend Bill, but too late for Senate action. The *Nation* had contended that the bill would not pass the House, unless the members firmly believed it would die or be amended to death in the Senate.[78] Cannon, "the sly conservative," had not opposed the bill. A Cannon-Aldrich agreement might have been the reason. "Such agreements at Washington are not recorded. But everyone

77. L. W. Busbey, *op. cit.*, 212-3.
78. "The Pending Step in Railroad Regulation," *Nation* LXXX (February 9, 1905), 108.

knows that they happen," Aldrich's biographer has observed.[79]

In his message to Congress in December 1904, the President had indicated a new concern for railroad legislation. Previously when a rate had been challenged by the Interstate Commerce Commission the old rate remained in force through a long judicial process to determine its reasonables. Roosevelt's message called on Congress to give the Commission power to decide, "subject to judicial review," what constituted a reasonable rate, the ruling to take effect immediately and to prevail "unless and until it is reversed by a court of review."[80]

The Esch-Townsend Bill in passing the House on February 9, 1905, by a vote of 326 to 17, received hearty support from the Democrats. It would have invested the Interstate Commerce Commission with the right to specify reasonable railroad rates to replace the ones determined by it to be unjust and unreasonable. A transportation court composed of five circuit judges was to review the decisions of the Commission. The Democratic efforts in securing the bill's passage in the House were such that the party's orators even expressed admiration for President Roosevelt during the debate. William Jennings Bryan also joined in the chorus of approval.[81] The *Nation,* as usual, found fault; it said the passage of the Esch-Townsend Bill by the House "marked one more step in its legislative degradation. . . . Even the President at whose behest it was passed says he is most anxious to have it 'perfected.' This is his way of complimenting the House. Any sort of ragged and limping measure is good enough for the representatives."[82]

79. Nathaniel W. Stephenson, *op. cit.,* 257. John Morton Blum, *op. cit.,* 80-81, suggests that Roosevelt and Cannon had a tacit understanding. The President was not to press hard for tariff revision. In return for this favor the Speaker was to work for a railroad law.

80. James D. Richardson, *Messages and Papers of the Presidents,* X, 809-10.

81. Henry Litchfield West, "American Politics," *Forum* XXXVI (April, 1905), 486-7.

82. "A Legislative Grimace," *Nation* LXXX (February 16, 1905), 127.

One measure that had not been good enough for them was William Randolph Hearst's railroad bill. The wealthy publisher, who represented his New York district as a Democrat, had favored a special court with power to modify an I.C.C. order and thus to act as a legislative rather than as a judicial body. Hearst's bill would also have required railroads to furnish freight cars to shippers on the demand of the shippers or be hailed before the I.C.C. to answer for charges of discriminatory practices.[83] The publisher gave the impression through his newspapers that he was an exceedingly active member of Congress. The reverse was true for he was seldom present. When his bill came up, he was absent. John A. Sullivan, a fellow Democrat from Massachusetts, asked in vain for an explanation of the bill's terms, calling attention to the fact that "although a year has passed the gentleman has not taken the opportunity to explain his own bill on the floor of the House, which I for one would have welcomed." The House greeted his remarks with applause, but the next day's *New York American* made some deft comments about the lack of congressional ability of "a bold, red-nosed young man, whose name it seems, is Sullivan."[84]

On February 13, 1905, Sullivan raised a question of personal privilege in the House. Speaker Cannon egged on the battling Democrat, making no attempt to conceal his grinning delight. Sullivan made some slighting remarks about "yellow journals" and referred to Hearst's "contemptible mental and moral equipment" as being insufficient for the office of President to which he aspired. Hearst had a few compliments to pay Mr. Sullivan, also. He put in an appearance in the House, and under unanimous consent, Cannon having delightedly quashed points of order, denied that he had ever intended to attack Sullivan. If he had, he said he could have mentioned the

83. *Congressional Record,* 58-3, 2009-11.

84. Oliver Carlson and Ernest Sutherland Bates, *Hearst, Lord of San Simeon,* 120-22.

fact that Sullivan had been convicted of manslaughter in 1885.[85]

Insignificant as this unseemly exchange was in itself, it provides a clue to Speaker Cannon's strategy in handling the Democratic minority. He followed the old maxim, divide and rule. While John Sharp Williams was the Democratic floor leader from 1903 to 1909, James E. Watson, Republican whip and a crony of Uncle Joe's, induced the Speaker to confer upon Williams the unprecedented right to name the minority members of the different committees of the House. The Speakers had previously exercised that privilege, but Cannon was swayed by Watson's argument that if Williams were permitted to name committee members, he would become involved in all sorts of petty difficulties with his followers, and the solidarity of the Democratic opposition would be weakened. His prediction was correct. Williams, exercising his appointive power, eventually demoted two Missourians, Dorsey Shackleford and David De Armond, because they did not vote as regularly with the Democrats as he wanted them to. Neither took their demotions in good grace. They roused other Democrats to oppose the minority leader, and once De Armond even engaged Williams in fisticuffs. The Watson-Cannon strategy was an apparent success.[86] However, anti-Williams Democrats subsequently were among the leaders in the attempts to restrict Speaker Cannon's powers.

Uncle Joe and John Sharp Williams, despite their mutual devotion to partisanship, were fast friends. On one occasion when they were engaged in a heated argument, Williams remarked with a smile: "We are just reasoning together in brotherly love."[87] One observer remarked that no matter how hot the partisan encounter betwen the two men became, "an occasional smile dissipated the thought

85. *Ibid.*, 122-3; 126-9.
86. James E. Watson, *As I Knew Them*, 285-6.
87. *Congressional Record*, 58-2, 5035.

that superheated zeal had buried friendship."[88] A favorite Williams joke on Cannon was that one day when he walked into the Speaker's private conference room, Cannon absentmindedly thought Williams was a Republican and began in strictest confidence to discuss committee appointments with him. After a few minutes, Uncle Joe realized what he was doing, and both men enjoyed a hearty laugh.[89]

Cannon was unusually successful and popular during the 58th Congress which ended with T.R.'s first term. Shortly before the House adjourned on March 4, 1905, Representative Henry S. Boutell, an Illinois Republican, made a laudatory address, thanking the Speaker for the way in which he had conducted his office, and presented him with a loving cup. John Sharp Willams paid tribute to Cannon "in recognition of kindly services and kindly feeling already extended and already appreciated" on both sides of the House. Champ Clark added a word. "Historians of our times," he affirmed, "will record the fact that the Fifty-eighth Congress was celebrated above all its predecessors for all its extraordinary kindness which prevailed among its members."[90]

As Theodore Roosevelt's first term drew to a close, Speaker Cannon was secure in his chair; he was consulted with deference by the President and praised by his own colleagues in the House.

---

88. De Alva Stanwood Alexander, *History and Procedure of the House of Representatives,* 209.
89. George Coleman Osborn, "Joseph G. Cannon and John Sharp Williams," *Indiana Magazine of History,* XXXV (June, 1939), 288.
90. *Congressional Record,* 58-3, 4038-40.

CHAPTER FOUR

The Era Of Good Feeling Vanishes

John Sharp Williams: "Mr. Speaker, I will always think you are as fair as I believe you will be."
Speaker Cannon: "John, I'm going to be as fair as I can consistent with the exigencies of American politics."

New York Times, April 29, 1904

The chief issues before the country in 1905, as Theodore Roosevelt began his second term as President and Uncle Joe Cannon his second term as Speaker, were railroad regulation and that well-worn perennial, the tariff. These issues, together with continuing problems of finance, conservation, and labor, placed a strain on the Roosevelt-Cannon relationship, so that the two men and their respective followers came to a parting of the ways by 1908, thus, preparing the way for Cannon's later battle with the Insurgents. The aggressive, ever-strenuous President pressed for reform, even scolding Congress when he did not get what he wanted. The cautious, veteran Speaker —especially during the 60th Congress, showed less and less enthusiasm for Roosevelt's proposals.[1]

1. James Bryce, *The American Commonwealth* I, 209, explains this predicament: "The President himself, although he has been voted into office by his party, is not necessarily its leader, nor even one among its most prominent leaders. Hence he does not sway the policy of those members of Congress who belong to his own side. No duty lies on Congress to take up a subject to which he has called attention as needing legislation; and the suggestions which he makes, year after year, are in fact frequently neglected, even when his party has a majority in both Houses, or when the subject lies outside party lines."

With the Congress out of session until December, Roosevelt was not idle. In a speech before the Iroquois Club of Chicago on May 10, he expressed the belief that the Interstate Commerce Commission should be armed with full power to fix railroad rates. The review of its actions by the courts was to be limited to the single function of seeing that railroad property was not actually confiscated.[2] Just before leaving on a tour around the world in September, 1905, William Jennings Bryan had given the President some free counsel: "It will embarrass you to have strong party leaders against you; you may have been embarrassed by having so many Democrats cooperate with you; but you must reconcile yourself to both."[3] Roosevelt obviously did not reconcile himself to being embarrassed in the advanced position he had taken on rate-fixing in his Chicago speech. In a public address on October 19, 1905, he hinted that he would accept only a part of the power he had sought. Even before Congress convened, he was talking of compromise.[4]

Upon the assembling of Congress in December 1905, the President devoted many more paragraphs of his annual message to railroad reform than he ever had before. He wrote:

> The immediate and most pressing need so far as legislation is concerned, is the enactment into law of some scheme to . . . secure to the government such supervision and regulation of the rates charged by the railroads of the country engaged in interstate traffic as shall summarily and effectively prevent the imposition of unjust and unreasonable rates.[5]

This plea was balanced characteristically by his further statement:

2. Nathaniel Stephenson, *Nelson W. Aldrich,* 277.
3. *The Commoner,* September 29, 1905, quoted in Paxton Hibben, *The Peerless Leader, William Jennings Bryan,* 264..
4. Mathew Josephson, *The President Makers,* 1896-1919, 227.
5. James D. Richardson, *Messages and Papers of the Presidents,* XI, 1135.

I do not believe in the government interfering with private business any more than is necessary. Let me most earnestly say that these recommendations are not made in a spirit of hostility to the railroads. . . . This legislation should be enacted in a spirit as remote as possible from hysteria and rancor.[6]

Taking cognizance of the pleas of reformers like Dr. Harvey W. Wiley, Roosevelt came out in favor of pure food legislation near the end of his message, recommending "that a law be enacted to regulate interstate commerce in misbranded and adulterated foods, drinks, and drugs. Such a law would protect legitimate manufacture and commerce, and would tend to secure the health and welfare of the consuming public. Traffic in foodstuffs which have been debased or adulterated so as to injure health or deceive purchasers should," he insisted, "be forbidden."[7]

Strangely missing again was a statement on the tariff. For reasons that are not entirely clear, Roosevelt apparently deleted a statement on the tariff from his message. According to N. W. Stephenson, Senator Albert B. Cummins, the Iowa Republican associated with the low-tariff "Iowa Idea," saw a statement to the effect that a special message would be devoted to the tariff and approved it. But the actual message to Congress did not contain the statement. Senator Cummins is supposed to have reproached the President, whereupon T. R. readily admitted that Senator Aldrich and Speaker Cannon had told him that they would not allow his railroad legislation to go before Congress unless he abandoned tariff revision. He had, therefore, deleted the tariff reference, for he was very keen on getting a railroad bill passed.[8] When Roosevelt's actions on the tariff question in 1904 are recalled, this version seems credible. Besides the outspoken opposition of men like Aldrich and Cannon, tariff revision was made

6. *Ibid.*, XI, 1135.
7. *Ibid.*, XI, 1170.
8. Nathaniel W. Stephenson, *op. cit.*, 254.

very unlikely by the "serious obstacle" of "general prosperity."[9] Robert M. LaFollette contended that T.R. gave Cannon and Aldrich the very support they needed to maintain their standpat position on the tariff. He touched the subject, said LaFollette, "now and then with a deftness that enabled him to escape, for the time, being classed as a standpatter himself."[10] Cannon clinched the matter by adhering to the advice of conservative colleagues.[11] He took great care in assigning GOP members to the new Ways and Means Committee so that it would consist only of avowed opponents of revision.[12]

Roosevelt's second administration did not have an auspicious beginning in the House. The closing hours of debate on the first Panama Canal appropriations disclosed a remarkable state of bitterness. Several of the House leaders, including Hepburn, Payne, Grosvenor, and Dalzell, held an "indignation meeting" in the Speaker's room. They were agitated about looseness in the expenditures for the canal and were particularly angry over the Canal Commission maintaining a $10,000 a year press agent. Speaker Cannon was not successful in quieting the turmoil, and even was moved to say that he found it "extremely hard" to stand by the President. The result was a reduced appropriation, with the sweeping stipulation that the expenditures of the Canal Commission must undergo the close scrutiny of Congress.[13]

To hear the *Nation* tell it, such conflict was inevitable and the country was about to see "a severe test of the President's political generalship." The paper made the suggestion that Roosevelt had not sufficiently weighed an old political truth. "This is that an Administration, no

---

9. Henry Litchfield West, "American Politics," *Forum* XXXVII (October, 1905), 156.
10. Robert M. LaFollette, *Autobiography,* 713.
11. Charles H. Grosvenor to Joseph G. Cannon, May 21, 1905, Cannon Papers.
12. Henry Litchfield West, "American Politics," *Forum* XXXVII (January, 1906), 299.
13. *Chicago Chronicle,* December 8, 1905.

matter how strong it may seem in popular support, no sooner begins to live than it begins to die. . . . Political interest soon centres elsewhere. Who is to be the successor?"[14] It is of incidental interest to note that Cannon's colleagues had already told him that his chances for the Presidency in 1908 were better than those of anyone else.[15]

Early in 1906 the Democratic *New York World* believed that Roosevelt himself was in favor of Cannon for 1908.[16] Soon afterwards, the independent *Chicago Evening Post* noted a movement sweeping Congress for Cannon as the next GOP candidate for President.[17]

Meanwhile, the most engrossing topic, in the 1st session of the 59th Congress, was the proposed railroad legislation. No one could truthfully say that the House dawdled in dealing with it. On January 27, 1906, Chairman Hepburn of the Committee on Interstate and Foreign Commerce, with the unanimous recommendation of his eighteen man committee, reported a railroad bill to the floor. The report emphasized that the railroads themselves were responsible for the legislation: "It is proper to say to those who complain of this legislation that the necessity for it is the result of misconduct of the carriers. . . . If carriers in good faith had accepted existing statutes and obeyed them, there would be no necessity for increasing the powers of the Commission or the enactment of other coercive measures."[18]

The most important point in the Hepburn Bill was its giving the Interstate Commerce Commission the power to investigate complaints that a rate was unfair or a regulation unjust, and "to determine and prescribe" a reasonable rate or "to fix and determine" a just regulation. An order embodying a decision of the Commission was to go

14. "Congress on Roosevelt's Hands," *Nation* LXXXII (January 18, 1906), 46.
15. Charles H. Grosvenor to Joseph G. Cannon, May 21, 1905, Cannon Papers.
16. *New York World*, March 12, 1906.
17. *Chicago Evening Post*, May 24, 1906.
18. 59th Congress, 1st Session, *House Report* 591, 3.

into effect in thirty days unless set aside "by a court of competent jurisdiction." All railroad terminal and storage facilities were to be brought under the Commission's jurisdiction; so-called "midnight tariffs" were to be outlawed by a provision calling for thirty days public notice of rate changes; and provision was made for standardized railroad bookeeping procedures.

The debate in the House on the Hepburn Bill was characterized by an atmosphere of good feeling. William Adamson, Democrat from Georgia, acknowledged the magnitude of Republican efforts in the House for rate regulation since 1904. He even ventured to say that "In many personal respects there are some really good Republicans despite the vicious doctrines of their abominable party."[19] Attempts to amend the bill by members of both parties—to give the Interstate Commerce Commission jurisdiction over express companies, telephone, telegraph, and sleeping car companies, to abolish free passes, and to allow rates to be investigated upon the motion of the Commission—were without avail. The bill was rushed to passage on February 8, 1906, by a vote of 346 to 7. The great majority of the Democrats—120 out of 137—joined 226 Republicans in favoring the measure. Republicans provided the 7 nays.[20]

The *Nation* called the Hepburn Bill, a "slovenly bill," put through the House in a hurry to oblige the President who wanted the measure taken up in the Senate early in the session. "Any old bill" was good enough for the House. Indirectly, the paper intimated that the result showed masterful direction, if not wisdom, on the part of Cannon's majority.[21] Uncle Joe used the result to show that the Speaker was "the servant of the House, nothing more, nothing less." He also pointed out that the House was a place of free speech and action, that it came closer

19. *Congressional Record,* 59-1, 1771.
20. *Ibid.,* 59-1, 2256-70; 2303.
21. "How not to Legislate," *Nation* LXXXII (February 15, 1906), 130.

to representing "enlightened public opinion" than it ever had before.[22]

The speed and decisiveness of the House action put the Senate on the spot. On February 23, Senator Aldrich, the real power of his chamber's Committee on Interstate Commerce, sought to destroy the bill by adroitly giving the job of piloting it through the Senate to a Democrat, the tempestuous Senator Tillman from South Carolina, who was definitely not in the good graces of the White House.[23] Roosevelt regarded this action as "simply childish."[24] Debate dragged on for weeks and weeks—eleven altogether. Ohio's Joseph Foraker made eighty-seven speeches against it; some fifty amendments were offered; "Pitchfork Ben" Tillman, a self-proclaimed "corn field lawyer" fought for it until Roosevelt suddenly "dropped his pilot" and shifted his support to a Republican William B. Allison on the touchy subject of judicial review. A bitter exchange followed between the Rough Rider and the South Carolinian, but finally the bill passed on May 18, 1906, by a vote of 71 to 3.[25] After more weeks of House-Senate conferences, the Hepburn Bill became law on June 29, 1906. It is understandable that Theodore Roosevelt, plagued by delay and bickering in the Senate, could be grateful to the House, and especially to the Speaker, for their part in lending to his administration an air of positive accomplishment.

In the midst of the Senate debates, Roosevelt had unburdened himself to William Howard Taft:

> I do not at all like the social conditions at present. The dull, purblind folly of the very rich men; their greed and arrogance, and the way in which they unduly prospered by the help of the ablest lawyers, and too often through the weakness or shortsightedness

22. *New York Herald,* March 4, 1906.
23. N. W. Stephenson, *op. cit.,* 293-6.
24. Theodore Roosevelt, *Autobiography,* 436.
25. *Congressional Record,* 59-1, 7088.

> of the judges or by their unfortunate possession of meticulous minds; these facts, and the corruption in business and politics have tended to produce a very unhealthy condition of excitement and irritation in the popular mind, which shows itself in part in the enormous increase in socialistic propaganda. Nothing effective, because nothing at once honest and intelligent, is being done to combat the great amount of evil which, mixed with a little good, a little truth, is contained in the out-pourings of the Cosmopolitan, of McClure's, of Collier's, of Tom Lawson, of David Graham Phillips, of Upton Sinclair.

Roosevelt said he wanted to still the unrest before it could take the shape of a political campaign. He indicated that Taft would be the "best possible leader" for 1908.[26]

Immediately, Roosevelt's administration, besides pushing the Hepburn Bill, gave moral support to Congressional attempts to secure pure food and meat inspection laws. T.R.'s efforts met with difficulties, one of them being that Speaker Cannon was blissfully unaware of the social crisis that worried the President. Uncle Joe thought that American civilization, based on "the hustling of the human unit," was "a great success from every standpoint." In fact, he saw "very little unrest in the country just now. I know how hard a few demagogues are working to discredit the prosperity of the nation, but the people are too busy, too prosperous, to make calamity-howling a success. This country is not going backward; it is going forward."[27] Years later he fondly recalled the good old days: "We had no trouble about pure laws or canned goods, for the meat came from the hog pen or the pasture where the cattle and sheep grew fat, the butter from the family churn, and the canned berries were homemade." [28]

Prior to 1906 the federal government did not have ef-

---

26. Theodore Roosevelt to William Howard Taft, March 15. 1906, Roosevelt Papers.
27. *New York Evening Post,* June 19, 1906.
28. L. W. Busbey, *Uncle Joe Cannon,* 36.

fective means for inspecting food and drugs for possible adulteration or for inspecting the sanitation standards of the meat packing industry. What powers the government possessed were either investigative in nature or were concerned with safeguarding the farmer and the export trade and not the general public. The Sherman Act of 1902, for example, made illegal the false branding of food and dairy products as to the state or territory in which they had been produced. Also, in its Agricultural Appropriation Act for 1902, the Congress had authorized the Secretary of Agriculture to investigate the coloring, preservatives and other substances added to foodstuffs: From this provision Dr. Harvey Wiley's "poison squad" came into being. The shocking disclosures it made, and the muckraking of Samuel Hopkins Adams and Upton Sinclair helped to focus public attention on the need for federal regulation of the food and meat packing industries.[29]

Twice the House had passed a pure food bill drawn up by Colonel Hepburn only to have it die in the Senate.[30] Hepburn's bill had aimed to prevent the "adulteration, misbranding, and imitation of foods, beverages, candies, drugs, and condiments" by regulating their production in the District of Columbia and the states and territories and by regulating their flow in interstate commerce. The bill required that packages be labeled, and it made the shipment, receipt, or sale of adulterated foods or drugs in interstate commerce punishable by fine or imprisonment for a second offense knowingly committed.[31] Senator Aldrich led the opposition to a pure food bill. In one of his forays, he argued that the Democrats were trying to trap the Republicans into passing a law which might send dozen of small grocers to prison and cause irreparable damage to the GOP. The Senator posed a ques-

29. Mark Sullivan, *Our Times,* II, 520-4. In *The Jungle,* Sinclair aimed at the public's heart on behalf of socialism; by accident he hit its stomach.
30. *Congressional Record,* 57-2, 458; 58-2, 940.
31. *Ibid.,* 57-1, 184.

tion: "Are we going to take up the question as to what a man shall eat and what a man shall drink, and put him under severe penalties if he is eating or drinking something different from what the chemists of the Agricultural Department think it is desirable for him to eat or drink?"[32]

In the 59th Congress, a powerful friend of this type of legislation in the White House, and the support of public sentiment which had been built up over the years, were strong enough to keep pure food bills from being blocked by the sort of objection Aldrich had raised.[33] This time the Senate led the way; on February 21, 1906, by a vote of 63 to 4, it passed a pure food bill authored by Senator Weldon B. Heyburn of Idaho. Republicans like Aldrich lost their talking point when the bill was amended to provide specifically that, if a retailer could furnish a certificate from the manufacturer guaranteeing that a product was not adulterated, he was in the clear. Southern Democrats accounted for the 4 negative votes.[34]

In the House, it was agreed that a vote on pure food would be taken on April 10, but an appropriation was under discussion at that time, and in the following weeks, bills of higher privilege kept intervening. Friends of pure food legislation were becoming anxious.[35] The *Chicago Tribune* of May 24, 1906 reported that the bill was sleeping to death in the House. Its editor believed that Hepburn and James R. Mann, leading Republicans on the Committee on Interstate and Foreign Commerce, sincerely desired a pure food law. But he thought many members had been frightened by lobbyists and wanted to dodge a vote on the issue.[36]

Theodore Roosevelt had been active in the meantime. Aroused by the unflattering picture of the Chicago stock-

32. *Congressional Record,* 58-3, 263.
33. Mark Sullivan, *Our Times,* II, 531.
34. *Congressional Record,* 59-1, 2773.
35. John Ely Briggs, *William Peters Hepburn,* 282.
36. *Chicago Tribune,* May 24, 1906.

yards which Upton Sinclair had painted in *The Jungle,* the President started his own investigation of the packers.[37] He also prompted Albert J. Beveridge, Republican Senator from Indiana, to introduce a bill empowering the federal government to inspect thoroughly all the processes of the packing houses.[38] Beveridge introduced his bill on May 21, and then as a Senate amendment it was attached to the session's agricultural appropriation bill.[39] This amendment required that all labels on meat products be dated and the cost of government inspection be borne by the packers. Nevertheless, the entire bill passed without a dissenting vote.[40] In the House, it was referred to the Committee on Agriculture of which James W. Wadsworth of New York was the chairman.

Roosevelt promptly wrote Wadsworth, urging the adoption of the Beveridge amendment. The President said that his investigators, Charles P. Neill and James B. Reynolds, had made a report which disclosed a "hideous" situation in Chicago's packing houses. He noted that the packers, through Louis Swift, had promised to remedy all wrongs if the report was not made public. However, the report would be made public if meat inspection legislation that was really in the interest of the stock growers and the packers could not be secured in any other way.[41]

Through his secretary, William R. Loeb, the President queried Speaker Cannon as to whether the pure food bill was going to pass the House. The Speaker replied in noncommittal fashion that the pure food bill was on the Calendar; the House could consider it any day a majority wished to do so. Uncle Joe said he had not canvassed the House on the subject but thought the pure food bill would

37. Mark Sullivan, *Our Times,* II, 537.

38. John A. Coffin, "The Senatorial Career of Albert J. Beveridge," *Indiana Magazine of History* XXIV (December, 1928), 244.

39. *Congressional Record,* 59-1, 7127.

40. *Ibid.,* 59-1, 7421.

41. Theodore Roosevelt to James Wadsworth, May 26, 1906, Roosevelt Papers.

pass when brought to a vote.[42] A reply from Representative Wadsworth on the meat inspection amendment was even less satisfactory. Wadsworth suggested that the government and not the packers should bear the cost of inspection. Roosevelt thought that would be a "ruinous" alteration of the Beveridge amendment. He said that the Secretary of Agriculture, James Wilson, had convinced him the point was important. He saw no other choice except to send the Neill-Reynolds report to Congress.[43]

Roosevelt did just that on June 4. The Neill-Reynolds report was definitely not complimentary to the packers' sanitary methods.[44] Owing to the President's persistence, it seemed certain that both the pure food and meat inspection bills would have to be voted on. The only hope of the opposition was to make them as harmless as possible.[45] Representatives of the packing industry scoffed at the report as an "hysterical outburst." They were disgruntled because the President had seen fit to make it public and they predicted ruin for themselves, and urged Congress to go slow. Neill and Reynolds simply answered that they had reported what they had seen and were not responsible for the agitation caused by the report's release.[46]

The President's action indirectly compelled action on the pure food bill in the House. James R. Mann immediately introduced a resolution calling upon the Committee on Rules for a special order to allow consideration of the bill for two days. Writing in the *Chicago Tribune,* John O'Laughlin reported that Speaker Cannon had consented to action on both pure food and meat inspection bills. In doing so, Uncle Joe announced that the majority of the House had had the power for weeks, upon the action of any member, to consider the pure food bill. What did he have to say about statements that he was opposed to the

42. Joseph G. Cannon to William R. Loeb, May 30, 1906, Roosevelt Papers.
43. Theodore Roosevelt to James Wadsworth, May 31, 1906, Roosevelt Papers.
44. *Congressional Record,* 59-1, 7800-2.
45. Mark Sullivan, *Our Times,* II, 544.
46. *Chicago Tribune,* June 5, 1906.

bill? Nothing! Action spoke louder than words. What about meat inspection? He was informed that the Agriculture Committee was giving it careful consideration and was sure that proper legislation for the benefit of all concerned would be enacted.[47]

The *Racine* (Wisconsin) *Times* gleefully editorialized on the subject, "Cannon Smoked Out." The paper pointed out that the pure food bill had not been considered by the House prior to the President's bold action. Who was responsible? None other than "the absolute master of the House," Speaker Cannon. The members were mere puppets, and if one of them had moved to bring up the pure food bill, he would have been stigmatized as disloyal. Besides, no member could have obtained recognition for making such a motion to the Speaker. The *Racine Times* therefore concluded: "The very fact that no such motion has been made speaks eloquently of the influences that have been at work to prevent action."[48]

Chairman Wadsworth's Agriculture Committee, after holding hearings on the Beveridge meat inspection amendment, finally rejected it by a vote of 9 to 7.[49] Instead, a substitute which said nothing of dated labels and put the cost of inspection on the government was sent to the floor.[50] This brought a warm exchange of letters between Roosevelt and Wadsworth, the President bluntly telling the Congressman: "The more closely I investigate your proposed substitute, the worse I find it."[51]

After the adverse committee action, Roosevelt held a conference with Speaker Cannon. This caused the House minority leader, John Sharp Williams, to observe drily that the pure food and meat inspection bills could not be

---

47. *Chicago Tribune,* June 5, 1906.
48. *Racine* (Wisconsin) *Times,* June 6, 1906. For the attack on Cannon and his defense, "Speaker Cannon's Contentment with Present Foods," and "Speaker Cannon's Reply to His Critics," *Literary Digest* XXXII (June 16 and June 30, 1906), 894-5; 960.
49. Mark Sullivan, *Our Times,* II, 546.
50. *Congressional Record,* 59-1, 8720; House Report, 4953.
51. Theodore Roosevelt to James Wadsworth, June 14, 1906, Roosevelt Papers.

defeated "because the two ruling authorities under this boasted American form of free government—to wit, the President of the United States and the Speaker of the House of Representatives—have consulted together about it and determined upon and prescribed exactly what should be done."[52]

Evidently the prescription was not written by Theodore Roosevelt. On June 20, the meat inspection bill with the Wadsworth amendment attached passed the House without a record vote.[53] The Senate concurred with the House, Senator Porter J. McCumber openly admitting defeat for the administration when he declared: "We have met the enemy and we are theirs."[54]

The *Nation* mournfully related that the President had made "a plain surrender on points which he had declared essential; but by this stooping he conquered, in the sense that he got a law, which, but for his feverish activity, we should not have seen at all."[55]

The President's consultation with Cannon may however, have influenced the Speaker to induce his Rules Committee, finally, to send the pure food bill to the floor on June 20.[56] In fact, Uncle Joe sponsored the necessary special rule, which the House adopted by a vote of 142 to 72.[57] The *Chicago Interocean* declared that the Speaker's action disproved charges against him. He had been all along in favor of getting the pure food bill before the House. Poor management on the part of the bill's sponsors, explained the *Interocean,* had been responsible for the delay. No one believed in pure food more thoroughly than Cannon.[58] The bill passed on June 23 by a vote of

52. *Congressional Record,* 59-1, 8723.
53. *Ibid.,* 59-1, 8729.
54. *Ibid.,* 59-1, 9661.
55. "The Muck Rake Congress," *Nation* LXXXIII (July 5, 1906), 4.
56. John Ely Briggs, *op. cit.,* 283.
57. *Chicago Tribune,* June 21, 1906.
58. *Chicago Interocean,* June 21, 1906. Harvey W. Wiley in his *Autobiography,* 228, 231 says that he believed Cannon "was never entirely won over to the wisdom of such legislation." Wiley gives considerable credit to James R. Mann, but minimizes President Roosevelt's role.

241 to 17, all the negative votes being cast by southern Democrats.[59] For a change, the *Nation* was not critical. Its editor observed that the pure food laws gave the year 1906 a more lasting distinction than even the Hepburn Act could have.[60]

Mindful of the approaching Congressional elections, Joe Cannon stated that the legislative achievements of the first session of the 59th Congress surpassed anything he had seen during his thirty years in Congress. Apparently the Republicans intended to wage their campaign by "pointing with pride."

II

During his campaign for re-election to the Congress in 1906, Cannon encountered stern opposition from organized labor, as it was personified by Samuel Gompers, the patriarch of the American Federation of Labor. To put it mildly, the two were not congenial. Gompers was displeased because Cannon had successfully blocked a literacy test for immigrants in the session just concluded. He also considered Uncle Joe to be "the strategic center of opposition to labor" in the House.[61]

In 1906, with the assistance of Andrew Furuseth, Gompers had drawn up a document called "Labor's Bill of Grievances." It was received with attention and concern by President Roosevelt, who was particularly disturbed by the charge that the government was negligent in enforcing the eight hour law for its own workers and on its contracts. But Gompers and his delegation did not receive a very gracious reception at the Speaker's room in the Capitol. Gompers read the Bill of Grievances: in reply, Cannon asserted that the committees of the House were selected as fairly as possible. Gompers objected that

59. *Congressional Record,* 59-1, 9075-6.
60. "The Year of the Food Laws," *Nation* LXXXII (June 28, 1906), 522-3.
61. Samuel Gompers, *Seventy Years of Life and Labor,* II, 171-2; 239.

labor legislation was being suppressed by unsympathetic committees; whereupon, Cannon declared in emphatic language that Gompers was not "the whole works in the country" and abruptly ended the interview.[62] Cannon's trusted lieutenant, James E. Watson, fearing unfortunate political repercussions, tried in vain to shut off Uncle Joe's tirade against the influential labor leader.[63]

In an attempt to change the *status quo* in the House, Gompers determined upon political action. He decided to engage in the 1906 election campaign in Maine against Charles E. Littlefield, Republican from the sixth district. Gompers held Littlefield, a member of the House Judiciary Committee, directly responsible for killing a bill which would have specifically exempted labor organizations from prosecution under the Sherman Act. A. F. of L. organizers were sent to Littlefield's district to compete against a battery of Republican orators—William Howard Taft, Henry Cabot Lodge, Albert J. Beveridge, James E. Watson, and Joseph G. Cannon. In his autobiography, Gompers complained that Uncle Joe had been especially abusive. He noted with satisfaction, however, that Littlefield's majority was cut from 5000 to 1000.[64]

Cannon, in fact, had not pulled his punches in Maine. He told his Yankee listeners that Gompers had come into Littlefield's district not because the Congressman had failed to represent them, but because he had failed to represent Mr. Gompers, a citizen of New York, who demanded that Congress enact his own will into law. Gompers had read him out of civilization, too, but Uncle Joe said he would rather keep his own self-respect and the regard of law abiding folks than sacrifice the country to the un-American propositions of Mr. Gompers.[65]

Gompers recalled that no other Congressmen of Little-

62. *Ibid.*, II, 242-4
63. James E. Watson, *As I Knew Them*, 98-9.
64. Samuel Gompers, *op. cit.*, II, 238-9; 244-5.
65. The Maine Campaign of 1906, Cannon Papers.

field's ultra-conservative type had requested his aid. But Republican leader William T. Cobb, the Governor of Maine, wrote to Cannon: "That old pirate, Gompers, can't get much satisfaction out of his cruise in Maine waters."[67] Roosevelt agreed with Cannon that "The Maine election was a triumph." But he wished Republican candidates would "quit attacking Gompers." Otherwise, "owing to the imperfections of human nature," the average laboring man would get the impression that Gompers was being attacked as their representative. He ventured advice: "Put all the emphasis on what we have done for labor."[68] Cannon agreed with the President that Gompers should not be "magnified by name or by personal attack" unless it became absolutely necessary late in October. He said that there were enough members of the Federation in his district to defeat him if they voted together solidly.[69] Four or five thousand of them could be formidable; he was glad the railway unions were not federated under Gompers. Even so, John McNamee, the Democratic editor of the *Locomotive Fireman's Magazine* of Indianapolis, had attacked him personally. But Cannon felt safer when he recalled that in the session of Congress just concluded, he had supported the Employer's Liability Act for railroad workers, in fact, had recognized a motion for the suspension of the rules in order to get it passed. In his view, said Uncle Joe, Gompers, who sought the enactment of "class legislation" and proposed to blacklist all who did not assent to his demands, was one of the worst enemies that organized labor could have.[70] Incidentally, William Howard Taft apparently agreed, calling Gompers a "bumptious demagogue."[71] Cannon was thank-

---

66. Samuel Gompers, *op. cit,* 245.
67. William T. Cobb to Joseph G. Cannon, September 11, 1906, Cannon Papers.
68. Theodore Roosevelt to Joseph G. Cannon, September 17, 1906, Cannon Papers
69. Joseph G. Cannon to Theodore Roosevelt, September 22, 1906, Cannon Papers.
70. Joseph G. Cannon to Theodore Roosevelt, September 14, 1906, Roosevelt Papers.
71. William Howard Taft to Theodore Roosevelt, November 4, 1906, Roosevelt Papers.

ful indeed that John Mitchell of the mine workers did not sympathize with Gompers' attacks in the name of organized labor against GOP Congressional candidates.[72]

Both Uncle Joe and Jim Watson worried lest Theodore Roosevelt neglect his duty on behalf of Republican candidates for Congress. Watson urged T. R. to get into the campaign, and the President was glad to oblige.[73] To Henry Cabot Lodge, Roosevelt wrote on August 9, 1906: "I shall convulse the googoos and mugwumps with horror by taking the chance to write a letter making as strong a plea as I know how for the election of a Republican Congress."[74] His endorsement of GOP candidates appeared the next day in the form of a letter to Watson. He wrote:

> With Mr. Cannon as Speaker, working hand in hand and in hearty fashion with the Senate, Congress has accomplished a literally phenomenal amount of good work. It has shown courage, good sense and patriotism that it would be a real and serious misfortune for the country to fail to recognize. . . . A change would substitute purposeless confusion for the present orderly progress along the lines of a carefully thought out policy.[75]

T. R. had told Senator Lodge: "The labor people are utterly unreasonable." He wrote again to say that in his letter to Watson he had "strengthened the part about labor where I thought Cannon took a very manly stand and was entitled to any backing I could give him."[76] But Roosevelt had some misgivings, for he told the Secretary of Agriculture, James Wilson, "I think more wisdom on the part of Speaker Cannon and the Labor Committee in Congress would have averted a good deal of trouble."[77]

---

72. Joseph G. Cannon to William R. Loeb, September 22, 1906, Roosevelt Papers.
73. James E. Watson, *op. cit.*, 73-5.
74. Henry Cabot Lodge, ed., *Selections from the Correspondence of Theodore Roosevelt and Henry Cabot Lodge,* 1884-1918, II, 224-5.
75. Theodore Roosevelt to James E. Watson, August 10, 1906, Cannon Papers.
76. Henry Cabot Lodge, ed., *op. cit.*, 225; 228.
77. Theodore Roosevelt to James Wilson, September 11, 1906. Roosevelt Papers.

Cannon was properly appreciative of the Watson letter. He wrote Roosevelt that it would "do more to assure success to the party in November than all the speeches to be made by those of us who are to be actively engaged in the work of the campaign."[78] William Howard Taft considered the letter "admirable."[79]

Since the Democrats were still their main foe, the Republicans were bedeviled again by the vexatious tariff issue. During the Spring of 1906, the *Washington Post* published a letter on the subject which Cannon had written to John N. Taylor of an Ohio pottery firm. With surprising resignation Uncle Joe had stated:

> I am satisfied that there will be no tariff revision this Congress, but it goes without saying that the desire for a change which exists in the common mind will drive the Republican party, if continued in power, to a tariff revision. I do not want it, but it will come in the not distant future.[80]

Theodore Roosevelt as usual was more concerned than Cannon about revision in the immediate future. Before publishing his endorsement of Republican candidates he told Lodge: "I am glad that the idiot revision feeling is dying out in Massachusetts. It is not dying out in certain regions in the West, however, probably having arisen somewhat later in that section." He intended to say in his letter that the GOP believed in protection, but, of course, was willing to undertake revision "whenever it becomes evident to the American people as a whole that the damage thereby done will be offset by the advantage gained." Roosevelt thought such a statement "preferable to the more naked standpat declaration which Cannon and the leaders of the lower House seem to prefer."[81] In his

78. Joseph G. Cannon to Theodore Roosevelt, August 13, 1906, Roosevelt Papers.
79. William Howard Taft to Theodore Roosevelt, August 14, 1906. Roosevelt Papers.
80. *Washington Post,* April 5, 1906.
81. Henry Cabot Lodge, ed. *op. cit.,* II, 225.

letter to Watson, he indicated that the party stood "unequivocally" for a protective tariff, but that the door was always open for revision.[82]

Having made his own statement, the President wrote at length to Cannon urging the Speaker to "soften down" his own speeches on the tariff, for the term "stand-pat" might irritate too many people.[83] But for the third time in three years where the tariff was concerned, Uncle Joe forced his views on the White House. From his home in Danville he wrote Roosevelt that a "promise now to revise would bring us defeat" in the approaching elections.[84] When Roosevelt's apprehensions that failure to make this pledge would result in a Democratic victory were not realized, he eventually admitted that Cannon had been right: "For the last two years I have accepted your view as to just what we should say on the tariff—or rather as to what we should not say—and I am satisfied that it was wiser than the course I had intended to follow."[85]

In making his own speeches during the campaign, Cannon followed his own inclinations. Before the Republican convention of the 18th Illinois district at Danville, he declared: "The remarkable prosperity under the Dingley law has not been for one class, but for all the people." He used the weight of census statistics to bolster his argument.[86] The *Democratic Campaign Book* pointed out, on the other hand, that the Speaker's statistics showed an increase of 9.4% in average yearly wages between 1890 and 1905 and an increase of 58.7% in the value of manufactured products for the same period. It concluded that the statistics proved the prosperity of the trusts but not the prosperity of the wage-earners. "Mr. Cannon and other Republican orators should confine themselves to

82. Theodore Roosevelt to James E. Watson, August 10, 1906, Cannon Papers.
83. Theodore Roosevelt to Joseph G. Cannon, August 15, 1906, Cannon Papers.
84. Joseph G. Cannon to Theodore Roosevelt, August 17, 1906, Roosevelt Papers.
85. Theodore Roosevelt to Joseph G. Cannon, March 2, 1907, Roosevelt Papers.
86. Speech of August 16, 1906, at Danville, Cannon Papers.

glittering generalities and attempt to prove nothing."[87]

Senator Beveridge was also critical of Cannon's Danville speech. The Indiana Republican wrote to T. R.:

> Mr. Cannon, in his speech at Danville, has utterly missed the meaning of the times. He entirely fails to comprehend the great movement of the American millions which you are leading; he is utterly ignorant of the spirit that is now spreading over this nation. I am sorry, a good deal sorrier than I can say. For I had come to like him tremendously and admire his immense strength of character and mind.

Beveridge thought that nearly all of the older politicians were "like a bunch of belated travelers," who stood waiting to catch a train when as a matter of fact the train had already passed.[88] Roosevelt replied sympathetically that he had been desirous of revising the tariff. "But I confess I do not see how we are going to accomplish this just at this time unless there is a change in the temper of the people, as reflected by their Congressmen."[89] To Leslie Shaw, he wrote that the tariff issue could be met for 1906 "simply by not saying 'stand-pat' in an offensive way."[90]

The *Nation* provided an eloquent editorial on the Speaker:

> His downright and square cut ways are in refreshing contrast with the tricky facilities of the ordinary politician. On the tariff, Mr. Cannon is positively delightful. Here, at any rate, is one sincere believer in it as the source of every blessing. Others may hedge and blush and hem and haw, but your Uncle Joe roundly tells you that 'since the enactment of the first revenue under Washington down to the

87. *Democratic Campaign Book* for 1906, 64-5.
88. Albert J. Beveridge to Theodore Roosevelt, August 22, 1906, Roosevelt Papers.
89. Theodore Roosevelt to Albert J. Beveridge, August 23, 1906, Roosevelt Papers.
90. Theodore Roosevelt to Leslie Mortimer Shaw, September 11, 1906, Roosevelt Papers.

> present time, the periods of prosperity have been under protection, and the periods of adversity have been under the policy of free trade or tariff for revenue only.' This, of course, he devoutly believes that if he hangs a horseshoe on his apple tree at Christmas, he insures a good crop in October. . . . If he stands pat on the tariff, he also stands pat on equity and the principles of law and justice older than the Constitution and underlying it. For that kind of stand-patter the country has urgent need, and may well admire and applaud one of that rare breed among politicians, when it is lucky anough to find him.[91]

The socialist-accented *Arena* filed a vigorous dissent to that line of reasoning: "At almost every point Speaker Cannon has courted the favor of privileged interests in the great battle being waged between the people and the oppressive public-servic corporations, monopolies and trusts. He has seemed determined to out-Aldrich Aldrich in his subserviency to plutocracy." The magazine was certain that his "insolent contempt for the reasonable demands of labor" would boomerang as "the American toilers" became aroused and exerted their strength at the polls against "the arrogant demands of the feudalism of wealth."[92]

Behind the scenes rumors spread that Uncle Joe was going to be the GOP presidential candidate in 1908. T.R., in a moment of weakness not duplicated by the second Roosevelt, had publicly and rather emphatically announced on November 8, 1904, that he was not in the running for the nomination in 1908. At that time he had declared: "On the 4th of March next I shall have served three and a half years and this three and a half years constitutes my first term. The wise custom which limits the President to

91. "Flatfooted Mr. Cannon," *Nation* LXXXIII (August 23, 1906), 156.
92. "Speaker Cannon as the Friend of the Privileged Interests," *Arena* XXXVI (September, 1906), 307-8.

two terms regards the substance and not the form, and under no circumstances will I be a candidate for or accept another nomination."[93]

The party convention in Cannon's own Congressional district endorsed Uncle Joe as the fittest available candidate. The Speaker was wary; he simply stated that no man could refuse the party's nomination, but that it was not to be had for the seeking.[94] The *Washington Post* reported that at the conclusion of a two hour conference at Sagamore Hill between the President and H. C. Loudenslager, W. B. McKinley, James S. Sherman, and Cannon, all members of the Congressional Campaign Committee, Roosevelt had personally told Cannon he would be the next President of the United States. Whereupon Uncle Joe had countered by saying that Roosevelt would have to accept the nomination again.[95] James E. Watson has told a similar story with the setting changed to a fall dinner at the White House.[96]

In any event, Cannon was disturbed by a Berryman cartoon in the *Washington Star* which represented Roosevelt telling him that he would be the next President, assuring him that the cartoon had "no foundation in fact." He did not have "the Presidential bee" nor did he wish to embarrass the administration in the 1906 elections or those who did have "the Presidential bee." "I do not believe for a moment," he said in conclusion, "that you would think I was either knave or fool enough to in any way be privy to inspiring the cartoon."[97] Roosevelt replied in a jocular vein. Of course, he put no stock in the cartoon. "I know your attitude absolutely. All you are trying to do is from the stand point of the welfare of the country and the party, and to strengthen all the factors that can

93. Theodore Roosevelt statement, November 8, 1904, Cannon Papers.

94. *New York Tribune*, August 17, 1906.

95. *Washington Post*, August 17, 1906.

96. James E. Watson, *op. cit.*, 88-9.

97. Joseph G. Cannon to Theodore Roosevelt, August 23, 1906, Cannon Papers.

be brought into play for success in November. You have done your part up to the handle. More power to your elbow."[98]

The Roosevelt-Cannon mutual admiration society worked overtime in 1906. Cannon told his constituents: "In the Executive Department of the Government the record of the party has been brilliant, courageous, and honest, and the name of 'Roosevelt' has become a synonym for all those qualities throughout the realms of civilization."[99] Roosevelt avowed that he had

> no stouter friend than the Speaker of the House. . . . It seems to me that not only as good Republicans but as good citizens we ought to feel that it would be a veritable calamity to have Mr. Cannon, not beaten—as I do not suppose that is possible — but not re-elected by an increased majority, so that his influence will not be impaired. I need not say to you that it is a simple absurdity to portray him as an enemy of labor. People might just as well call him an enemy of capital because he helped pass the interstate commerce bill this year, or favored the employers' liability bill. He is a patriotic American. He is for every man, rich or poor, capitalist or labor man, so long as he is a decent American, and he is entitled to our support because he is a patriotic man.[100]

In accordance with his custom, Cannon made a tour on behalf of other Republican candidates. At Detroit on October 15 he put on a crowd-pleasing performance full of homely anecdotes as well as denunciation of the Democrats.[101] But Roosevelt was not pleased with another of

---

98. Theodore Roosevelt to Joseph G. Cannon, August 25, 1906, Cannon Papers. In a letter to Whitelaw Reid (July 27, 1906, Roosevelt Papers) T.R. had indicated his low opinion of William Jennings Bryan and concluded that "he is so cheap that I think we can beat him with Taft, Root, or Cannon."
99. Speech of August 16, 1906, at Danville, Cannon Papers.
100. Theodore Roosevelt to E. E. Clark, September 5, 1906, Roosevelt Papers.
101. Speech of October 15, 1906, at Detroit; Edwin Denby to Joseph G. Cannon, October 26, 1906, Cannon Papers.

his efforts. He wrote to Lodge on October 25, 1906: "Cannon came to New York where he made a two and a quarter hours' speech on the tariff, the history of the Republican party, the full dinner pail, and various other topics about which the people in New York this year are no more concerned than they are with the embargo or the Dred Scott decision. He half emptied a huge hall, and the meeting was a . . . fizzle."[102]

From Illinois, William Howard Taft reported to the President that the situation looked very good. He did not think there was the slightest danger that Uncle Joe would be defeated. "The report that Uncle Joe was in danger seems to have stirred up a great deal of feeling in his district, and to insure a better vote than otherwise might have been given," Taft wrote.[103] He was angered by "the utterly absurd position" taken by Bryan and other Democrats that a Democratic House was necessary if Roosevelt's policies were to be given continued support. "Every effort to separate you from the lower House, is, as I have had the occasion to say from the stump many times, one of the jokes of a very peculiar campaign."[104]

The election returns were hardly a fizzle. In his 18th Illinois district, Cannon won handily. He garnered 22,804 votes against 12,777 for his Democratic opponent, Charles G. Taylor. Two other candidates accounted for 3,448 votes.[105] President Roosevelt wired: "Three cheers for Uncle Joe and for the people who had the good sense to stand by him."[106] Although the Republicans had to take a reduction in the House, they elected 222 members, the Democrats 164, a net loss of 28 for the GOP. In the Senate,

102. Henry Cabot Lodge ed., *op. cit.*, II, 253.

103. William Howard Taft to Theodore Roosevelt, October 31, 1906, Roosevelt Papers.

104. William Howard Taft to Theodore Roosevelt, November 7, 1906, Roosevelt Papers.

105. See Appendix for results of Cannon's elections.

106. Theodore Roosevelt to Joseph G. Cannon, November 7, 1906, Roosevelt Papers.

they gained four seats which gave them a total of 61 out the 92.[107]

III

Roosevelt's annual message delivered in December, 1906 to the lame duck session of the 59th Congress placed him far ahead of his party. Among other things, he proposed the enactment of a graduated income tax on the ground that "the man of great wealth owes a peculiar obligation to the state, because he derives special advantages from the mere existence of government."[108] The *Nation* had some pertinent comments on his behavior. "Ordinary statesmen are content to gain a painful inch at a time," the paper said. "But Mr. Roosevelt outlines legislation which would convulse the country and occupy Congress for years." Was there a reasonable prospect that any of his vast schemes would be carried out? None whatever. The long session of Congress meeting in December, 1907, would be careful in a presidential year. The short session, December, 1908 to March, 1909, would pass with most of his proposals not even debated. "It is to future contests that Mr. Roosevelt is plainly looking forward."[109]

The cordiality between the President and the Speaker soon vanished. It had never been sincere. "Too long had the proud head of Congress bowed to the imperial will in the White House," declares Pringle. The revolt began in 1907, with Cannon at the head of the rebel forces. "The President was no longer the potent influence he had been for the simple reason that he would go out of office on March 5, 1909."[110] The question of whether Cannon would be a candidate in 1908 was not answered; but there could be no doubt that he would be able to find support.

---

107. *Historical Statistics of the United States,* 293.
108. Henry Litchfield West, "American Politics," *Forum* XXXVIII (January, 1907), 291-2.
109. "The President's Programme," *Nation* LXXIV (June 13, 1907), 534.
110. Henry F. Pringle, *Theodore Roosevelt,* 476.

The 222 GOP representatives constituted the basis for a strong machine.[111]

Roosevelt tried to keep up the pretense after the 1906 election that an era of good feeling between himself and the Speaker was still possible. He wrote to Uncle Joe "as a Nestor in the Republican party and one of the few big men who can still speak first hand of Lincoln," that the Republican Club of New York wanted him to speak at their Lincoln Birthday banquet. "I spoke there two years ago myself, which you must not hold against the club because it could not help itself."[112] He pleaded for the Speaker's good will: "I do not usually feel inclined to try to influence your judgment in matters of home legislation, for my experience has been that your judgment is rather more apt to be sound than mine in such matters. . . . Now, Uncle Joe, stand by me if you can."[113]

Incidentally, the growing hostility toward Theodore Roosevelt was not limited to the legislative branch. At Vicksburg, Mississippi, in October, 1907, the President dared to recommend that the Constitution be interpreted liberally. Though heartily agreeing that the Constitution represented "a fixed series of principles," he held that "it must be interpreted not as a strait-jacket, not as laying the hand of death upon our development, but as an instrument designed for the life and healthy growth of the Nation." Sometimes executive officers and legislators were tempted "to yield too much to an improper public clamor." But he feared the temptation for judges was just the reverse. Supreme Court Justice Brewer was one who levelled a rebuke in the President's direction. "The Constitution," Justice Brewer declared, "is not a criminal code. It is a theory of government and is not to be read in favor of anybody." Likewise Supreme Court Justice Harlan

---

111. *Chicago Tribune,* February 10, 1907.

112. Theodore Roosevelt to Joseph G. Cannon, December 14, 1906, Roosevelt Papers.

113. Theodore Roosevelt to Joseph G. Cannon, March 2, 1907, Roosevelt Papers.

expressed regret over the trend toward centralization in government that Roosevelt apparently approved.[114]

Whether Joe Cannon was ever a serious candidate for the Presidency in 1908, and if so, whether his aspiration affected his loyalty to the Roosevelt administration, must remain a riddle as far as the written evidence is concerned.[115] A careful reading of Cannon's papers simply discloses that a large number of influential Republican politicians were interested in his candidacy. While Cannon's answers varied from time to time, there was a refrain in them to the effect that the party could go farther, do worse, and probably would. Most of the correspondence on the subject took place in 1907 before the 60th Congress convened for the first time. So it is possible that many of the assurances of support from Republican Congressmen were not entirely sincere. GOP adherents in Illinois, of course, could hope that Cannon might really be able to follow in the footsteps of "the First Railsplitter." James R. Mann, a Representative of Chicago's Hyde Park district, was strong for Cannon.[116] So was Senator Shelby M. Cullom, a party patriarch in Illinois who had authored the original Interstate Commerce Act. Cullom believed that the President was determined to nominate either himself or Taft, but that the state ought to go unanimously for Uncle Joe.[117] Cannon was certain that it would.[118] He also fancied that "some of the other state delegations might go that way if the President should not have the nomination forced upon him."[119] Taft, in his judgment, had "the respect and regard of the people, but would have no considerable following for the nomination if he were not believed to be the President's choice."[120] In another letter,

114. Henry F. Pringle, *Theodore Roosevelt,* 477.

115. L. W. Busbey, *Uncle Joe Cannon,* xx-xxii, indicates that Cannon "did not consider himself intellectually unfit to be President."

116. *Chicago Interocean,* May 25, 1907.

117. Shelby M. Cullom to Joseph G. Cannon, April 25, 1907, Cannon Papers.

118. Joseph G. Cannon to Wesley L. Jones, May 3, 1907, Cannon Papers.

119. Joseph G. Cannon to F. S. Brien, May 6, 1907, Cannon Papers.

120. Joseph G. Cannon to David J. Foster, May 9, 1907, Cannon Papers.

by means of an anecdote, he indicated the time was not ripe for the formation of an organization to seek the nomination.[121] He wrote that he would welcome their support if convention sentiment leaned toward him.[122]

The *New York Evening Post* saw signs that "reactionary sentiment" within the GOP was turning toward Cannon. The paper said the reactionaries desired Uncle Joe because they knew that he wore "the face of the reformer but has the heart of a reactionary."[123] At Springfield, Illinois the state House of Representatives accorded him a reception. He was introduced by Speaker Shurtleff as the next President. The *Chicago Interocean,* a Cannon advocate, found significance in the fact that Uncle Joe did not express objection to the appellation, but beamed smilingly on the gathering.[124]

Charles H. Grosvenor, a long time colleague, told Cannon in October, 1907, that his chances of being nominated were as good if not better than those of anyone else.[125] William S. Greene, a member of Congress from Massachusetts, declared only two things stood in the way of his triumphant nomination and election, his age and his profanity. The former could not be helped, while the latter should not really count against him, because it was not real irreverence but merely a habit of speech.[126] The Illinois Congressional delegation endorsed the Speaker at a meeting in Chicago's Auditorium Hotel during October, 1907. When told what his brethren had done, Uncle Joe threw up his arms and said: "Well, boys will be boys. Do as you please."[127] The *Decatur Review* commented drily that the "boys" had not found Cannon's age (71) to be a disqualifying factor. On the contrary, they believed

121. Joseph G. Cannon to W. H. Wade, June 29, 1907, Cannon Papers.
122. Joseph G. Cannon to Elmer J. Burkett, July 3, 1907 and to Charles E. Townsend, July 14, 1907, Cannon Papers.
123. *New York Evening Post,* May 3, 1907.
124. *Chicago Interocean,* May 9, 1907.
125. Charles H. Grosvenor to Joseph G. Cannon, October 12, 1907, Cannon Papers.
126. *New York Sun,* January 8, 1908.
127. *Washington Herald,* October 29, 1907.

that a man of his age could never embarrass them with a wish for a third term.[128] The possibility that the convention might go "lickety brindle to Cannon" or another well known conservative worried the editor of the *Emporia Gazette*, William Allen White, who conveyed his fear to Theodore Roosevelt.[129]

The campaign for Cannon continued to attract attention in the early months of 1908. William F. Draper of the American Protective Tariff league recognized a good friend when he saw one and assured Uncle Joe that he was the League's favorite candidate.[130] But a Cannon organization was lacking as the *Chicago Interocean* was well aware.[131] Uncle Joe wrote to B. M. Chiperfield, March 10, 1908: "Frankly, if there is any real sentiment for me in Illinois what is needed is for those who do things and who are on the ground to organize that sentiment and see that it materializes. It seems to me, that if Illinois shall present in good faith my name to the Convention it will have more than an even chance of being successful."[132]

When the power of the Roosevelt-Taft combination became all too evident, Cannon changed his tune. He wrote to Federal Judge P. S. Grosscup of Chicago: "I have been somewhat embarrassed by the connection of my name with the nomination for the Presidency. So far as I see I have no prospect of success, and I had no desire for the nomination."[133] The Cannon for President campaign was finally responsible for a song called "Grand Old Uncle Joe," for a number of magazine articles, some favorable and some not, and for ovations and complimentary votes in the Convention for Uncle Joe.[134]

---

128. *Decatur Review,* October 30, 1907.
129. William Allen White to Theodore Roosevelt, November 22, 1907, White Papers.
130. William F. Draper to Joseph G. Cannon, January 17, 1908, Cannon Papers.
131. *Chicago Interocean,* February 11, 1908.
132. Joseph G. Cannon to B. M. Chiperfield, March 10, 1908, Cannon Papers.
133. Joseph G. Cannon to P. S. Grosscup, April 13, 1908, Cannon Papers.
134. H. S. Boutell, "Speaker Cannon and the Presidency," *Independent* LXIV (April 23, 1908), 894-99; H. S. Boutell, "Joseph Gurney Cannon," *North*

Of more immediate concern to Cannon in 1907 was the Speakership. The *Washington Post* suggested that President Roosevelt was determined to make Theodore Burton of Ohio Speaker of the House on the pretext that Uncle Joe had not been thoroughly in accord with his policies.[135] Charles H. Grosvenor assured Cannon that nothing the President could do would keep Uncle Joe from being elected Speaker for the third time.[136]

Trade unionists thoroughout the country were urged to campaign against Cannon's re-election in a circular issued by the American Federation of Labor over the signature of Samuel Gompers.[137] Entrenched in his position as he was, it is doubtful whether Cannon was ever worried. When the Congress met in December, 1907, he was re-elected to his office without a protesting Republican vote. The *Milwaukee News* chortled that Samuel Gompers' widely advertised fight against Uncle Joe's re-election had not succeeded "in drawing of any blood from the Cannon cuticle." The paper suspected that as a politician Mr. Gompers was a "blank cartridge."[138]

In accepting the GOP caucus nomination the Speaker directed some verbal shots at the President. Mr. Roosevelt had come out in favor of an income tax and an inheritance tax. Cannon wanted neither of them. "In my judgment," he said, "it is not wise to increase the revenue of Government, nor is it necessary or advisable to transfer burdens from the local and state treasuries to the Federal Treasury—to foster a centralizing power and responsibility which of necessity develops quite enough."[139]

In his annual message delivered to the new 60th Con-

American Review CLXXXVII (May, 1908), 641-47; Sydney Brooks, "Presidential Possibilities," *Living Age* CCLVII (June 6, 1908), 579-89; Alfred Henry Lewis, "Some Presidential Candidates; Speaker Joseph Gurney Cannon," *Human Life* (April, 1908), 9-10 and 32-33.

135. *Washington Post,* May 14, 1907.
136. Charles H. Grosvenor to Joseph G. Cannon, May 15, 1907, Cannon Papers.
137. *Chicago Tribune,* October 31, 1907.
138. *Milwaukee News,* December 3, 1907.
139. *New York Sun,* December 3, 1907.

gress, Roosevelt outlined enough topics to keep the legislators busy for many months. Among other things, he suggested federal licensing of corporations, federal supervision of the issuing of railway securities and the legalizing of pooling agreements, federal income and inheritance taxes, federal investigation of labor disputes and laws to regulate the employment of women and children, the establishment of a postal savings system and the expansion of parcel post, the creation of forest reserves in the White Mountains and the Southern Appalachians, and the admission of wood pulp free of duty.[140]

When the Congress met, however, the country was in the middle of a financial panic, with the result that a large part of the first session was devoted to the discussions of cures and preventives for panics. In his message the President had urged Congress to do something to achieve a more elastic currency—as he had before—but he did not specify what he wanted. Though he continued to call for action, he does not appear to have taken an active part in framing banking and currency legislation to meet the emergency.[141]

Most radical and far reaching of the Republican proposals was the Fowler Bill, emanating from the New Jersey Congressman's Committee on Banking and Currency. As introduced on January 8, 1908, his bill included such unrelated provisions as the unification of national banks into groups for mutual supervision, the replacement of the existing currency secured by U. S. bonds by a currency based on commercial paper, and the guarantee of bank deposits.[142] From the very provisions of the bill it can be deduced easily that Speaker Cannon was firmly opposed to it.

---

140. Henry Litchfield West, "American Politics," *Forum* XXIX (January, 1908), 314.
141. Lawrence Chamberlain, *The President, Congress and Legislation,* 311.
142. A. P. Andrew, "Currency Legislation of 1908," *Quarterly Journal of Economics* XXII (August, 1908), 666.

In the Senate, meanwhile, discussion was focused on the Aldrich Bill, which had been introduced by the powerful chairman of the Finance Committee. His original bill would have allowed national banks to issue emergency notes against the bonds of the more substantial railroad and public utility companies. But Aldrich gave up that type of security on March 17, 1908, just before Robert M. LaFollette, the crusading Wisconsin Republican, could deliver a tirade against it.[143] National banks were still to be the issuing agents of emergency currency, but federal, state, and municipal bonds were to secure the notes.[144] On March 27, 1908, the Senate passed the Aldrich Bill, 42 to 16.[145]

Bitter hostility from the American Banker's Association and an unfriendly House leadership were too much for the Fowler Bill to overcome; and the House Committee on Banking and Currency promptly tabled the Aldrich measure. A special group of House Republicans led by Representative Vreeland of New York (and not including Fowler) drew up a brand new bill. It provided for an emergency currency based on commercial paper and for a National Currency Commission to study and report on a permanent measure.[146] After some parliamentary maneuvering, the House passed the Vreeland Bill on May 13th, 185 to 145, in a strictly partisan vote.[147]

The disagreement between the houses necessitated a conference from which the final Aldrich-Vreeland measure emerged. Speaker Cannon, significantly, omitted Fowler from the group of House conferees. Subsequently, at the beginning of the next Congress, he saw to it that the Committee on Banking and Currency had a new chairman. Fowler then threw in his lot with the growing Insurgent band and did his best to exorcise the demon Cannonism.

143. Robert M. LaFollette, *Autobiography,* 466.
144. *Congressional Record,* 60-1, 3421.
145. *Ibid.,* 60-1, 4025.
146. Lawrence Chamberlain, *op. cit.,* 312.
147. *Congressional Record,* 60-1, 6294-5.

The Aldrich-Vreeland Bill, incidentally, became law according to the prescription of the House and despite a dramatic filibuster by Senator LaFollette.[148] The bill received its final form in a private conference between Aldrich, Cannon, and Vreeland in Aldrich's rooms in the Arlington Hotel.[149]

Despite Presidential pressure the Congress tried to confine itself to masterly inactivity. The Speaker's equanimity was ruffled by the Democrats to a greater extent than usual. Their leader, John Sharp Williams, in order to direct attention to Congressional inactivity, began demanding roll calls "on every affirmative matter of legislation." Of course the Republicans lost no time in throttling his efforts as much as possible. Williams once objected: "We have gotten to the point where the procedures of this House lie within the secret conscience of the Speaker. There is no duty any more for him to communicate his reasons, his motives, or his feelings to the House." And at least once his friendship with Cannon suffered a temporary collapse. On April 18, 1908, the Speaker declared the House adjourned when Williams was on his feet clamoring for recognition. The angry minority leader refused the Speaker's proffered handshake as the members made their way out of the House chamber. But by the end of the Congress all was forgiven; Williams offered the usual vote of thanks to the Speaker.[150]

Suffragettes badgered the Speaker, who avoided a conclusive statement, but said that he did not think women wanted to vote. He doubted that anyone was entitled to more than one vote, and a woman would have her own and her husband's. In any case, Uncle Joe thought the suffragettes were wasting their time in Washington working for a Constitutional amendment. They should first

148. *Ibid.*, 60-1, 7078; 7260.
149. N. W. Stephenson, *Nelson W. Aldrich*, 330.
150. George Coleman Osborn, "Joseph G. Cannon and John Sharp Williams," *Indiana Magazine of History* XXXV (June, 1939), 289-90.

concentrate on increasing the list of three states which allowed them to vote.[151]

To a delegation from the Methodist Episcopal Church, headed by Governor J. Frank Hanly of Indiana, which wanted Congress to pass the Littlefield Bill on the liquor traffic, Cannon gave a little advice but no comfort. The delegation presented a resolution which stated that the liquor traffic had been excluded from seventy per cent of the U. S. territorial area containing a population of 38,000,000. But the effectiveness of state action was seriously impaired by the lack of federal legislation prohibiting interstate shipments of intoxicants into such territory. The Littlefield Bill which was before the Judiciary Committee was quite satisfactory to them on that point. All doubts of the measure's constitutionality should be resolved in behalf of the public welfare, said the delegation, which represented itself as voicing "the awakened conscience of a Christian people and the high resolve of millions of Christian freemen." Uncle Joe pointed out that he did care about the constitutionality of the Littlefield Bill even though the Methodist petitioners did not. He did not believe that Congress could prohibit the sale, use, or manufacture of liquor in any state. It might, he thought, prohibit a common carrier engaged in interstate commerce from being the agent of the vendor or the purchaser of the liquor. But the states, including Indiana, had not exercised their own police powers to the fullest extent possible. "I suggest with all becoming modesty to the various states, had we not better remove the beam from our own eyes before we seek to remove the mote from the eye of a neighbor?"[152]

Samuel Gompers, in an interview with the Speaker on March 19, 1908, spoke out against "the indifference if not actual hostility" which Congress had shown toward "the

151. *Chicago Interocean,* March 22, 1908.

152. *Congressional Record,* 60-1, Appendix 176-9. The interview took place on May 8, 1908. Eventually he voted for the 18th Amendment. *Record,* 65-2, 469.

reasonable and righteous measures proposed by the workers for the safeguarding of their rights and interests." Labor, "justly indignant," desired Congress to supply relief by passing a law specifically exempting labor unions from prosecution under the Sherman Anti-Trust Act so that the Danbury Hatter's decision could not set a precedent. Even monarchical England, said Gompers, had passed a Trade Disputes Act to relieve its workers from the effects of the Taff Vale Decision. The American republic could do no less. Gompers said he also wanted the passage of the Pearre Bill to regulate the issuance of injunctions. In reply, the Speaker said that he was only one Representative of almost four hundred. He believed the United States was blessed with the best form of government on earth, "and in the fullness of time," all laws conformed to popular sentiment. Referring to the Danbury Hatter's case in which the Supreme Court had ruled that a combination of labor unions attempting to boycott a dealer's goods was in restraint of trade in the meaning of the Sherman Act, Uncle Joe said he saw nothing in the decision which rendered labor unions unlawful. He told "Brother Gompers" that he, like every other citizen, had recourse to the ballot-box, and ended the interview by affirming his belief that an employer had the right to discharge a man for any reason including union membership.[153]

Nine bills were introduced in the 60th Congress for the establishment of forest reserves in the White Mountains and the Southern Appalachians. According to Gifford Pinchot, the Speaker's position was "not one cent for scenery."[154] The *Outlook* pointed out that such a project had been repeatedly recommended by the President and even had been unanimously approved by the House Agriculture Committee of the 59th Congress. But

153. *Ibid.*, 60-1, 3765-8.

154. Gifford Pinchot, *Breaking New Ground*, 240.

Speaker Cannon was opposed to it, and in the new Congress referred the bill to the Judiciary Committee, which was more likely to agree with his view. The committee was to decide upon the bill's constitutionality.[155] De Alva Stanwood Alexander of that committee claimed that the House and not the Speaker was responsible for referring the forestry section of the President's message to the Judiciary Committee and that the Speaker had not tried to influence the members of the committee.[156]

In an effort to get to the root of the matter, Henry A. Barker of the American Civic Association wrote a forceful letter to the Speaker. Barker thought that Cannon, "a man of directness," would like to know that Republicans favorable to the forest reserves doubted that the question of constitutionality could be determined until too late in the session for action. Had the committee been instructed by Cannon to delay its decision?[157] Uncle Joe replied that he was "too busy with real matters of legislation" to waste time answering Barker's allegations.[158]

The belief that the Speaker could practically pass the bill if he so desired persisted among the proponents of conservation. After the Judiciary Committee pronounced the bill constitutional as far as it was concerned, Cannon was told that he alone was thwarting the will of the people and assisting in the destruction of the forests and other natural resources.[159] A bill, providing for the new reserves and named for John W. Weeks of Massachusetts, did pass the House on March 1,1909, 157 to 147,[160] But it was too late for Senate action.[161] Not until March, 1911, after Cannon had gone through the attack of the

155. "Government by Oligarchy," *Outlook* LXXXIX (May 2, 1908), 12.
156. "The Speaker, Committees, and the House," *Outlook* LXXXIX (May 16, 1908), 129.
157. Henry A. Barker to Joseph G. Cannon, April 9, 1908, Cannon Papers.
158. Joseph G. Cannon to Henry A. Barker, April 13, 1908, Cannon Papers.
159. William North Rice to Joseph G. Cannon, May 14, 1908, Cannon Papers.
160. *Congressional Record*, 60-2, 3566.
161. *Ibid.*, 60-2, 3749-51.

Insurgents and was about to retire as Speaker, did the Weeks Bill finally become law.

In the presidential year of 1908 the tariff issue as usual caused a good deal of commotion. President Roosevelt had asked for the repeal of the duties on wood pulp, most of which came from Canada, the intent being to lower the price of newsprint. Almost without exception the newspapers of the country, though many of them were ultra-protectionists on everything else, were anxious to have the tariff on their chief raw material abolished. To accomplish that end, the American Newspaper Publisher's Association headed by Herman Ridder tried to cultivate the good will of Speaker Cannon.

Uncle Joe was not at all sure that the placing of wood pulp on the free list would materially affect the price. Mr. Ridder was demanding that he pass the bill, but without the cooperation of the Ways and Means Committee and the Republican majority in the House, of course, that was impossible. Even if the bill should pass the House, he wrote, "it would be subject to unlimited amendment in the Senate, where it would either sleep the sleep of death or precipitate a revision of the tariff on the eve of the campaign."[162]

Cannon, therefore, decided to declare his own kind of war on the print paper trust so-called. On April 2, 1908, he introduced two resolutions in the House, one directing the Department of Justice to report what steps had been taken to dissolve the trust, and the other calling on the Secretary of Commerce and Labor to report any investigation made by its Bureau of Corporations into the workings of the paper companies, especially International Paper of New York. The Speaker told the House that the duty on wood pulp and newsprint since 1890 had been 15% *ad valorem*. Newspaper publishers and Mr. Ridder claimed

162. Joseph G. Cannon to L. J. White, March 28, 1908, Cannon Papers.

that prices had been advanced more than equal to the duty. If this were true, a trust conspiracy and not the tariff was the reason.[163]

The newspapers and the Democrats were not put off so easily. Herman Ridder wrote to Cannon that the ranking Republican members on the Ways and Means Committee, John Dalzell and Sereno E. Payne, had declared that under no circumstances would they permit the Stevens Bill, which placed wood pulp and newsprint on the free list, to be reported from their committee. But eighty Republicans and all the Democrats in the House—an absolute majority—had pledged themselves in writing to support the principles contained in the Stevens Bill. "I am sure that the Hon. Joseph G. Cannon, the Speaker, who is a broad minded man will favor this proposition to bring the matter before the House and allow a vote to be taken thereon."[164]

According to the recollections of James E. Watson, Mr. Ridder, who was also treasurer of the Democratic National Committee, was intent on driving a wedge right through the middle of the Republican party. So intent was he that, in return for Cannon's allowing the subject of free wood pulp and newsprint to be brought up in the House, he intimated that the publishers could make Uncle Joe the next President. Flattery got Ridder nowhere. The Speaker reminded him that he was hardly in a position to be giving away the Presidency.[165]

But Uncle Joe did modify his tactics. He engineered the appointment of a special committee to investigate the International Paper Company. The committee's membership included four Republicans and two Democrats. James R. Mann, Cannon's professional objector on the floor,

163. *Chicago Tribune* and *Chicago Interocean,* April 3, 1908.
164. Herman Ridder to Joseph G. Cannon, April 9, 1908, Cannon Papers.
165. James E. Watson, *As I Knew Them,* 116-8. Busbey, *op. cit.,* 282-292, repeats this story at considerable length. Ridder always denied there was any truth in it. Blair Bolles, *Tyrant from Illinois,* 116, uncritically accepts Cannon's version.

was named chairman. Democrats David DeArmond and John Sharp Williams charged in vain that the Speaker's new move was a pretense to avoid action.[166] The American Newspaper Publisher's Association protested against the creation of the investigating committee as a "subterfuge . . . inspired in bad faith."[167] The *Chicago Tribune* editorialized that the GOP House leadership had maneuvered itself into a bad spot. The paper observed that the Democrats were circulating a petition asking the Speaker to give the Stevens Bill the right of way. "The responsibility is clearly up to the Speaker and the committee on rules for refusing to take any action on the recommendation of President Roosevelt and the repeated petitions and demands of newspaper editors and managers of the whole country."[168]

Medill McCormick, chairman of a special committee from the American Newspaper Publisher's Association, Herman Ridder, and others began the presentation of their arguments to the House itself with a lively interlude in the Speaker's room. Herman Ridder and Uncle Joe locked horns. Ridder claimed the Speaker was much too persistent in holding up the Stevens Bill; Cannon boiled over and charged, in language needing fumigation, that Ridder was indulging in a campaign of deliberate misrepresentation. James R. Mann gave assurances of fair play.[169]

As a means of obtaining a positive demonstration of the attitude of House Republicans toward the Stevens Bill, the publishers requested the Speaker to allow the bill to be discussed informally at a conference of the majority members to be held on the currency question. Cannon flatly refused to entertain their request. He asserted the tariff would not be taken up at the conference. That was a matter for the Mann Committee and would not be

166. *Chicago Examiner*, April 22, 1908.
167. E. H. Baker to Joseph G. Cannon, April 23, 1908, Cannon Papers.
168. *Chicago Tribune*, April 25, 1908.
169. *Chicago Tribune*, April 26, 1908.

discussed informally or otherwise until the Committee reported.[170]

John Sharp Williams then took up the attack. In the course of a cleverly humorous and satirical speech on April 29, 1908, the minority leader unrolled and displayed a petition to the Speaker bearing the signatures of 164 of the 166 Democratic members. The petition requested Cannon to recognize any Representative to move to discharge the Ways and Means Committee from further consideration of and to suspend the rules and pass the Stevens Bill, or any other bill having the effect of placing wood pulp and newsprint on the free list. Williams noted that when the remaining two Democratic signatures were added, only thirty Republicans would be needed to swell the strength of the petition to majority strength. Since almost thirty Republicans had introduced free paper bills, in good faith of course, it should be easy to get their signatures. The Speaker had said that a majority of the House would always be heeded. Williams argued:

> So if you put thirty names to our 166 and constitute 196, a majority of the House of Representatives, I know that the eminently good natured man who presides over this House, who is so tolerant of opposition, so patient whenever there is a stumbling block across his pathway, will bow in his most elegant manner with the gesticulation that is peculiar to him, and say: 'Gentlemen, a majority of the Representatives of the American people have a right to their way and I will recognize somebody.'"[171]

Williams' exhortation caused the independent *Chicago Evening Post* to comment on the degradation of the House. The *Post* said that Williams, despite his buffoonery, had forced upon the country "the almost incredible spectacle of 164 duly elected representatives of the people pleading

170. *Chicago Tribune,* April 28, 1908.
171. *Chicago Tribune,* April 30, 1908.

in vain for the mere opportunity to present to their fellow legislators in any shape or form a legislative proposal which they unitedly favored." The paper had a gloomy conclusion: "With solemn humbug, with party buncombe, with ancient political cant Speaker Cannon has completed the wretched work of turning the free legislative assembly of Democracy into a shameless autocracy. He himself, single and unaided," said the *Post,* "now dares to speak, think, and act for 386 men. . . . The rule of the majority, a fundamental principle of the nation, he disregards with a cool impudence that would not be tolerated in the Russian duma." [172]

For Victor Lawson's *Chicago Record-Herald,* Walter Wellman wrote that the GOP was in grave peril because of the "well-nigh inexplicable attitude of Speaker Cannon and the other House leaders on the wood pulp question." If they dared to treat the newspapers in such fashion on the eve of a Presidential campaign, what would they do to the representatives of other industries after the election was over?[173] Wellman reported that the President had invited Cannon to the White House and told him bluntly that he would be responsible for the Republican defeat at the polls unless he did something for the public interest. T. R. particularly wanted the Stevens Bill passed. Uncle Joe argued that it was not necessary to pass a bill just because the newspaper publishers wanted it passed. The country would declare that the Republicans had discriminated in favor of the newspapers, and the party would have to bear the righteous indignation of the voters.[174]

Late in May, 1908, James R. Mann's select committee of six submitted majority and minority reports. The majority reported that the price of paper would not be affected to any considerable degree by the passage of the

172. *Chicago Evening Post,* April 30, 1908.
173. *Chicago Record-Herald,* May 4, 1908.
174. *Chicago Record-Herald,* May 6, 1908.

Stevens Bill. Nor was there any combination in restraint of trade in the paper industry. The minority report concluded that paper and pulp should be placed on the free list and that a good case for unlawful combination in violation of the Sherman Act could be made.[175] There the matter rested.

Mr. Roosevelt's letters to the Speaker, often indicating presidential impatience, were another annoyance that Cannon had to take. Roosevelt feared that the Interstate Commerce Commission would be handcuffed by too small an appropriation, thus bringing discredit on the administration responsible for the passage of the Hepburn Act, and he told the Speaker so in frank language.[176] But the President was especially insistent in pressing upon Congress his demand for four new battleships and the establishment of a base at Pearl Harbor. He wrote: "I am acting with a view to the emergencies that there is a reasonable chance may arise within the next decade or two." Considerations of economy should not be allowed to offset the far greater need of guaranteeing "the national honor and interest."[177] If Cannon knew "the stormy time" he had been having on the Speaker's behalf, he would look favorably on the request.[178] In the end, only two battleships (and an appropriation for Pearl Harbor) were authorized, but the President believed he had won. "I knew I would not get two and have those two hurried up unless I made a violent fight for four."[179]

The exigencies of a campaign year made Joe Cannon strive for harmony within the party. At a Gridiron dinner early in 1908, the President aimed a few well-chosen words at Senators, especially Joseph B. Foraker of Ohio, who lacked respect for the executive branch of the govern-

---

175. *Chicago Evening Post,* May 28, 1908.

176. Theodore Roosevelt to Joseph G. Cannon, April 30, 1908, Roosevelt Papers.

177. Theodore Roosevelt to Joseph G. Cannon, February 29, 1908, Roosevelt Papers.

178. Theodore Roosevelt to Joseph G. Cannon, March 23, 1908, Roosevelt Papers.

179. Theodore Roosevelt to Henry White, April 17, 1908, Roosevelt Papers.

ment. Foraker, no shrinking violet, suggested rather forcefully that the President should have more respect for Senators. Uncle Joe finally intervened as peacemaker with humorous remarks to the effect that the world would go on turning even without that particular roomful of very important persons. There was no use getting excited.[180]

But President Roosevelt could write to Theodore Jr. on May 12, 1908, and really mean it when he said: "I am now ending my experience with Congress for the year, giving and taking heavy blows."[181] The President was less than enthusiastic about the record of Congress. He told Whitelaw Reid on May 25, 1908:

> Congress is ending, by no means in a blaze of glory. The leaders in the House and Senate felt a relief that they did not try to conceal at the fact that I was not to remain as President, and need not be too implicitly followed; and they forgot that the discipline they have been able to keep for the last six years was primarily due to the fact that we had a compact and aggressive organization, kept together by my leadership, due to my hold, and the hold the policies I championed had upon the people. Accordingly they have seen their own power crumble away under their hands and both the House and Senate are now in chaos. All opposition to Taft has died down and he will be nominated easily. But in electing him we shall have no help from the record of the present Congress. The election must be won upon his own personality; upon the general Republican achievement of the past twelve years; and, by no means least, upon the rather absurd attitude of the Democracy.[182]

The *Arena* took an extremely critical position on the

180. Henry L. Stoddard, *As I Knew Them, Presidents and Politics from Grant to Coolidge,* 330-1.
181. Theodore Roosevelt to Theodore Jr., May 12, 1908, Roosevelt Papers.
182. Theodore Roosevelt to Whitelaw Reid, May 25, 1908, Roosevelt Papers.

work of Congress and especially that of the House. The magazine spoke of Cannon and his lieutenants receiving "princely salaries" from the "industrial autocracy" for zealous and effective services rendered in accomplishing what was really "a record of shame." It said that "flagrant defiance" of the popular will was a typical Cannon attitude.[183]

There were some, to be sure, who were pleased with the record of Congress. Charles H. Grosvenor told Speaker Cannon:

> You have had a contest in Washington with elements that were new and awful and I sincerely believe that you have achieved greater renown in the management of the things that you have done, than in any previous campaign of your life.[184]

Uncle Joe, on his part, was willing to go into the 1908 election on his record. He considered the LaFollette-Victor Murdock type of Republican "worse Populists than Bryan himself and more dangerous. . . . I am being magnified far beyond my merit, and magnified for a safe and sane party organization and party policy:" He was determined to keep his own "self respect, without apologizing for the legislation that has been enacted or being intimidated by the howl of the enemy, who, lacking merit, seek by damnable iteration to make the people believe a lie."[185]

If a politician is loved by his constituents for the enemies he has made, "Dear Old Uncle Joe" should have been assured of an unprecedented majority in 1908. Muckraking journalists were abroad in the land telling their readers that he was a cynical and tyrannical old czar. Not only had Cannon been contemptuous of them, but he had dared to treat the whole newspaper fraternity in cavalier

183. "Speaker Cannon and the Destruction of Popular Rule in the House of Representatives," *Arena XL* (July, 1908), 89-91.
184. Charles H. Grosvenor to Joseph G. Cannon, June 5, 1908, Cannon Papers.
185. Joseph G. Cannon to Frank P. MacLennan, April 3, 1908, Cannon Papers.

fashion. He had stirred up one hornet's nest after another: reformers who aimed at forest conservation or prohibition; Sam Gompers and the American Federation of Labor; and even the National Association of Manufacturers whose proposals for a tariff commission he had blithely ignored. He had dared to disregard almost all of the Rooseveltian policies supposed to be so dear to the hearts of so many people. He had roused the Democrats to unusual forms of opposition, and some members of his own party had concluded that his sterling qualities were fewer than they had once thought. They were becoming vocal in their opposition to his regime in the House. Evidently, at the age of seventy-two, Speaker Cannon had reached the most eventful part of his career.

CHAPTER FIVE

The Incorporation of Taft, Cannon And Company

"Anyone who thinks you can run a free government of 80,000,000 of people without party organization, is mistaken. When this government ceases to be a government of and by parties, it ceases to be a free government. It is the unwritten law of our country that when the majority has fairly expressed its will at the polls, the majority shall control until such times as the people have a chance to speak again."

Joseph G. Cannon in *The Hamiltonian* (A publication of the Hamilton Club of Chicago), IV September, 1903, Cannon Papers.

When the National Convention of the Grand Old Party met in Chicago on June 16, 1908, its "stand-pat" wing had several leading candidates for the presidential nomination. President Roosevelt, however, as early as 1907 had indicated that he would support his affable Secretary of War, William Howard Taft, for the nomination. Unless the Convention were to stampede for another man, the general expectation was that the presidential preference would be ratified in short order.

Senator Henry Cabot Lodge, a close personal friend of the President, acted as permanent chairman. While some members of the Taft family distrusted Lodge, his conduct was all that Roosevelt or Taft could have wanted. In his opening speech, Lodge called Roosevelt "the best abused and most popular man in the United States today." Pro-Roosevelt delegates and galleryites thereupon broke into a rousing demonstration for "four more years of Teddy," but Lodge threw cold water on their hopes. He announced that Roosevelt was retiring on his own volition, that his decision was "final and irrevocable." The next day, the names of Cannon, Vice-President Charles W. Fairbanks, Charles Evans Hughes, Philander C. Knox, Joseph B. Foraker, Robert M. LaFollette and William Howard Taft were placed in nomination to the accompniment of the florid brand of oratory peculiar to American party conventions. Lodge then called the roll; Taft was nominated, as expected on the first ballot. President Roosevelt was pleased at the efficient way in which the gentleman from Massachusetts had handled the "peculiarly delicate and difficult work at Chicago."[1] The President fretted, however, about the nomination of Representative James S. Sherman of New York to be Taft's running mate. He told Lodge that Sherman's nomination would be helpful in New York but not in the Mississippi valley where, as a member of the House Rules Committee, he was identified with Cannon, "and I have been disturbed by the extent of the hostility to and the revolt against Cannon."[2]

During the convention Cannon made an off-hand statement to the press which is worthy of mention in view of his position and subsequent events. He said: "I should rather have people wish I were President than be President. As for the second place, I would not be Vice-President for a Vice-President can enter no caucuses and can name no committees."[3]

William Allen White recalled that while the delegates "obeyed vox populi, which was the bidding of Theodore Roosevelt in the White House," Joe Cannon and not

1. Karl Schriftgeisser, *The Gentleman from Massachusetts: Henry Cabot Lodge*, 231-2.
2. Henry Cabot Lodge, ed., *Selections from the Correspondence of Theodore Roosevelt and Henry Cabot Lodge*, 1884-1918, II, 301. Nicholas Murray Butler, *Across the Busy Years*, II, 239, says Sherman's nomination was made "in order to keep peace in the political family and at the urgent request of Speaker Cannon."
3. *Chicago Examiner*, July 18, 1908.

Taft had been the idol of the convention.[4] Besides securing the 58 favorite son votes of the Illinois contingent and influencing the vice-presidential nomination, Uncle Joe was able to instruct the platform committee concerning an anti-injunction plank. (He had no such luck on the tariff. The platform committed the party to revision.) Roosevelt had written to Lodge that as regards Labor he did not want a "Gompers Plank," or "a colorless plank," or a "National Association of Manufacturers' Plank." He wanted the party to take the position that was "right."[5] Uncle Joe, knew exactly what he wanted and his views prevailed. He argued: "The injunction is just as necessary to the laboring man as it is to the millionaire. When a man's property or his earnings, or his home are in danger of irreparable injury, the injunction is his only recourse. In all English speaking countries it has been a refuge and a protection to the poor and rich alike. We can't afford to meddle with it now." And the platform as adopted reaffirmed existing injunction law.[6] For his part in that result, Cannon received hearty congratulations from Nicholas Murray Butler, the politically aspiring Columbia University president, who wrote that Uncle Joe had "once more rendered to the Republican party and the nation a most conspicuous service."[7]

That master of personal journalism, Marse Henry Watterson, indicated in an editorial on June 20, 1908, what sort of a predicament he thought the Republicans were in. Calling Taft "the counterfeit presentment of Theodore Roosevelt," Marse Henry explored the possibility that the GOP was divided against itself. "It cannot at one and the same time keep step with Roosevelt the Radical, and Cannon, the Standpatter; with Tariff Reform and the Gospel of Protection; with the Trust of the East

4. William Allen White, *The Autobiography of William Allen White,* 401.
5. Theodore Roosevelt to Henry Cabot Lodge, June 16, 1908, Roosevelt Papers.
6. *Chicago Examiner,* July 18, 1908.
7. Nicholas Murray Butler to Joseph G. Cannon, July 19, 1908, Cannon Papers.

and the Farmers of the West; with the People and the System. In one word, Republicanism for all its arts and resources cannot serve both God and Mammon."[8]

Despite the fact that the Democratic headliner was William Jennings Bryan, up from the Chautauqua circuits for a third try at the Presidency, the campaign of 1908 was not particularly outstanding for its histrionics. It had none of the circus atmosphere of 1840, the grim tragic foreboding of 1860, or the oratorical fireworks of 1896. It takes two to make a fight. Bryan was willing and in good voice, but his jovial, massive opponent, much to the dismay of Theodore Roosevelt, preferred golf at Virginia's Hot Springs to vigorous campaigning. This is not to say that Taft did nothing in his own behalf. He did, and he struck hard blows at the Democrats, but his active entrance into the battle was belated.

The Democrats were never at a loss for words; they hurled much of their verbal barrage at Joe Cannon who was only too glad to reply in kind. Except for some bombast issued by the impatient tenant of the White House who was spoiling for action, or the ludicrous attempt to picture Taft as an un-Christian Unitarian monster as well as a faithful defender of the Pope, the most interesting part of the campaign concerned the Sage of Danville and his system called "Cannonism."

Believing they had an issue of great popular appeal, the Democrats harped on the theme that "Cannonism" prevented the rule of the people. Their national platform considered the subject at length:

> The House of Representatives was designed by the fathers of the Constitution to be the popular branch of our government, responsive to the public will.
>
> The House of Representatives, as controlled in recent years by the Republican party, has ceased to be a deliberative and legislative body, responsive to the

8. Arthur Krock, *The Editorials of Henry Watterson*, 104-5.

> will of a majority of its members, but has come under the absolute domination of the Speaker, who has entire control of its deliberations, and powers of legislation.
>
> We have observed with amazement the popular branch of our federal government helpless to obtain either the consideration or enactment of measures desired by a majority of its members.
>
> Legislative government becomes a failure when one member, in the person of the Speaker, is more powerful than the entire body.
>
> We demand that the House of Representatives shall again become a deliberate body, controlled by a majority of the people's representatives and not by the Speaker, and we pledge ourselves to adopt such rules and regulations of its members to direct its deliberations and control legislation.[9]

To that line of argument Uncle Joe invariably replied:

> Under the Constitution of the United States, the House of Representatives organizes itself, and any member of the House, of any party or no party, on any day, at any time, can halt any business before the House, and as a question of highest privilege offer a resolution and secure a vote on it to displace the Speaker of the House of Representatives and put some other member in his place.[10]

While such action was not as easy for the House to take as Cannon intimated, ironically the Democratic-Insurgent combination in 1910 was to show that Uncle Joe had been fundamentally correct.

One of the Speaker's trusted lieutenants, John Dalzell, provided a defense of the House rules suited to the Cannon taste. Dalzell wrote that the House had to have some order of business. The Rules Committee only made sug-

9. *Democratic Campaign Book of* 1908, 77.
10. *St. Louis Globe-Democrat,* August 20, 1908.

gestions; it did not dictate to the House, for its reports were of no consequence until they were adopted by a majority. The fact that their reports were almost invariably adopted evidenced the Committee's wisdom. Dalzell also defended the Speaker's power of appointment. He contended that committees could best be selected by "an authority that can with certainty be located and made to bear the burden of responsibility." Besides acting openly, the Speaker was vitally interested in the success of the administration as well as in his own reputation.[11]

Cannon had a personal fight on his hands as was indicated by the fact that he departed from previous custom and did most—though not all—of his campaigning near home. He disregarded the request from Frank H. Hitchcock, chairman of the Republican National Committee, that he devote as much time as possible to speaking engagements outside of Illinois.[12] James A. Tawney of Minnesota, noting that the public mind in his own district was unsettled, extended his sympathy to Uncle Joe because of the varied and intense attacks which had been launched against him. "The assault which has been made upon you," Tawney wrote, "is the most damnable piece of work that has ever been indulged in by the press or by any other interest."[13]

All the pressure elements to which Cannon had given brusque treatment were barking at his heels during the campaign. The *American Federationist*, official organ of the A. F. of L., issued an eight page pamphlet, "How Speaker Cannon Has Abused Labor." Taking its examples of the Speaker's alleged hostility to labor from the *Congressional Record*, the *Federationist* added a conclusion of its own: Uncle Joe was a "vindictive man of power."[14]

---

11. John Dalzell, "The Rules of the House of Representatives," *Independent* LXIV (March 12, 1908), 581.
12. Frank H. Hitchcock to Joseph G. Cannon, August 27, 1908, Cannon Papers.
13. James A. Tawney to Joseph G. Cannon, September 30, 1908, Cannon Papers.
14. "How Speaker Cannon Has Abused Labor," Cannon Papers.

On September 7, Labor Day, Samuel Gompers himself made the feature address at Danville's Lincoln Park. He spoke of the GOP platform plank on injunctions as "only a ragged knothole." Reading from William Hard's article in *Collier's,* Gompers agreed with the author's conclusion: "If we were offered the privilege of eliminating Aldrich, Rockefeller, or Cannon from influence in America, without hesitation we should choose Cannon as the most dangerous of the three." Gompers added a few words of his own: "I have no word of personal disregard or disrespect to speak of Mr. Cannon. I understand that genially and in a social way he is just all right. If you love him so much you will do the American people a great public service if you will keep him home with you."[15]

Cannon thought there were about 5000 "legal voters" among the labor unions of Danville and vicinity. He was "reliably informed" that Gompers had "over 40 foreign agents under his control trying to make things hot in the district by all means fair and foul—substantially foul."[16]

He was even more worried by the concerted campaign made against him by Methodist churchmen and the Anti-Saloon League which they dominated. The *Illinois Issue* of September 11, 1908, denounced Cannon's stand on liquor legislation. Its denunciation was fortified by an array of fifteen Methodist bishops.[17] On October 23, the paper devoted almost its entire eight page issue to Uncle Joe. It declared: "He is a living offense to the right minded people of this country."[18] The *Northwestern Christian Advocate* of September 9 discoursed on "Speaker Cannon's Autocratic Methods." The paper contended that he was "unsafe" because he would allow liquor dealers to nullify laws so that anarchy might triumph.[19] Dr.

---

15. September 7, 1908 Speech of Samuel Gompers at Lincoln Park, Danville, Illinois, Cannon Papers; *Danville Democrat,* September 8, 1908.
16. Joseph G. Cannon to William G. Beale, October 17, 1908. Cannon Papers.
17. *Illinois Issue,* September 11, 1908, Cannon Papers.
18. *Illinois Issue,* October 23, 1908, Cannon Papers.
19. *Northwestern Christian Advocate,* September 9, 1908, Cannon Papers.

D. D. Thompson, the editor of the *Northwestern Christian Advomate,* even ventured to address William Howard Taft on the subject. His letter elicited an astonishing reply from the GOP standard bearer. "Confidentially," wrote Taft, "the great weight I have to carry in this campaign is Cannonism, not only for the reason you suggest but for other reasons. . . . I should not be at all disappointed if a new Speaker were elected in the next Republican House, if it is to be Republican."[20]

Uncle Joe took to the platform to answer the prohibitionist charges. He said he was a "brother-in-law" of the Methodist church through his departed wife, and that he had no quarrel with the fifteen bishops who had attacked him. He represented only 200,000 of the 90,000,000 people in the country, and could never keep a majority from doing what it wanted to do. But the point was that the Littlefield Bill, which the Anti-Saloon people wanted, proposed to protect dry territory in one state against the shipment of liquor from another state. The federal government, in his view, could not do this. It could regulate but not prohibit interstate commerce.[21] The Speaker also encouraged members of the Judiciary Committee to make public statements that he had in no way interfered with action on the Littlefield Bill or packed the Committee with opponents of the Bill,[22] He wrote to Methodist Bishop Frank M. Bristol that he had not prevented the House from considering the Littlefield Bill, nor had he the power to do so. The rules of the House, the Committee on Rules, and the Speaker could not

20. William Howard Taft to Dr. D. D. Thompson, August 27, 1908, Taft Papers. Taft himself thought that the national GOP should have nothing to do with prohibition. Taft to Theodore Roosevelt, July 13, 1908, Roosevelt Papers.

21. Speech of October 3, 1908, at Onarga, Illinois, Cannon Papers.

22. Joseph G. Cannon to William G. Beale, October 17, 1908; Charles Q. Tirrell to the *Central Christian Advocate* enclosed in a letter to Cannon, October 19, 1908; John H. Foster, John Jenkins, Richard Wayne Parker, and Henry T. Bannon to Cannon, October 20, 1908; George Malby to Cannon, October 21, 1908, Cannon Papers.

prevent a majority of the House from taking up any measure and acting upon it at any time.[23]

Some Republican newspapers and politicians were reluctant to endorse Cannon, particularly if he were going to be a candidate for a fourth term as speaker. Thus, the *Chicago Tribune* was cool to Cannon. William G. Beale, a Chicago law partner of Robert Todd Lincoln and a *Tribune* legal adviser, became increasingly impatient with the paper's policy. Beale told Medill McCormick that the Tribune should support Cannon because "a vicious fight" was being made against him. "Ministers dominating politics, or other practical public matters," he wrote, "are about as undesirable as saloon keepers doing so–both ought to be relegated to the rear,– and with the fight of the ministers as well as the fight of Gompers, the *Tribune* should show no sympathy."[24] Cannon agreed with Beale that the *Tribune* could do "great good" for both the party and himself. He said it had been his "most efficient supporter" when he had first been elected Speaker. "If its antagonism is personal in its nature, I regret it, for I certainly have no desire to incur the personal enmity of anyone who controls the *Tribune's* policy."[25] Finally, though hardly with enthusiasm, the "Thunderer of the Prairie" obliged. It was for the re-election of Cannon because he was honest, capable, courageous, and efficient. "The district cannot decently desert him. The state cannot afford to let him go. The nation cannot completely fill his place." [26]

Various Republican members of Congress indicated they preferred to support someone other than Cannon for Speaker of the House in the 61st Congress. One of them was Edgar C. Ellis of Missouri.[27] Others included

23. *Danville Commercial News,* October 31, 1908.

24. William G. Beale to Joseph G. Cannon, October 16, 1908, Cannon Papers.

25. Joseph G. Cannon to William G. Beale, October 17, 1908, Cannon Papers.

26. *Chicago Tribune,* October 25, 1908.

27. *Kansas City Star,* September 28, 1908.

Representative J. F. Boyd[28] and George W. Norris, both of Nebraska. Norris said he was opposed to the re-election of Cannon as Speaker, because Uncle Joe was against any change in the rules which would take away or modify "the unreasonable and arbitrary power" possessed by the Speaker. Norris declared that a Speaker ought to be the servant of the House, doing its will, rather than controlling its action.[29] Cannon believed that the movement against him was directed by Victor Rosewater, editor of the *Omaha Bee* and a GOP National Committeeman from Nebraska. He wrote to Taft that the Speakership question promoted discord at a time when Republicans should be united against a common enemy.[30] Taft referred the complaint to Rosewater who declared it to be based upon fiction.[31]

As has already been indicated, William Howard Taft believed that Cannon was not an asset to his campaign. He wrote to his friend in the White House in late September: "The burden I have to carry in this campaign is largely Cannonism, and I don't propose to be involved in a bunko game with the public. My strong impression is that the people are insistent, as they ought to be, on a real revision, that we are not going to encounter the difficulties that we would have encountered in the last Congress had such a revision been proposed."[32] Taft was especially upset when he learned that Joe Cannon was going to campaign in Kansas. "The Republicans who are fighting for the success of the ticket," he wrote to Charles F. Brooker, "are either opposed to him or dread the effect of his support." Taft hoped Brooker might intercede with William B. McKinley, head of the Congressional Campaign Committee, to keep Cannon from going west of

---

28. *Norfolk* (Nebraska) *Daily News,* October 6, 1908.
29. G. B. Smith to Joseph G. Cannon, September 22, 1908, Cannon Papers.
30. Joseph G. Cannon to William Howard Taft, September 19, 1908, Cannon Papers.
31. William Howard Taft to Victor Rosewater, September 20, 1908, Taft Papers; Victor Rosewater to William Howard Taft, September 22, 1908, Taft Papers.
32. William Howard Taft to Theodore Roosevelt, September 21, 1908, Roosevelt Papers.

the Mississippi, and certainly not into Kansas or Nebraska.[33] He wrote directly to Uncle Joe that friends of the party in Kansas cautioned that everything was in good order and that no personal attacks should be made on Bryan.[34] When W. R. Stubbs, Republican candidate for governor in Kansas, wrote that Cannon's influence had been to the good after all, Taft breathed a sigh of relief.[35]

After surveying his and the party's chances, Taft told Roosevelt that he expected to receive between 275 and 300 electoral votes.

> Congress is going to be close with a small Republican majority, with enough men who will refuse to vote for Cannon to defeat him for Speaker. I feel as if this would be on the whole an excellent result. I am not at all anxious to have a large majority. I am quite content to get in by eight or ten votes, and shall be pleased if we can have such a Republican majority as will take the power away from Cannon, for I regard him as the burden we have had in the campaign and as an obstruction to all legislation of a progressive character that we really need.[36]

The President replied to Taft: "I feel just as you do about Cannon. . . . and the ideal result would be to have a Republican Congress with a majority so small that neither Cannon nor Tawney can be made Speaker."[37]

Roosevelt gave more than a merely formal amount of attention to the campaign. He said he wanted "to put more snap into the business."[38] But he told Lodge, "As for our enemies, Cabot, the simple fact is that dishonest men are naturally opposed to us."[39] T. R. did provide

33. William Howard Taft to Charles F. Brooker, September 12, 1908, Taft Papers.
34. William Howard Taft to Joseph G. Cannon, September 14, 1908, Taft Papers.
35. William Howard Taft to Joseph G. Cannon, September 20, 1908, Taft Papers.
36. William Howard Taft to Theodore Roosevelt, October 9, 1908, Taft Papers.
37. Theodore Roosevelt to William Howard Taft, October 12, 1908, Roosevelt Papers.
38. Theodore Roosevelt to Lawrence Abbott, September 22, 1908, Roosevelt Papers.
39. Theodore Roosevelt to Henry Cabot Lodge, September 25, 1908, Roosevelt Papers.

a statement on the necessity of electing a Republican Congress noticeably less strenuous than his letter to James A. Watson in 1906 had been. He paid tribute to the past accomplishments of the Republican Congress as "a record of substantial achievement. . . . To fail to elect Mr. Taft would be a calamity to the country; and it would be folly while electing him, yet at the same time to elect a Congress hostile to him, a Congress which under the influence of partisan leadership would be certain to thwart and baffle him on every possible occasion."[40] Nowhere in his short statement were there the specific words of praise that had embellished his statement two years before. He explained why to James S. Sherman: "I was not willing to say that I asked support for every nominal Republican Congressman, for there are three or four of them at least who, from the standpoint of the Republican party no less than of decent citizenship, are not entitled to any such support, men whose places it would have been a great advantage to us to have had filled by other people of almost any party during the last session of Congress." No inkling was given concerning the identity of the three or four. But he later wrote to Lodge:

> Cannon has proved such a load that they have had to cancel his engagements in the very doubtful districts, the candidates being afraid to have him come into their districts. The people at large, whatever their own morals, are bound at this moment that they shall be led only by leaders who on the elementary questions of public morality are sound — and they don't think some of our leaders are."[41]

Of course, Cannon was not without friends in his fight for re-election. The vast majority of the Republican Con-

40. Theodore Roosevelt to William B. McKinley, September 9, 1908, Roosevelt Papers.

41. Theodore Roosevelt to James S. Sherman, September 9, 1908, Roosevelt Papers. Roosevelt to Henry Cabot Lodge, October 21, 1908, Roosevelt Papers

gressmen were still on his side, though many of them found it politic not to say so until after election day. One who did speak out was Representative William S. Greene of Massachusetts. He stated that a House of 391 members could not transact business of national importance after the fashion of a New England Town Meeting. He emphasized the need for a definite center of responsibility and emphatically upheld Speaker Cannon.[42] J. Warren Keifer of Ohio, Speaker from 1881 to 1883 and back in Congress after a long absence, was sure that "disreputable assaults" had caused people generally to be interested in Cannon's success.[43] J. Adam Bede of Minnesota wrote in a similar vein.[44]

The election results showed that Taft had underestimated his own margin of victory. He received 321 electoral votes to 162 for Bryan; his popular margin was 7,678,908 to 6,409,104, not quite T.R.'s thumping victory of 1904 but a substantial one. Taft's professed hope for a narrow Republican majority in the House was not fulfilled. The party won 219 seats to the Democrats' 172.[45] Cannon wired the President-elect: "The people do rule."[46] Henry F. Pringle believes the Speaker's intent was satirical.[47] Cannon's own re-election was accomplished with his margin of victory slightly reduced from 1904. He received 29,170 votes, over one thousand less. H. C. Bell, his Democratic opponent, received 21,795 votes, and two also-rans, 2217. In 1904 his competition had garnered only 18,723 votes. Nebraska's George W. Norris had the closest call of his career. He defeated Fred Ashton, his Democratic opponent, by only 22 votes: Norris—20,649; Ashton—20,627. The presence of the state's favorite son, William Jennings Bryan, at the head of the Democratic

42. *Boston Transcript,* October 3, 1908.
43. J. Warren Keifer to Joseph G. Cannon, October 26, 1908, Cannon Papers.
44. J. Adam Bede to Joseph G. Cannon, October 29, 1908, Cannon Papers.
45. *Historical Statistics of the United States,* 289, 293.
46. Joseph G. Cannon to William Howard Taft, November 3, 1908, Taft Papers.
47. Henry F. Pringle, *The Life and Times of William Howard Taft,* I, 378.

ticket almost carried Ashton to victory and almost prevented Norris from leading the Insurgents in 1910.[48]

Theodore Roosevelt commented privately to President-elect Taft: "The returns of the election make it evident to me that you are the only one whom we could have nominated that could have been elected. Of course neither Cannon nor any other of the reactionaries would have stood a ghost of a chance."[49]

II

Since it appeared probable that Taft would convene Congress in special session soon after his inauguration, the Speaker's office had to be filled nine months earlier than usual. That detail was a matter for immediate attention. Charles N. Fowler of New Jersey, the chairman of the Committee on Banking and Currency who had been virtually ignored when the Aldrich-Vreeland Act was passed, bravely announced that he was a candidate for Speakership in the new 61st Congress.[50] The Cannon papers abound in post-election congratulatory telegrams from other GOP Congressmen. This evidently assured him that the consensus of Republican opinion in the House favored his re-election. He was sure that Fowler would not attract a great following.[51] Promises like Sereno E. Payne's that New York's 26 GOP votes would be solidly behind him for Speaker must have strengthened his confidence.[52]

Nevertheless, Joe Cannon's adherents resorted to extraordinary procedure on behalf of a Speaker already in office. James R. Mann sent out letters to Republicans

48. Richard L. Neuberger and Stephen B. Kahn, *Integrity: The Life of George W. Norris,* 35.
49. Theodore Roosevelt to William Howard Taft, November 10, 1908, Roosevelt Papers.
50. Charles N. Fowler to Arthur P. Murphy, November 6, 1908, enclosed in Murphy to Cannon, November 9, 1908, Cannon Papers.
51. Joseph G. Cannon to Arthur P. Murphy, November 8, 1908, Cannon Papers.
52. Sereno E. Payne to Joseph G. Cannon, November 9, 1908, Cannon Papers.

elected to the 61st Congress saying that the Illinois delegation intended to present Cannon's name to the party caucus for the Speakership. Their support was invited, and replies were requested.[53] About a week later Mann announced that more than one-half of the Republican members—elect had pledged themselves to Cannon for Speaker. Mann insisted that a responsible head of the House was necessary if a tariff bill were going to be passed. "The very men who are now loudest in their demands for the abolition of strict rules," he declared, "will be the first to beg for the reaffirmation of the old rules once the filibustering begins. . . . And all this talk about the tyranny of the Speaker is rot. I do not think any genuine move will be made to take away any of his power."[54]

Soon after the election Uncle Joe delivered a realistic speech in Cleveland in which he said that the Republican party would redeem its pledge for tariff revision by placing a "compromise" revenue law on the books. He said that he wanted to be Speaker but would be content as a member on the floor. Taft was shocked by Cannon's down to earth discussion of the intricacies of tariff making.[55]

The President-elect wrote a gracious letter to Theodore Roosevelt, telling the President: "You have always been the chief agent in working out the present state of affairs, and my selection and election are chiefly your work. . . . The great comfort I have in being under such heavy obligation to you is that I know the easiest way for me to discharge it is to make a success of my administration and to justify you in your wish and effort to make me your successor." The one disquieting phase of the election, Taft said, was that the administration could not take advantage of the opposition to Cannon. He would like to help in blocking Cannon's nomination for the

53. *Boston Transcript*, November 24, 1908.
54. *Chicago Interocean*, December 2, 1908.
55. Henry F. Pringle, *op. cit.*, I, 403-4.

Speakership if he could, but, he told T.R., "I want to take no false step in the matter, because to attempt to defeat 'Joe' and not to succeed would be worse than to let him get in and deal with him as best as I can."[56] Roosevelt apparently agreed with Taft on "the Cannon business." He declared: "If it is evident that four-fifths of the Republicans want Cannon I do not believe it would be well to have him in the position of the sullen and hostile floor leader bound to bring your administration to grief, even tho you were able to put someone else in as Speaker."[57] Elihu Root was even more opposed to an open war on Cannon. He advised the President-elect that "it would be very unfortunate to have the idea get out that you wanted to beat Cannon and are not able to do it. . . . I have treated all the newspaper talk about your going into a fight against Cannon as mere newspaper talk. . . . I hope you will find some way to dispel the impression that it tends to create."[58]

In Chicago, Cannon stated flatly that no man was big enough to dictate to the House; that body would elect its own Speaker without the advice or dictation of the executive branch of government. He said, however, that he had no intention of having the House run at cross purposes to the rest of the government. There would be "an honest revision of the tariff."[59]

In the meantime, Taft had decided on his course. He elected not to contest the Speakership. "I cannot take part in the movement to defeat Mr. Cannon for Speaker," he wrote, "however much such a movement would accord with my wishes or with the welfare of the Republican party. But I shall have certain constitutional functions to discharge with reference to the tariff bill which I shall

56. William Howard Taft to Theodore Roosevelt, November 7, 1908, Roosevelt Papers.

57. Theodore Roosevelt to William Howard Taft, November 10, 1908, Roosevelt Papers.

58. Elihu Root to William Howard Taft, November 23, 1908, Taft Papers.

59. *Chicago Interocean,* November 24, 1908.

not hesitate to exercise should it fail to redeem the promise of the platform."[60] To the anti-Cannon Congressman from Minnesota, Halvor Steenerson, Taft explained:

> I do not hesitate to say that a new Speaker would give assurance to the country of good faith in the following of the Roosevelt policies and of the revision of the tariff, which may not follow the election of Mr. Cannon, but it is the members of the House who do the electing, and I would be very severely criticized if I should attempt to use Executive power to control the election in the House. . . . I must abide the election and then do the best I can afterwards.[61]

He was indignant when friends were disturbed that he had "consented" to a fourth term for Cannon. "The election of a speaker of the House is not within my consent. I have no jurisdiction in respect to the matter."[62] In a more realistic mood, he observed: "There is some doubt whether I could have beaten Cannon if I had gone in and used all the influence of a new executive, because he is pretty thoroughly entrenched in the affection and friendship of the old members who remain, and because the association growing out of appointments in Committees would make the recipients of his favors reluctant to leave him."[63] According to Henry F. Pringle, "No sane president-elect could have taken a course different from this one by Taft." But he made a mistake when he informed newspaper reporters that he had seen Cannon and was confident of the Speaker's good faith. That action "sent a chill of discouragement over the valiant but futile band of House insurgents." They soon were to grow bitter and make unjust accusations.[64]

---

60. William Howard Taft to E. H. Hinshaw, November 24, 1908, Taft Papers.
61. William Howard Taft to Halvor Steenerson, November 30, 1908, Taft Papers.
62. William Howard Taft to George S. Harding, December 6, 1908, Taft Papers.
63. William Howard Taft to William Worthington, December 5, 1908, Taft Papers.
64. Henry F. Pringle, *op. cit.*, I, 406-7.

Foiled in his attempt to secure a House management more to his liking, Taft, more determinedly than ever, stuck to his guns on the subject of tariff revision. He thought Cannon backed by his "nest of standpatters" was unduly cynical in that regard. "I don't care how he feels or how they feel in the House," he told Theodore Roosevelt, "I am not going to be made the mouthpiece of a lie to the people without disclaiming my responsibility. If they will play fair, I will play fair, but if they won't then I reserve all my rights to do anything I find myself able to do."[65] He expressed the hope that he was going to succeed in respect to revision. "It may be that it will ultimately defeat my administration, but I shall much prefer to go down upholding the proposition that we must comply with our party promises, than to go down, as we certainly would go down, if I were to yield by approving which was nothing but a humiliating compromise with the reactionaries on this subject."[66]

The opening of the lame duck session of the 60th Congress in December, 1908, found old friends exchanging pleasantries and Republicans indulging in self-congratulation. Anticipating the strife that was to come, the House parliamentarian, Asher C. Hinds of Maine, issued an eleven page typewritten defense of the rules which he said were subject to great misunderstanding. The House was highly efficient and maintained absolute control over its business. If the Speaker could refuse recognition to a member desiring unanimous consent, so could any other member of the House do likewise by objecting: there was no tyranny there. Victor Murdock, the Kansas Insurgent, was unimpressed. He promised undying warfare on Speaker Cannon and changes in the rules.[67]

Taft was favorable to a rules change: "The taking away of the committees from the speaker would reduce the

65. William Howard Taft to Theodore Roosevelt, November 25, 1908, Taft Papers.
66. William Howard Taft to William Worthington, December 5, 1908, Taft Papers.
67. *New York Herald*. December 8, 1908,

speakership to an almost judicial position, and I am rather inclined to think that would be better. I doubt, however, whether the Speaker would consent to it."[68] He believed he could down Cannon and Aldrich; if not, the result would be a broken party and the Democrats in power.[69]

Over a month after the event, Joe Cannon wrote Theodore Roosevelt that "more than any other agency" Roosevelt had contributed to the party's electoral success. The Speaker particularly praised T.R.'s vigorous letters against Bryan.[70] Roosevelt replied: "I am very greatly pleased by your letter. It is a generous and manly letter for you to have written; and I do not know whether to be most pleased at what the letter contains, or with the mere fact of your having been willing to write it."[71]

Formal cordiality was about all both men could afford by this time. The Speaker was not consulted about President Roosevelt's last annual message to Congress as he had been for all others in the past. He was surprised to find that the message contained what he believed was an assault on the Congress, and especially on the House.[72] The President had been angered by an amendment of James A. Tawney's to an appropriation bill in the previous session which limited strictly the activities of the Secret Service. The House reacted, swiftly. It adopted unanimously a resolution by James Breck Perkins, a New York Republican who was the chairman of the Foreign Relations Committee, that a select committee be named to arrange a suitable retaliation on the President. Also on the select committee besides Perkins were Republicans Edwin Denby of Michigan and John W. Weeks of Massa-

68. William Howard Taft to H. E. Pollard, December 22, 1908, Taft Papers.

69. William Howard Taft to W. R. Nelson, January 5, 1909, Taft Papers.

70. Joseph G. Cannon to Theodore Roosevelt, December 11, 1908, Roosevelt Papers.

71. Theodore Roosevelt to Joseph G. Cannon, December 14, 1908, Roosevelt Papers.

72. L. W. Busbey, *Uncle Joe Cannon,* 231-2.

chusetts, and Democrats John Sharp Williams and James Lloyd of Missouri.[73]

The Perkins Committee reported unanimously that the President should be requested to furnish the House with any information in his position that justified the language used in his message. The House agreed to the report. The President still had a chance to make peace with the legislators if he chose to do so. Cannon went to the White House and came near to a personal quarrel with the President. Roosevelt intimated that L. W. Busbey, who in 1903 before he became Cannon's secretary had written a newspaper article criticizing the Secret Service, had inspired the House to limit the activities of the service.[74] Roosevelt did not make peace but sent an even more sharply worded message to the House on January 4, 1909. He quoted liberally from Busbey's article and among other things conferred membership in the Ananias Club on Representative Tawney.[75] Cannon thought this the "weakest political move" T.R. had ever made. The House promptly referred his second message to the Perkins Committee which recommended that it be laid on the table. The House adopted the recommendation almost unanimously. It was the first time since Andrew Jackson's administration that the House had refused to accept a message from a President.[76]

In a letter to Kermit, the President wrote: "Congress has been having a brainstorm . . . both Houses have held a can-can over the secret service. Personally I doubt if they have gained very much . . . and I do not see how the House can get away from what I have said about it."[77] Roosevelt was determined to be "full President right up to the end—which hardly any other President ever has been." He thought he could "hold Congress down" during his

73. *Chicago Interocean*, December 12, 1908.
74. L. W. Busbey, *op. cit.*, 234; 237-8.
75. *Chicago Examiner*, January 5, 1909.
76. L. W. Busbey, *op. cit.*, 240-1.
77. Theodore Roosevelt to Kermit Roosevelt, January 10, 1909, Roosevelt Papers.

last month in office. "But they have been anxious to see it they could not do me up this winter."[78]

They still tried. On February 9, 1909, the President sent the report of his Country Life Commission to Congress. In an accompanying message he asked for $25,000 to print and circulate the report and to prepare for publication the other data collected by the Commission. Congress not only refused to appropriate the money but prohibited the continuation of the work. The instigator of that turn of events was James A. Tawney, a good friend of Cannon but thought by Roosevelt to be "one of the most efficient representatives of the cause of special privilege in the House." By Tawney's amendment to the Sundry Civil Bill the President was forbidden to appoint any more commissions unless specifically authorized to do so by Congress. As almost his last official act, Theodore Roosevelt told the Congress that he believed the Tawney amendment was unconstitutional, and that if he were remaining in office, he would refuse to obey it.[79]

On that querulous note, the master of the big stick bid farewell to Congress and went off to Africa where at least the animal life could not return his fire.

III

Besides trying to make life miserable for the man in the White House, the GOP leaders of the lame duck session of the 60th Congress had to mend their own fences. Upstarts in their own ranks, as well as the Democrats, forced the party's elders and Joe Cannon to take heed of their demands. The first full scale debate on the rules of the House and the powers of the Speaker since the days of "Czar" Reed was in prospect. From the sidelines, political scientists had already presented divergent views.

78. Theodore Roosevelt to Theodore Roosevelt Jr., January 31, 1909, Roosevelt Papers.

79. Theodore Roosevelt, *Autobiography,* 416.

Leading cheers for reform was J. Allen Smith of the University of Washington. In his book, *The Spirit of American Government* published in 1907, Smith argued that the power exercised by the Speaker and the Committees imposed an "effectual restraint" upon individual members and the majority as well. "There is no way," he wrote, "in which the House can override the veto of a committee or that of a speaker, since even when the rules are suspended no measure can be considered that has not been previously reported by a committee, while the speaker can enforce his veto through his power of recognition. Both the committee and the speaker have what is for all practical purposes an absolute veto on legislation." Smith believed that the system encouraged "log-rolling, causing members to vote for bills which they would prefer to vote against in order to secure support for bills in which they were interested—even to the extent that bills passed when a majority were really opposed to their enactment." In his opinion the system did not permit "public opinion to exercise an effective control over the proceedings of the House."[80]

On the other side was Woodrow Wilson, a scholar at Princeton. In his *Congressional Government* published in 1885, Wilson had pointed out that when a bill "goes from the Clerk's desk to a committee room, it crosses a parliamentary bridge of sighs to dim dungeons of silence whence it will never return."[81] But Wilson favored the Speaker's control of the House. "You must have leaders in a numerous body—leaders with authority; and you cannot give authority in the House except through the rules. The man who administers the rules must be master, and you must put this mastery into the hands of your very best party leader."[82] He did not see "how else business

80. J. Allen Smith, *The Spirit of American Government,* 199-202.

81. Woodrow Wilson, *Congressional Government,* 69.

82. Ray Stannard Baker and William E. Dodd, ed., *The Public Papers of Woodrow Wilson,* I, 334.

could go forward in an assembly which would otherwise be a mere mass meeting."[83] But, wrote Wilson in 1908, the Speaker was not an autocrat. That term "has really no place in our political vocabulary." The Speaker was the instrument of the majority; he was obeyed because the majority chose to follow his leadership. As for the rules of the House, Wilson declared:

> The rules are of its own making, and it can unmake them when it pleases. It can override the Speaker's decisions, too, and correct its presiding officer as every other assembly can. It has simply found it most convenient to put itself in the Speaker's hands, its object being efficiency not debate.[84]

As has already been noted, practical politicians of a reforming bent had been attacking the rules long before Cannon emerged as their archfoe. On the Republican side, as early as 1893 Colonel Pete Hepburn had told the House; "Each constituency is the equal of every other and through its Representative is entitled to the same right as every other." The power of the Speaker to disfranchise a constituency by refusing to recognize a member was contrary to the spirit of the Constitution.[85] At the beginning of the 56th Congress he had contended for a general decentralization of power with respect to committees and for a Rules Committee, enlarged in size and composed solely of members of the majority, that was independent of the Speaker.[86] Francis Cushman of Washington had joked: "The Calendar! That is a misnomer. It ought to be called a cemetery. For therein lie the whitening bones of legislative hopes."[87] But the time was not then ripe for revolt.

83. *Ibid.*, I, 349.
84. Woodrow Wilson, *Constitutional Government in the United States*, 95.
85. *Congressional Record*, 53-1, 1043; 1144-5.
86. John Ely Briggs, *William Peters Hepburn*, 313.
87. *Congressional Record*, 57-1, 4320.

Cannon's first two terms as Speaker had been characterized by quiet on the rules front, partly due to the fact that he enjoyed an extraordinary degree of popularity among his colleagues. But he utilized the same resources which other Speakers had developed in over a century of practice. With increasing frequency he politely ignored men rising for recognition on the floor who had not previously visited the Speaker's room and confided their plans to him in advance. Gradually he drew the reins of leadership tighter, not forcing legislation through a protesting House but assisting in holding from the floor bills to which he and his associates objected. He summarily removed several recalcitrant members from committee chairmanships and filled key committees with loyal supporters.[88]

Of course not all of Cannon's committee changes were made arbitrarily; some were made at the request of the members themselves. But Changwei Chiu, in a study of the matter, has noted that from the 58th to the 61st Congress there were 470 Republican places on the ten major House committees—Agriculture, Appropriations, Banking and Currency, Judiciary, Interstate and Foreign Commerce. Military Affairs, Naval Affairs, Post Office and Post Roads, Rivers and Harbors, and Ways and Means. In his four terms as Speaker, Cannon made forty-one changes or removals in regard to those committees. In the 59th Congress, for example, he appointed James A. Tawney to be chairman of the Appropriations Committee although that gentleman had never served on the committee. In the 60th Congress with James W. Wadsworth, previous chairman of the Agriculture Committee, out of Congress, Uncle Joe passed over E. S. Henry of Connecticut and Gilbert N. Haugen of Iowa, who were next in line by seniority and appointed Charles F. Scott, a Kansas Regular to that position. Henry's views on meat inspection, pure

88. Kenneth W. Hechler, *Insurgency,* 30.

food, and other legislation ran counter to Cannon's, and this may have figured in his decision.[89]

A partisan of Uncle Joe's like James E. Watson believed that the Insurgent Republicans were hostile to the Speaker "wholly because of blighted personal hopes and ambitions and not because they were actuated by any principle." He believed that Norris of Nebraska was especially embittered because he had not been named to the Judiciary Committee, that Victor Murdock of Kansas was disappointed because he had not been chosen for the Appropriations Committee. On the other hand, the Democrats were in the fight, not against the Speaker as an individual, but against the system. Led by Champ Clark and David DeArmond of Missouri and Oscar W. Underwood of Alabama, they were mainly interested in reaping advantages for their party.[90] Clark admitted as much. He said: "I seized with delight the growing dissatisfaction among the Republicans in the House over the rules, as a wedge with which to weaken and finally split the Republican party wide open."[91] In the view of Kenneth W. Hechler: "It was 'Uncle Joe' Cannon's economic and social philosophy that first aroused the western Congressmen against his autocracy. The question of power in itself did not greatly excite the average Congressman; but power exercised for reactionary economic and social ends seemed downright pernicious."[92]

The fires of Insurgency smouldered throughout the 60th Congress. In the first session John N. Nelson of Wisconsin attacked the Speaker's personal power, calling it "the sword of Damocles hanging over the head of every member who dares rebel against the established order." Applause greeted his remark that "President Roosevelt has

---

89. Chang-wei Chiu, *The Speaker of the House of Representatives Since 1896*, 76-7; 70.

90. James E. Watson, *As I Saw Them*, 114-5.

91. Champ Clark, *My Quarter Century of American Politics*, II, 259-60.

92. Kenneth W. Hechler, *op. cit.*, 31.

been trying to cultivate oranges for many years in the frigid climate of the Committee of Rules, but what has he gotten but the proverbial lemons?"[93] Victor Murdock voiced a demand for a larger Committee on Rules which would be appointed by the vote of the entire House and hold public sessions.[94]

In the second session of the 60th Congress it was Colonel Hepburn, by then a seventy-six year old lame duck for he had not been re-elected in 1908, who fanned the flames. On December 11, 1908, twenty-five Insurgents gathered in his committee room to begin the organized fight to change the method of procedure in the House. Hepburn presided at the meeting. Four days later the first skirmish on the floor took place. A resolution was offered proposing that 8 members, 5 chosen by the Speaker and 3 by the minority, should be appointed to report by February 1, 1909 any changes in the rules which seemed desirable. Sereno E. Payne raised a point of order. Cannon sustained him and was upheld, 149 to 136.[95]

The Insurgents warmed to their task. John M. Nelson of Wisconsin wrote an article about the Speaker for *LaFollette's Magazine* entitled "The American Frankenstein." Nelson fervently hoped that Taft would contest the power of the Speaker. A sample of Nelson's prose is indicative of the strength of his feelings. "No tale spun by popular fancy in the childhood of a race about some mythical giant, vampire, or troll," he declared, "has more in it of the extraordinary or the incredible than the actual portraiture of this extra-constitutional creature—the autocrat of Congress." President Taft would have to take a hand, and "nothing better could happen for the progressive movement than a contest between the Speaker and the President."[96]

---

93. *Congressional Record,* 60-1, 1652.
94. *Ibid.,* 60-1, 2837.
95. John Ely Briggs, *op. cit.,* 320.
96. John M. Nelson, "The American Frankenstein," *LaFollette's Weekly Magazine,* I (January 23, 1909), 6; 14-5.

On February 9, 1909, twenty-nine Insurgents went into action again. They submitted a three part resolution, the brain-child of Norris, to their colleagues. The resolution called for the abolition of the Speaker's powers to appoint committees, the institution of a Rules Committee composed of 9 from the majority and 6 from the minority chosen by the House from fifteen geographical areas, and the establishment of "Calendar Tuesday," on which day the committees would be called in alphabetical order for the presentation of legislation.[97] At this juncture Champ Clark decided that the Democrats should join the Insurgents in active collaboration.[98]

Hepburn delivered his farewell address on February 19, 1909. He ridiculed the idea that the Insurgents were assaulting the so-called Reed Rules. He said the Reed Rules had been designed to stop filibustering and that purpose had been accomplished. He did not want to change them; he wanted to check the "undue and overgrown power of the Speaker." Colonel Pete said he was against the system, not the man. "If we are to have a benevolent despot, then the benevolent gentleman who is our despot would be my choice." But he declared that according to practice no member was able to deliver the message of his constituents except with the consent of "the gentleman from the Danville district," for the recognition procedure made every member "a mendicant at the feet of the Speaker."[99]

The Regulars, after a decent interval, counter-attacked. On March 1, 1909, John Dalzell, Cannon's right hand man on the Rules Committee, offered a reform resolution for a "Calendar Wednesday" instead of the Insurgents' "Calendar Tuesday." Dalzell's resolution sought to achieve a call of committees once a week on "Calendar Wednes-

97. House Resolution 551, 60th Congress, 2nd Session. "Calendar Tuesday" could be set aside only by a two-thirds vote of the House.
98. *Congressional Record,* 60-2, 2653-55.
99. *Congressional Record,* 60-2, 2653-55.

day" except during the last two weeks of each session. The call could not be dispensed with except by a majority vote. Although the suggestion for a "Calendar Day" had originated with the Insurgents, whose purpose was to reduce the Speaker's power over the committees of the House, the Regulars adopted the principle for themselves as a way of meeting the least objectionable of the Insurgent demands. Their sincerity in doing so was suspect.[100]

The debate on the subject was short by the design of the House leaders; the alliance of the Insurgents and Democrats became clear, however, when John Sharp Williams assigned 11 of his 20 minutes to Insurgents Norris, Hepburn, Murdock, and A. P. Gardner of Massachusetts. Norris referred to "Calendar Wednesday" as "the most comical parliamentary joke that has ever come down the pike. In its application it is a homeopathic dose of nothingness. Are we men or is this kindergarten?" Murdock declared: "This is a Trojan Horse . . . and sticking out of the paunch of that horse I think I see several notable cold feet."[101] The roll call vote showed 168 in favor of "Calendar Wednesday," 163 against it—including 26 of the 29 Insurgents.[102] Thus the Insurgent menace was scotched temporarily. But Cannon and his loyal supporters, with a slightly reduced majority, could look forward to another contest when the special session of the 61st Congress met on March 15, 1909, for the purpose of considering a revision of the tariff.

President Taft, supremely anxious to have a tariff bill passed that would be a credit to his administration, believed that he had to regard "the Republican party as the instrumentality through which to try to accomplish something." However much he sympathized with the Insur-

100. *Ibid.*, 60-2, 3567, Chang-wei Chiu, *The Speaker of the House of Representatives Since* 1896, 234-236.
101. *Congressional Record*, 60-2, 3570.
102. *Ibid.*, 60-2, 3572.

gents, he could not sacrifice his program to stand out against the other 190 Republicans in the House. He had to rely on party discipline, and it was not his business to quarrel with Speaker Cannon. He predicted that when the special session convened, Cannon would be able to find enough Democrats to join him so that the Insurgents would be defeated on the rules.[103]

E. C. Higgins's new *Success Magazine* on March 10, 1909, published the result of a poll of its 20,248 lifetime subscribers in every state of the union with regard to the election of the new Speaker and the House Rules. The magazine's final report on four questions included the tabulation of 11,956 replies, and indicated, to the editor's satisfaction, a tide of 20 to 1 against "Cannonism."[104]

The result of the Speaker's election, however, had been a foregone conclusion for several months. When the House convened on March 15, 1909, the Republicans again showed their faith in Danville's grand old man. The tally for Speaker showed: Cannon, 204; Clark, 166; Esch, 1; Norris, 2; Cooper, 8, Hepburn, 1. The Insurgents not only had to accept Uncle Joe for a fourth term, but they could muster only twelve votes against him.[105]

Dalzell then presented the usual motion that the rules of the previous Congress be re-adopted. But Champ Clark

---

103. William Howard Taft to W. D. Foulke, March 12, 1909, Taft Papers. *LaFollette's Weekly* I, (March 13, 1904), 4, trumpeted that the people had "commisioned" Taft "to drive on—carefully, conservatively, cannily, diplomatically, slowly, it may be, but to *drive on.*"

104. *Success Magazine*, March 10, 1909.

The Questions	*Yes*	*No*	*Not Voting*
1. Should Cannon be re-elected Speaker?	549	11,045	325
2. Should the Speaker choose committees?	369	11,361	215
3. Would you favor the placing of this power in the hands of a special committee chosen by the House?	11,453	241	241
4. Would you favor "Calendar Tuesday?"	11,546	129	265

105. *Congressional Record*, 61-1, 18.

forced a roll call, and by a vote of 193 to 189, the rules of the 60th Congress were not re-adopted.[106] Clark promptly offered a resolution to deprive the Speaker of the power to appoint committees and to set up a fifteen man Committee on Rules.[107] His resolution specifically named the members of the new Rules Committee to consist of six Democrats, five Regular Republicans, and four Insurgent Republicans. When a vote was taken on Clark's resolution, sixteen Democrats bolted and joined the Cannon forces, resulting in Clark's defeat, 203 to 180.[108]

At this juncture, John Fitzgerald, a Tammany Democrat, came to the rescue of the Regulars. His proposals, offered as an amendment to the old rules, did not hamper the Speaker's control of the Rules Committee or his power to appoint committees. But they did improve existing arrangements, providing for a unanimous consent calendar which disposed of the necessity of the daily trek to the Speaker's office for minor bills, and for a strengthened "Calendar Wednesday" by raising the requirement for setting it aside from a majority to a two-thirds vote.[109] A hot debate followed, after which a vote was taken. Fitzgerald's rules won out, 211 to 172. This time twenty-three Democrats joined the Regular Republicans.[110]

Apparently, as Kenneth W. Hechler, the chief authority on Insurgency has demonstrated, a deal had been consummated between Cannon and Tammany Democrats who were desirous of securing tariff favors.[111] James R. Mann later assumed full responsibility for the "deal." He denied that the Democrats had received any rewards; they had voted with the Regulars because of "a mutual desire to have the rules perfected for legitimate business pur-

106. *Ibid.*, 61-1, 21.
107. *Ibid.*, 61-1, 22.
108. Kenneth W. Hechler, *op. cit.*, 57.
109. *Congressional Record*, 61-1, 22.
110. *Danville Commercial News*, March 16, 1909.
111. Kenneth W. Hechler, *op. cit.*, 59-61; See also, H. Parker Willis, "The Tariff of 1909," *Journal of Political Economy* XVIII (January, 1910), 8-9.

poses."[112] Congressional comments on the result at the time varied. Insurgent A. P. Gardner stated that while the Insurgents had been seeking better things, progress had been made. But Victor Murdock declared: "We are conducting an insurrection. . . and I will continue to fight." Regular James R. Mann was closest to the truth: "The rules of the House have not been changed to an appreciable extent." [113]

The new minority leader, Champ Clark, believed that his part in the unsuccessful attempt had so angered Cannon that the Speaker, "as a punishment," had taken away the privilege previously granted to John Sharp Williams of making minority committee appointments.[114] Otherwise, Uncle Joe seemed to bear his slight curtailment of power with good grace. He said he welcomed the adoption of the Fitzgerald rules as a relief from the "drudgery" of reading hundreds of bills and also from "the sham autocracy" of his position. No longer could members write to their constituents that the tyrannical old Speaker would not recognize them to pass a pet bill. By way of defense Cannon also noted that most of the legislation credited to the Roosevelt administration had been passed under special rules.[115]

Taft told an Insurgent group led by A. P. Gardner that he had no intention of turning the House over to a coalition composed of the Democrats and a few Republicans.[116] He found "the solution of the difficulties in the House . . . extremely satisfactory."[117] But he wrote to Theodore Roosevelt: "I have no doubt that when you return you will find me very much under suspicion by our

112. *Chicago Record-Herald,* November 20, 1909. A House Democratic caucus adopted a resolution denouncing the bolting Democrats who voted for the Fitzgerald amendment. *LaFollette's Weekly* I (April 3, 1909), 5.

113. *Chicago Tribune,* March 16, 1909.

114. Champ Clark, *op. cit.,* II, 271.

115. Joseph G. Cannon, "The Power of the Speaker," *Century* LXXVIII (June, 1909), 312; 309.

116. Archie Butt, *Taft and Roosevelt: The Intimate Letters of Archie Butt,* I, 5-6.

117. William Howard Taft to Horace Taft, March 16, 1909, Taft Papers.

friends in the West." That was because he could not countenance an insurrection within the party. He had "to sit steady in the boat" and do what he could to help Cannon and the majority of the party. "Cannon and Aldrich have promised to stand by the party platform and to follow my lead. They did so I believe for you in the first Congress of your administration and this is the first Congress of mine." Taft further said that he wanted Theodore to know that he did nothing without considering what Roosevelt would have done under the same circumstances. In fact, Taft said he had difficulty in overcoming the habit of addressing Theodore as "My Dear Mr. President." Upon seeing press reports of the activities of the President, he did not readily identify them with himself.[118]

The modification of the House rules, though slight by Insurgent standards, was generally hailed by the press as a settlement that would prevail—at least for the duration of the 61st Congress. But the feeling against Cannon had not evaporated, Edwin Maxey, writing in the *Forum,* argued that the House rules were well adapted to securin the will of the majority. "The rules of the House," he said, "ought not to be held accountable for the fact that Joseph G. Cannon has an arbitrary and imperious cast of mind." The logical remedy was a change of Speakers.[119] The Insurgents, playing the roles of idealistic crusaders for democracy in the national legislature, generally stopped short of such a conclusion. Norris, in particular, disclaimed any intention of engaging in a personal attack on the Speaker. But as time wore on and the tariff debates ruffled tempers, it became more difficult for the crusaders and their Democratic allies to keep ideals separate from political opportunism.

---

118. William Howard Taft to Theodore Roosevelt, March 21, 1909, Taft Papers.
119. Edwin Maxey, "The Power of the Speaker," *Forum* XLI (April, 1909), 349.

IV

The special session of the 61st Congress labored from March to August, 1909, and brought forth the Payne-Aldrich tariff. William Starr Myers, historian of the GOP, believes that the tariff law was the turning point in the Taft administration. In his view, had Taft been a Roosevelt with brilliant powers of leadership, he might have vetoed the law, appealed to the people and strengthened his hold on their affections. Then, in all probability, he would have been able to defeat standpat leaders in Congress and proceed to a triumphant re-election in 1912 with Theodore Roosevelt as an enthusiastic supporter. The Republican party would have experienced "a veritable rebirth" and would have changed to meet modern conditions.[120] In reality, had Taft been a Roosevelt, he might have taken Joe Cannon's advice as T.R. always had and dodged the tariff issue artfully for four more years.

In accordance with campaign pledges and at the insistence of the President, the Republican Congress set about revising the Dingley tariff which had been in effect since 1897. Taft played much more than a passive role in the proceedings, but he did his work behind the scenes. This strategy created an impression of disinterestedness or even indifference that was misleading.[121] Sereno E. Payne's Ways and Means Committee had held hearings during November and December, 1908; they had drafted a reasonable tariff bill which placed lumber, hides, and petroleum on the free list, although woolen and cotton goods kept the same rates thanks to powerful lobbying. But the original Payne bill never saw the light of day. The House leaders used tariff concessions as a bargaining point to consolidate their position against the Insurgents before the 61st Congress convened. When the House Ways and Means

120. William Starr Myers, *The Republican Party, A History*, 393.

121. Lawrence Chamberlain, *The President, Congress, and Legislation*, 101-2.

Committee reported a tariff bill on March 16, 1909, it bore little resemblance to the original Payne bill.[122]

The three weeks debate in the House featured "a series of oratorical shots in the air." Payne's speech was a stereotyped defense of protection; Champ Clark's reply was wandering and pointless. The whole performance was "a gloomy episode" for the purpose of making good with constituents.[123] But the GOP leadership did not have everything its own way. The Speaker simply ignored the fledgling Congressman from Tennessee, Cordell Hull, who wanted to offer an income tax amendment.[124] However, the persistent Norris disrupted the machinery, and on the eve of the final vote, protested the clause in the tariff bill which raised the petroleum duty to 25% *ad valorem,* He offered an amendment reducing the duty to 1% *ad valorem.* Speaker Cannon ruled him out of order and made a speech in favor of the higher duty. With particular reference to the expanding oil fields in Illinois, Uncle Joe declared: "Gentlemen, is it not well enough to see when you seek to punish somebody that you claim is bad that you do not, like Samson pull down the pillars and have the temple fall upon you." The adoption of the Norris amendment would let in practically free refined oil from Mexico "and still the gentleman from Wisconsin (Cooper) and others flap their wings and crow and crucify the people while they demagogue in denouncing the wicked Standard Oil." Despite the Speaker's pleas, the House voted for the Norris amendment.[125]

Otherwise the Payne Bill passed the House on April 10, 1909, as it had been reported from the Ways and Means Committee. The vote was 217 to 171. At Taft's request, coal, hides, and iron were on the free list. The

122. H. Parker Willis, "The Tariff of 1909," *Journal of Political Economy* XVIII (January, 1910), 3-9.

123. *Ibid.,* 10-11.

124. Harold B. Hinton, *Cordell Hull,* 125.

125. *Chicago Interocean,* April 8, 1909.

tariff on lumber remained; advances in duties were provided for hosiery and gloves. Raymond wrote in the *Chicago Tribune*: "It is at least to the credit of Speaker Cannon and his lieutenants that they have been brave enough to assume responsibility for the whole Payne Bill including gloves, hosiery, and everything else."[126]

The Senate Finance Committee under the leadership of Senator Aldrich restored the duties on iron, hides, and coal, and increased those on lumber and cotton goods when it reported the Payne Bill to the Senate floor on April 12, 1909. Debate was enlivened by the Insurgent Republicans in the Senate. Several of them were ardent protectionists and even voted for specific increases in duties when they happened to affect products from their home states. Senators Dolliver, Bristow, LaFollette, Beveridge, and Cummins were the vociferous quintet who provided well marshalled arguments on behalf of "the rights of the ultimate consumer." Much to the discomfiture of the Aldrich coterie, the Insurgents and Democrats introduced an amendment calling for a personal income tax. By forming a temporary coalition they had enough votes to put it through. But President Taft came to the rescue of the Regulars. On June 16, 1909, in a special message to Congress, he expressed strong opposition to the income proposal. He made two specific recommendations: the immediate enactment of a tax upon the net in come of corporations and an amendment to the Constitution so as to permit an unapportioned tax upon individual incomes. This suggestion split the coalition and saved the Regulars. A mild corporation tax—1% of net earnings above $5000—was drafted by Senator Root of New York and Attorney General Wickersham and adopted by the Senate.[127] H. Parker Willis, believing that Taft had saved the Regulars from "a humiliating defeat," wrote

126. *Chicago Tribune,* April 10, 1909.
127. Lawrence Chamberlain, *op. cit.,* 104-6; Herbert S. Duffy, ***William Howard Taft,*** 235-6.

that "had he intervened for lower duties at this time, there is little doubt that he could have got them. But it was unofficially stated that no action would be taken until the bill had reached the Conference Committee. The crucial moment was allowed to slip by."[128]

The Senate bill had several other special features: a provision that the President could invoke an increase of 25% against countries discriminating against United States trade; a provision that the President was to be allowed a staff of experts to aid him in assembling data relevant to the tariff; and a provision specifically repealing the reciprocity feature of the Dingley tariff. Altogether the Senate added 847 amendments to the House bill, more than half of them increases. Many of the increases were dictated by special interests. The woolen and cotton industries of New England for which Senator Aldrich pleaded were especially successful. But Aldrich was not provincial, working out convenient arrangements for exchanging support with Senators from other sections of the country. After eleven weeks of debate, the revised bill passed the Senate by a vote of 45 to 34 on July 8, 1909.[129]

In the meantime, Taft had grown more and more distrustful of the Insurgents. He wrote that the extreme supporters of Mr. Roosevelt who liked to call themselves "progressives" were very suspicious of him because he was consorting with anti-Roosevelt men like Cannon and Aldrich. "What a fool I would be if I joined, or permitted myself to countenance the yelping and snarling at Cannon and Aldrich, which these so-called progressives and their amateur political newspaper correspondents are insisting upon as a mark of loyalty to the Roosevelt policies, and to the carrying out of which I am pledged."[130] Yet the President surely was aware that Cannon was a hard bargainer. Aldrich tried to intervene with Taft on the

128. H. Parker Willis, *loc. cit.*, 28-9.
129. Lawrence Chamberlain, *op. cit.*, 106-7.
130. William Howard Taft to Horace D. Taft, June 27, 1909, Taft Papers.

glove schedule which Cannon insisted must remain high, because he was committed to Representative Lucius Littauer of New York on the matter, that gentleman having helped him attain the Speakership. The President was indignant and called the high glove schedule "the most bare-faced piece of personal legislation that he had ever heard of and that the reason which Cannon gave made it all the more impossible for him to agree with it."[131]

Speaker Cannon was determined to choose men for the Conference Committee who were above suspicion of insurgency. He selected John Dalzell of Pennsylvania, Joseph W. Fordney of Michigan, Samuel W. McCall of Massachusetts, Henry S. Boutell of Illinois, and William Calderhead of Kansas, besides Sereno E. Payne. The Senate delegation consisted of Boies Penrose of Pennsylvania, Shelby M. Cullom of Illinois, Eugene Hale of Maine, and Julius Caesar Burrows of Michigan, besides Nelson W. Aldrich. "It would probably have been impossible to select a Conference Committee that was more disposed to the maintenance of high rates and protective arrangements of every kind. The Conference Committee began its work on July 12 and concluded it on July 29."[132] In Taft's view, Cannon had not played "square" with him.[133] He thought, however, that "Joe" had only aroused the indignation of the House, and that the members were more inclined to stand by Payne rather than by the rest of the Committee.[134]

"There is no doubt," wrote H. Parker Willis, "that the President's influence, whatever it was, generally tended toward the reduction of duties and the elimination of vicious provisions, but it was exerted so mildly and with so little insistence that, until the very end of the discussion, hardly any attention was paid to it by the men who were

131. Archie Butt, *Taft and Roosevelt: The Intimate Letters of Archie Butt*, I, 154-6.
132. H. Parker Willis, *loc. cit.*, 29-30.
133. William Howard Taft to Horace Taft, August 11, 1909, Taft Papers.
134. William Howard Taft to Mrs. Taft, July 25, 1909, Taft Papers.

engaged in framing the final draft."[135] At the last moment Cannon and the high tariff Senators yielded to the threat of a veto, and Taft believed he had won a total victory. He obtained free hides, and reductions on glass, lumber, coal, and iron ore. In addition, petroleum was put on the free list, decreases were effected for iron and steel goods, increases for silk and cotton goods. The woolen schedule remained the same. In the final Conference Report the House acquiesced completely in 522 of the Senate amendments to the original Payne bill, the Senate yielded on 124, and the remaining 201 amendments were compromised. The victory rested with Aldrich, Cannon, and high protection. But nobody was really satisfied.[136]

The Conference Report was approved by the House on July 31, 1909, 195 to 183, and by the Senate on August 5, 1909, 70 to 22. It was a far cry from the downward revision Taft had promised during his campaign and in his inaugural address. "Taft signed the bill because he believed that with all of its shortcomings it contained some genuine improvements over the existing law. Should he veto it, he reasoned, it would destroy the Republican party for some time to come and throw the responsibility of shaping tariff policy into the hands of the Democrats whom he believed totally incapable of producing a law that would work."[137] The President, himself, felt that he had defeated Cannon and Aldrich,[138] But Joseph R. Grundy, a wool manufacturer who was a Republican power in Pennsylvania, forwarded to Uncle Joe his "sincere appreciation for all that you accomplished by your splendid stand for protection to American industries during the special session."[139] James W. Van Cleave of

135. H. Parker Willis, *loc. cit.*, 31-2.
136. George Mowry, *Theodore Roosevelt and the Progressive Movement*, 63-4.
137. Lawrence Chamberlain, *op. cit.*, 109.
138. William Howard Taft to Horace Taft, August 11, 1909, Taft Papers.
139. Joseph R. Grundy to Joseph G. Cannon, August 10, 1909, Cannon Papers.

the NAM wrote: "May the Lord give us many years of your leadership in the House of Representatives."[140] Woodrow Wilson said of Cannon and Aldrich: "They have executed their purposes, not wisely, but too well. A day of judgment is at hand."[141]

All Illinois Republicans in the House except James R. Mann endorsed the Conference Report. Mann openly opposed it on the ground that the compromise rate on print paper—$3.75 per ton—was too high. Cannon was hardly enthusiastic; on the surface nothing was done in the whip and spur line. For publication Uncle Joe said that the Payne-Aldrich tariff protected established industries, but that under its provisions new industries would not be established. Nevertheless, the tariff law would not be "substantially changed for many years."[142]

One of the Insurgents who dodged back to the Regular side in the final vote on the tariff was Henry Allen Cooper of Wisconsin.[143] But Cooper was a little too late in trying to get on good terms with the House leadership. He had always professed his friendship for Taft. But the President had hardly been pleased when Cooper dodged a vote on the appropriation for the presidential traveling expenses and told the clerk when he was leaving the House that the appropriation was "a steal" and that there were a great many men of ability who would be willing to pay their traveling expenses out of a salary of $75,000 a year. The President wrote in July, 1909: "I would much prefer to have had Cooper vote against the bill, but he didn't do that and ran away instead. Such a policy on his part reconciles me to the dull thud with which he will strike the bottom of an unimportant committee in the next assignment of committees by the Speaker, in-

140. James W. Van Cleave to Joseph G. Cannon, September 17, 1909, Cannon Papers.
141. Woodrow Wilson, "The Tariff Make-Believe," *North American Review* CLXL (October, 1909), 542.
142. *Chicago Record-Herald,* July 31, 1909.
143. *Chicago Tribune,* August 1, 1909.

stead of being put at the head of the Insular Committee."[144]

Some House leaders warned the Speaker that a serious blunder would be committed if the Insurgents were punished. They contended that such a course of action would arouse public opinion and make martyrs of the Insurgents who were looking for another excuse to make war upon the rules again. But Uncle Joe's feelings toward the Insurgents were such that "if he followed his impulse," the *Chicago Tribune* reported, "they would be assigned to such committees as ventilation and acoustics, and the disposition of useless papers in the executive departments."[145]

Almost simultaneously with the final passage of the Payne-Aldrich tariff on August 5, Cannon announced the committees for the 61st Congress. Three Insurgents, Charles N. Fowler, A. P. Gardner, and Henry Allen Cooper lost their chairmanships. Vreeland of New York succeeded Fowler on Banking and Currency, Rodenberg of Illinois succeeded Gardner on Industrial Arts and Expositions, and Olmstead of Pennsylvania replaced Cooper on Insular Affairs. James R. Mann, although not the ranking member of the Interstate and Foreign Commerce Committee, was elevated to the chairmanship vacated by Hepburn. Altogether the Illinois GOP delegation with eight chairmanships fared very well.[146] Besides Taft's endorsement for Cooper's removal, Uncle Joe had the support of the Regulars for his action with regard to Fowler. Charles H. Grosvenor assured him that Fowler had been an absolute failure as chairman of the Banking and Currency Committee.[147]

Of the three who were deposed, Fowler was the most bitter. In an open letter of August 23 to the Speaker, he

---

144. William Howard Taft to Mrs. Taft, July 17, 1909, Taft Papers.
145. *Chicago Tribune,* July 19, 1909.
146. *Chicago Record-Herald,* August 6, 1909.
147. Charles H. Grosvenor to Joseph G. Cannon, August 25, 1909, Cannon Papers.

did not mince words. He argued that it was Cannon's own currency record that was at fault. In 1877-78 Cannon had voted for the Bland silver bill; in 1893 he had twice voted against the repeal of the Sherman Silver Purchase Act. Fowler said that his own bill (1907) which Cannon thought was "damned asset currency" was sound by comparison. As the result of Insurgency and the creation of a calendar day, Fowler gloated that members would no longer

> be compelled to crawl upon their bellies, like cringing lizards, to crave the indulgence of a recognition of the Speaker, which being granted, calls for gratitude, and carries with it an obligation, an appreciation of which must be shown of course, at the proper time, or the recipient is written down as an ingrate.

Fowler said that he had appreciated the probable consequences of his actions for some time. "Do you suppose that I was not aware of your ignorance, prejudice, inordinate conceit, favoritism, putrid preferences," he asked, "and that like all such characters possessing absolute power, malice is the mainspring of your every action under such circumstances? Do not forget that I chose my course in plain sight of your political guillotine, and the political carcasses of those you had decapitated; but that it had no terror for me . . . you revel in a glut of brutal power like Nero to terrorize your subject." Fowler added that Insurgency was always possible for the Speaker. He could and did plot against the House itself, the party platform, and even the President. Unless "Cannonism" were destroyed root and branch it would bring defeat to the Republican party.[148]

The recipient of Fowler's vituperation was vacationing at Mackinac. Hurt and angry, he managed to read the

---

148. *Chicago Tribune,* August 25, 1909.

whole letter without emitting one solitary "damn." He made it clear for publication that he was perfectly willing to be judged by his colleagues in the House for his action in not appointing Fowler to the Banking and Currency Committee; he would not answer the letter formally, for Fowler was a "damned joke." Privately, he exploded in unprintable language concerning Fowler's character.[149]

"I shall try to get up a speech for Winona to express my views," wrote President Taft on September 6, 1909 to Minnesota's stalwart Regular, James A. Tawney. The President was very reluctant to give up his golf, but he was determined that the West hear his story on the Payne-Aldrich tariff. His main speech was delivered in Insurgent country at Winona, Minnesota, on September 17, 1909. He declared that the Republican platform had not promised to revise all duties downward. Personally, he had favored free lumber and lower wool schedules. But there were many decreases, and on the whole, the Payne-Aldrich tariff was the best tariff bill the Republican party had ever passed.[150]

Uncle Joe wrote his estimate of the effects of the speech to Tawney:

> I read with pleasure Taft's speech at Winona. It seems to me it was a very politic, forceful, square speech, and it ought to have the effect of strengthening the Republican party all over the country. Of course the Bryan party and the assistants of that organization will denounce it, and those who claim to

149. *Ibid., LaFollette's Weekly* I (August 14, 1909), 4 commented on the Cannon policy of punishing Insurgents: "Cannon may fondly dream that the scourge of obscurity which he visited upon these insurgents will destroy them and their kind, and that never again will he find his throne of power trembling beneath him. . . . But by doing so he went a long way toward bringing about his own downfall. . . . Cannon's revenge is likely to cost him more dearly than anything else he has ever done."

150. William Howard Taft to James A. Tawney, September 6, 1909, Taft Papers; *Chicago Tribune,* September 18, 1909. (Taft said that of the 2025 items in the Dingley law, 220 had been increased, 654 decreased, and the remainder, 1150, was unchanged.)

> be Republicans but constantly seek to betray the party will, it seems to me, be driven to forsake their position heretofore taken or to openly join the enemy.[151]

Tawney agreed with this line of reasoning. "It has done the Republican party of Minnesota more good," he said, "than any utterance of any public man. And the Minnesota insurgents are in a quandary now to know just where they are at."[152] The speech evidently had a different effect on Kansas Insurgents. William Allen White wrote: "The fellows who were insurgent are still insurgent, only more so. I do not know of a man who has been led to even flicker on account of the President's attitude. He has lost and the insurgents have gained, for they are now in the attitude of being persecuted by those in high authority."[153]

The *Chicago Interocean* called the speech "almost epoch making." The paper thought Taft had delivered a "knock out" to the Insurgents.[154] The *Chicago Tribune* admitted the speech had been politically courageous. But since the wool schedules among others had been retained in all their "pristine iniquity" to satisfy New England, the *Tribune* declared: "There is a certain inconsistency in the President's attitude, the inconsistency of a superlatively honest man seeking to reconcile his theoretical view of the tariff with the tariff which the standpatters of his party forced upon him."[155] Taft had little patience with the views of Medill McCormick and the *Chicago Tribune.* He intimated that they had never consistently helped anyone, and were of no help to the Republican party.[156]

The President contended that no criticism of the In-

151. Joseph G. Cannon to James A. Tawney, September 18, 1909, Cannon Papers.
152. James A. Tawney to Joseph G. Cannon, September 21, 1909, Cannon Papers.
153. Walter Johnson, ed., *Selected Letters of William Allen White,* 1899-1943, 102.
154. *Chicago Interocean,* September 19, 1909.
155. *Chicago Tribune,* September 19, 1909.
156. William Howard Taft to W. B. McKinley, October 4, 1909, Taft Papers.

surgents had been intended in his Winona speech. And he told William Dudley Foulke:

> The alliance between Mr. Cannon, Senator Aldrich and myself is one of the easy accusations to make; but as I am engaged in trying to lead a party to take up certain measures and pass them . . . I can not avoid the charge of cooperation with those who are in leadership in each House. If those who are very free in their criticism could for a moment in a judicial way put themselves in the position of one charged with responsibility for affirmative action, they might be able to make useful suggestions to help one laboring under a considerable burden; but the millenium is not reached, and those of us with responsibility must struggle on and do the best we can.[157]

Yet the President was disturbed about Uncle Joe. He wrote to Philander Knox:

> There is only one feature of the situation that I look forward to with considerable concern, and that is the continuation in politics of Cannon. I think he has been sufficiently honored to justify him in now retiring and in announcing his retirement, at least from the Speakership contest, in advance of the next general election. . . . Should you get an opportunity in certain Senatorial and other quarters to make the suggestion that now is an appropriate time in advance of the beginning of the session, for Cannon to announce his retirement from the Speakership, if not for the contest for the next Congress, I think it might be well to do so.[158]

Incidentally, Henry Cabot Lodge wrote to Theodore Roosevelt at this time that in order to save the House in 1910,

---

157. William Howard Taft to William Dudley Foulke, November 18, 1909, Taft Papers.
158. William Howard Taft to Philander C. Knox, October 24, 1909, Taft Papers.

the Republicans must have the assurance that Cannon was not going to stand for Speaker again.[159]

Archie Butt, the President's military aide, was perturbed by the disparity between Taft's private attitude toward Cannon and his public actions. He recorded that Taft simply hated Uncle Joe and yet had flattered him openly on his western trip, was photographed with him, and appeared to endorse him whenever they spoke together.

> He is doing all he can to encompass his defeat to Congress and the Speakership, yet he constantly gives him strength by appearing to approve both him and his actions. . . . If by saying the word publicly that would defeat Cannon, I believe he would say it, so sincere is his dislike of the Speaker, but he does not feel that he is strong enough to say it, so he takes the opposite tack, hoping to aid in his defeat by private innuendo.[160]

Thus, before the first regular session of the 61st Congress convened in December, 1909, the Taft administration was on the defensive. The Insurgents played skillfully to the public impression that the reluctant incorporation of Taft, Cannon, and Company constituted the formation of a combination in restraint of the public interest. Their cause grew stronger with the passage of time.

---

159. Henry Cabot Lodge, ed., *Selections from the Correspondence of Theodore Roosevelt and Henry Cabot Lodge*, 1884-1918, II, 354.

160. Archie Butt, *Taft and Roosevelt: The Intimate Letters of Archie Butt*, I, 201, 222.

CHAPTER SIX

MARCH, 1910 — THE INSURGENTS WIN A ROUND

"Adam and Eve were insurgents and ate of the forbidden fruit expecting to become Gods. They only learned to see their own nakedness. Judas was an insurgent and sold his master for 30 pieces of silver; I have no doubt he would have been applauded by the newspapers of Jerusalem had there been any in that day."

Joseph G. Cannon in an undated manuscript, Cannon Papers.

"It's a damned good thing to remember in politics to stick to your party and never attempt to buy the favor of your enemies at the expenses of your friends."

Joseph G. Cannon in L. W. Busbey's *Uncle Joe Cannon,* 269

There was no lull before the storm. In the weeks between Taft's political tour of the West and the opening of Congress in December, 1909, hopes of peace within the Republican party were dashed. Insurgents sniped at Cannon and the venerable though no longer venerated Speaker fired back. "No man who knows Mr. Cannon," declared Medill McCormick, "can doubt his courage, and many are inclined to view that he is prepared to follow the line laid down for himself, whether it separates him entirely from the Republican party or not."[1]

1. Henry Beach Needham, "Insurgents vs. Aldrich, Cannon et al." *Everybody's* XXII (January, 1910), 109.

Irvine L. Lenroot, Wisconsin Insurgent, predicted in an address called "The New Patriotism" that Cannonism was doomed, that Uncle Joe would never be Speaker of the House again. He asserted that Wisconsin alone would increase its Insurgent delegation from three to eleven at the next election.[2] William Allen White made a discovery: "Emma Goldman, in her palmiest days, never made so many anarchists as Cannon."[3] Herbert Parsons, New York Republican, charged publicly that Cannon's re-election as Speaker for the 61st Congress could be ascribed to treason on the part of upstate New York Republicans. Cannon replied that the Speaker's job had never been in danger; he knew nothing about New York politics, had enough to take care of in his own district. "I don't make a hullabaloo about such things," said Uncle Joe. "When I first used to go hunting as a boy along the Wabash I saw one kind of an animal that I never had seen before, and kicked at it. I was weeks in recovering. . . . And since that time I never have kicked at that kind of an animal—in private life or in politics."[4]

Uncle Joe really broke out his colors while speaking before the Mayor's Association of Illinois at Elgin on October 19, 1909. Standing on tip-toe and waving his arms, he ripped into the Insurgent hosts. He declared that the time had come to decide whether seven Insurgent Senators and twenty Insurgent Congressmen constituted the Republican party. He cried out to his audience: "Behold Mr. Cannon, the Beelzebub of Congress! Gaze on this noble, manly form—me, Beelzebub—me, the Czar!"[5]

The Speaker's challenge was quickly accepted. Wisconsin's "Fighting Bob" LaFollette replied: "He cannot gavel through his classification of Republicans as he gavels through his schemes in Congress. The voters of the Re-

2. *Spokane Spokesman-Review,* October 20, 1909.
3. *Topeka State Journal,* October 20, 1909.
4. *New York Times,* October 4, 1909.
5. *Chicago Tribune* and the *Chicago Interocean,* October 20, 1909.

publican party will decide as to who are Republicans and who are not." The Senator said he would "never believe in the identity of the party of Lincoln with the party of Cannon. . . .His pronunciamentos are but the snarlings of a grim old wolf who hears the beaters in the woods and scents them closing in. He is still at large but the days of his depredation within the sheepfolds of the people are surely numbered."[6]

Senator Albert B. Cummins of Iowa defied Cannon to do his worst. The Insurgents, Cummins said, intended to reduce Cannon's influence to the point where he would find it necessary to consult instead of command.[7] And still Victor Murdock tried to put over the fiction that the Insurgent attack on Cannon was not personal.[8] He said that the House Insurgents had a three-point program which included the creation of a committee on committees similar to the one in the Senate, the omission of the Speaker from membership on the Rules Committee, and modification of the rule of recognition.[9]

Cannon's major answer to his tormentors was delivered in a prepared speech on November 26, 1909 at Kansas City, Missouri. With specific references to Senator Bristow of Kansas and to Senator LaFollette, he demonstrated that these two gentlemen along with other Insurgents had voted with the Regulars on Payne-Aldrich tariff schedules that protected the products of their constituents and with the Democrats on schedules that protected the products of other sections of the country. Uncle Joe said he could not—nor did he have the disposition—to read men out of the Republican party. They could read themselves out if their actions did not correspond to Republicanism. He invoked Taft's Winona speech as a definitive statement of

6. Press release enclosed in D. R. Anthony to Joseph G. Cannon, October 31, 1909, Cannon Papers.

7. *Chicago Tribune,* November 7, 1909.

8. *Chicago Tribune,* November 1, 1909.

9. *Chicago Tribune,* November 24, 1909.

party policy; he used some statements made by William Jennings Bryan as a member of the 53rd Democratic Congress in favor of a powerful Rules Committee; he made some pointed references to Lucifer, the first Insurgent, and to Bryan as the guiding spirits of the Insurgents.[10]

The *New York Tribune* opined that Cannon was "confusing the issue." The paper argued that the Insurgents were not aiming at doing away with the Committee on Rules or abridging its necessary powers. They simply wanted to take away from the Speaker the right to appoint that Committee and vest the right in the House itself. Such a change would correct the abuse of an overconcentration of power in the Speaker's hands, but it would not impair the rights of the majority, as represented on the Rules Committee, in controlling the business of the House. It was possible, indeed, that the House would develop greater efficiency if it learned to depend more on itself and to accept fuller responsibility for its own policies and actions.[11]

In Washington for the opening of the 61st Congress, Speaker Cannon wrote to the editor of the *Northwestern Christian Advocate*: "The country may not for long remember the name of the present Speaker of the House of Representatives, but in all charity I hope and am sure that it will not remember for long the writers who are willing through some imaginary prejudice against the man to slander the whole legislative department of the government."[12] He gave a statement to the press: "Cannonism in its true sense is Carlisleism, Reedism, Hendersonism, Crispism and the ism of all the Speakers who have presided over the House of Representatives for the past thirty-six years, the time I have been in Congress." Uncle Joe

---

10. 61st Congress, 2nd Session, *Senate Document* 163, 6-15.
11. *New York Tribune,* November 27, 1909.
12. L. W. Busbey to Charles M. Stuart, December 8, 1909, Cannon Papers.

declared that he intended for the administration to make progress without compromising with the Insurgents.[13]

Victor Murdock, the indefatigable Kansan, gave a slightly different definition of Cannonism:

> It is a condition obtaining in the House of Representatives inimical to popular government and offensive to the spirit of progress. Cannonism is founded in the belief that the popular desire is unsafe. Its invariable practice is to wear out or confuse the public wish by delay. The system it employs is to concentrate all the power of the representative body in the person of one man — the Speaker. Joseph G. Cannon gives to all the people what measures of representation he desires and he is accountable to the people of only one of 391 districts, the Danville, Ill. district.[14]

James R. Mann, a staunch regular although he had voted against Payne-Aldrich, came to Cannon's defense. Mann asserted that it simply was not true that the Speaker, through the Rules Committee, controlled the House. At two sessions, the 60th Congress had passed 629 public bills and resolutions, but the Rules Committee had acted only 21 times, and most of its reports had not referred to any pending bill. Of the 629 measures passed, not a single one was voted on under an order or report from the Rules Committee. Mann concluded:

> On the whole, the rules of the House probably are the best considered, the most scientifically constructed and finely adjusted rules governing any parliamentary body on earth. But there never has been and never will be any set of rules by which each one of the 400 members of the House can at any time bring

---

13. *Chicago Interocean,* December 2, 1909.
14. *Chicago Tribune,* December 6, 1909. George W. Norris, "The Secret of His Power," *LaFollette's Weekly Magazine* II (January 8, 1910), 8 argued that the authority to make committee assignments was the source of Cannon's power and that it was essential to the Insurgent cause that he be deprived of it.

each one of the 30,000 bills before the House for immediate consideration and disposal.[15]

The *Chicago Tribune* reported that Uncle Joe called at the White House and made his peace with Taft.[16] It was an uneasy peace. The President, in the middle of a withering crossfire, wanted harmony in the GOP at the expense of both the Insurgents and Cannon. On December 20, 1909, he wrote to Otto Bannard: "These gentlemen who profess to be Republicans and will yet do everything to bring the Democratic party into power cannot expect me to assist them with patronage, and I hope to make this as plain as I can before I get through." Taft asserted that he hoped "to separate the sheep from the goats." But he also wanted to get rid of Uncle Joe. "Walter I. Smith is the man whom I would select for Speaker if we can only get Uncle Joe out of the way—and I think we can. If he shall succeed in continuing at the top during the present Congress," said Taft indulging in wishful thinking, "he owes it to the public to relieve those who are his warm friends from the incubus of his future candidacy; and I believe this to be the opinion of those who are closest to him, Jim Sherman, Jim Hemenway, Jim Watson, and everyone with whom I have talked, of the Speaker's closest friends feel this way."[17]

The new year, 1910, did not begin auspiciously for Taft and the Regulars. The January 9th newsletter of the Republican Congressional Campaign Committee announced that the Committee would oppose the principles of Insurgency in the fall elections and would advocate the election of "regular and loyal" Republicans.[18] But the Insurgents were not idle. Norris addressed a blunt question to the President. Were his colleagues being penal-

15. *Chicago Evening Post,* December 6, 1909.
16. *Chicago Tribune,* December 6, 1909.
17. William Howard Taft to Otto Bannard, December 20, 1909, **Taft Papers.**
18. *New York Sun,* January 10, 1910.

ized in matters of federal patronage because of their war on Cannonism?[19] The President did not answer directly. He did say that those who felt no obligation in respect to the party platform could not complain if their recommendations were not given the customary weight.[20] Norris was not satisfied. He affirmed his own loyalty to party objectives, "respectfully" warned the President that it was "common knowledge" that the Speaker had so constituted the committees that most reform measures would be defeated.[21] In reply, Taft assured Norris that he would not seek to influence legislation by withholding patronage. He wished there were no patronage to dispense, but as long as there was he meant to see it go to those who favored the Republican administration so that patronage would not have the probable result of adding to the number of Democrats in Congress.[22]

"What I am laboring to do is to do something," Taft wrote a few days later to Guy W. Mallon. "And the idea that I am to stop and make an enemy of Cannon and make an enemy of Aldrich and make an enemy of those who in the present Congress have power to bring about the reforms which I am advocating, does not strike me with favor."[23] He was not going to be carried off his feet "by yelling by a lot of demagogues in respect to men who have done a great deal for the country . . . this reckless, violent, unmeasured abuse, . . . without definition or limit ought not to be encouraged and certainly will get no help from me."[24]

The nation's press was full of charges and countercharges and rumors of infinite variety. The Democratic *New York World* suggested editorially that "The Patronage Club would scarcely be an improvement, Mr. Pres-

19. George W. Norris to William Howard Taft, January 6, 1910, Taft Papers.
20. William Howard Taft to George W. Norris, January 7, 1910, Taft Papers.
21. George W. Norris to William Howard Taft, January 10, 1910, Taft Papers.
22. William Howard Taft to George W. Norris, January 11, 1910, Taft Papers.
23. William Howard Taft to Guy W. Mallon, January 13, 1910, Taft Papers.
24. William Howard Taft to Guy W. Mallon, January 17, 1910, Taft Papers.

ident, on the Big Stick . . . the business of coercing Congress is one of My Policies which Mr. Taft had better let alone." Cannon was quoted as having said, "I am not trying to run the President's end of the business . . . he is doing pretty well himself, thank you." A letter from Taft to Victor Rosewater, GOP National Committeeman from Nebraska, was made public. In it the President wrote of "a well founded custom" according to which the President, in making political appointments, "should act on the recommendation of the member of Congress in whose district they lie, if represented by a member of the same political party." But Taft declared the obligation was reciprocal. "The Republican Congressman is under a similar obligation to support Administration measures recommended by the President to carry out platform pledges on which both of us were elected. I have not turned down recommendations of insurgent Congressmen, but am simply preserving the *status quo* to impress them with their obligation." Norris retorted: "The fight of the insurgents in the House will continue against Speaker Cannon and the House rules, which he personifies. They will not, however, oppose any policy of the President so long as it is a Republican doctrine." But the independent *Washington Post* regarded "the Patronage Club" as a legitimate weapon:

> The 'insurgents' are shocked and surprised that practical methods should be used against them. They are invoking the Biblical argument that the President should turn the other cheek. But what responsible person ever expected the President to give the loaves and fishes to his opponent? Why should he? . . . His right to reward his supporters and deny comfort to his opponents cannot be questioned.[25]

One prominent Insurgent, A. P. Gardner of Massachu-

25. "Taking the Patronage Club to the Insurgents," *Literary Digest*, XL (January 15, 1910), 86-7.

setts, indicated that much of the talk about Taft wielding the bludgeon of patronage against the Insurgents was just that. In a letter of January 11, 1910, Gardner also said that he had abandoned all hope of Cannon withdrawing gracefully. "With regard to the question of withholding patronage from Insurgents because they are opposing Cannon," he declared,

> personally, I very much doubt the fact for various reasons. . . . We had a meeting of the Insurgents last night at which twenty men were present. A show of hands was called for to find out which Insurgents had had trouble with their patronage. Four hands went up, to wit: Cary, Lenroot, Norris, and Miller. Lenroot had had trouble about a census supervisor; Norris had had trouble about postmaster; and neither Cary nor Miller specified anything. Now I have the very highest confidence in Norris, and I am convinced that he thinks his insurgency is the cause of the trouble. Personally, I suspect that one of his Senators has put a finger in the pie, which, after all, a Senator has a perfect right to do inasmuch as the Constitution gives Senators a say in the appointment of officials. There may also be some such explanation in the Lenroot case: in fact, from time to time all Congressmen have trouble with their recommendations.

Gardner concluded: "If there is any truth in the report about patronage, it is certainly a singular fact that Murdock, Hayes, and Davis, who are as active insurgents as anybody, have had no trouble whatsoever."[26]

The Republican press was sharply divided on the question of what the party should do with Cannon. The *Chicago Tribune* foresaw defeat and wreckage for the GOP if he were not retired to pasture. The *Boston Transcript* politely invited him to resign. But Uncle Joe squelched their hopes: "I will say positively that I will not retire

---

26. Constance Gardner, ed., *Some Letters of Augustus Peabody Gardner,* 56-60.

from Congress until my constituents fail to give me a majority. My worst enemies have never accused me of cowardice, but if I retired under fire both my friends and my enemies would be justified in not only calling me a coward but a poltroon."[27] William Allen White, with a great deal of perspicacity, realized that Cannon's voluntary withdrawal would not affect the situation materially. "Cannon's retirement under fire," he told John Callan O'-Laughlin, "will only increase the clamor against the men who supported Cannon."[28]

Equally acute was an editorial, "The Speaker and the Rules," in the *Philadelphia Ledger* for January 17, 1910. The *Ledger* commented:

> The Insurgent Republicans obscure their own position by concentrating their hostility upon the person of Speaker Cannon. Mr. Cannon's individual character is not really a national issue. It might be an issue in his own district, but his constituents apparently like him. It might be proper issue also upon the occasion of an election for Speaker, but the fact that Mr. Cannon has been repeatedly chosen to this office by a majority of those most closely associated with him indicated that he cannot be quite as black as he is painted.

The *Ledger* considered Cannon no more autocratic than his predecessors under the system prevailing in the House. "Whether this is the best system or whether the rules might not be amended in the direction of greater freedom is a legitimate subject of debate. But the only way to amend them is by the votes of the majority of the House, and until the objectors can convert a majority to their way of thinking—or form a majority by leaving their own party and joining themselves with the minority —

27. "Republican Press on Party Rift," *Literary Digest* XL (January 22, 1910), 125.
28. William Allen White to John Callan O'Laughlin, January 19, 1910, White Papers.

it is only misleading to abuse the Speaker, who administers the rules as they are.[29]

II

As if the party's divergence on the Payne-Aldrich tariff and on Cannon and the House Rules were not enough, the Taft administration's difficulties were compounded by the Ballinger-Pinchot controversy,[30] Mark Sullivan has written of the chief forester: "As Pinchot sought heroes to worship, so did he seek demons to fight."[31] T. R. was his hero and Taft and Ballinger easily became his demons.

The Ballinger-Pinchot controversy was a bitter contention over the conservation of natural resources. Early in Taft's administration an order of Theodore Roosevelt's withdrawing from sale certain public lands in Wyoming and Montana containing water power sites was cancelled. Chief Forester Gifford Pinchot protested and publicly charged Secretary of the Interior Richard A. Ballinger with favoritism toward corporations seeking water power sites. Pinchot also defended L. R. Glavis, Land Office investigator in the Interior Department, who had been dismissed for accusing Ballinger of favoring the Cunningham syndicate's claim to valuable Alaskan mineral lands. Pinchot likewise was dismissed. Finally, a joint Congres-

---

29. *Philadelphia Ledger*, January 17, 1910.

30. Bibliography on the subject is extensive. Rose Mildred Stahl, *The Ballinger-Pinchot Controversy*, is an unbiased presentation. Alpheus T. Mason, *Bureaucracy Convicts Itself: the Ballinger-Pinchot Controversy* of 1910, is partial to Pinchot. As the title suggests, Harold L. Ickes, "Not Guilty! Richard Ballinger, An American Dreyfus," *Saturday Evening Post* CCXII (May 25, 1940), 9-11 and 123-128, is partial to Ballinger. Pinchot defends himself in *Breaking New Ground*. Henry F. Pringle, *The Life and Times of William Howard Taft*, is very partial to the President. Oswald Garrison Villard, *Fighting Years, Memoirs of a Liberal Editor*, and Mark Sullivan, *Our Times*, IV, provide enlightening accounts. The official record of the long investigation can be found in *Senate Document* 719, 61st Congress, 3rd Session. *Collier's* and *Hampton's* published sensational contemporary accounts. The *Outlook* and the *Nation* were more temperate in their week by week summaries. The writer here is interested chiefly in the part Cannon played in the controversy. He makes no attempt to assess the rights or wrongs of the complicated and acrimonious arguments.

31. Mark Sullivan, *Our Times*, IV, 387.

sional investigating committee exonerated Ballinger, but failing to get public confidence, the Secretary resigned. The incident widened the cleavage in the GOP.[32] Pinchot, said Mark Sullivan, had been guilty of "flagrant insubordination." And as late as April, 1910, T.R. wrote to Lodge: "I am not yet sure whether Taft . . . could have followed any course save the one he did."[33]

It was the matter of appointing the six House members of the Ballinger-Pinchot investigating committee that stirred up trouble for Czar Cannon. The Senate had already passed a concurrent resolution for the appointment of an investigating committee. When the resolution came up in the House, Norris made up his mind to try to take the appointment of the investigators from the Speaker and vest that privilege in the House itself. While the resolution was under consideration on January 19, 1910, John Dalzell was serving in the chair. But at one o'clock that staunch Regular went to lunch and relinquished the gavel to Walter I. Smith of Iowa, junior GOP member on the Rules Committee. Smith, not suspecting a plot, recognized Norris who offered his amendment to the resolution by the terms of which the House as a body would choose the investigators. With Insurgents—twenty-six of them—supporting the Norris amendment the Democrats supplied most of the coalition strength and passed it by the narrow margin of 149 to 146.[34] Heartened by their victory, the Insurgents met in Representative William Hubbard's office and decided that they would insist upon the appointment of one of their number, Edmond Madison of Kansas, to the investigating committee and would refuse to countenance the appointment of either Payne or Dalzell. At that juncture the

32. Glenn H. Benton, "Ballinger-Pinchot Controversy," *Dictionary of American History,* I, 148.

33. Mark Sullivan, *Our Times,* IV, 393; 396.

34. George W. Norris, *Fighting Liberal: The Autobiography of George W. Norris,* 109-10.

President intervened, concluding an agreement with Hayes of the Insurgents and Dwight of the Regulars which assured the Insurgents that their views concerning the GOP representation on the investigating committee would receive full consideration in a party caucus. They succeeded in getting their man Madison on the joint investigating committee.[35]

Wrote the *Literary Digest* after the defeat of the Regulars: "Just as Robespierre, after dealing out life and death with despotic hand, had his own convention turn upon him and hurry him to the fatal knife, so the Czar of the House of Representatives now sees his own party haling him to the fate to which he has sent the victims of his displeasure." In the Republican press, Cannon was not openly condemned, an ominous silence generally prevailed. The *Louisville Herald* observed that the handwriting on the wall was "so legible for the eyes of a certain gentleman from Danville, Ill., as to be no longer obscure even to him."[36] The *Springfield Republican* pointed out that there was no case on record since 1789 in which a Speaker had been rebuked so convincingly by the House. That was an "unenviable distinction" for Joe Cannon.[37] A *Chicago Tribune* poll of GOP editors west of the Alleghanies showed 2653 against Cannon's re-election as Speaker, only 546 for him. Defenders of the Payne-Aldrich tariff were outnumbered, 2686 to 812. Presidential preferences for 1912 showed 1093 for Taft but 1360 for T.R.[38] The Regulars could take little comfort in any of this news.

Moreover, the Insurgents continued on the attack. Norris wrote in *LaFollette's Magazine*:

---

35. Kenneth W. Hechler, *Insurgency*, 64-5.

36. "Cannon Viewed By His Own Party," *Literary Digest* XI (January 29, 1910), 169.

37. "The Insurgents and Speaker Cannon," *Current Literature* XLVIII (February, 1910), 127.

38. *Chicago Tribune*, February 14, 1910.

> So far as the enactment of legislation is concerned the House of Representatives bears about as much relation to the National Government as the appendix does to the human body – it has no well recognized function. For all practical purposes our National Government, like Gaul of Old, is divided into three parts: the Senate, the President, and the Speaker. This perversion of the real intent and object of the Constitution has been brought about so gradually and so quietly that until recently the people have not understood the method of its accomplishment.

Cannonites like James R. Mann, forced on the defensive, took refuge behind the line that the issue was Cannon or Chaos.[39]

As far as the Speaker was concerned, Chaos was already reigning. Said he:

> It is impossible to tell what a day may bring forth in the House of Representatives. While we have a nominal majority of 46, we never know whether we have a real majority for the followers in the House of LaFollette, Cummins, and Bristow, so far as their cowardice will let them, are ever ready to cooperate with the Democratic minority, and one can never tell when they will perform.[40]

From his desk at the *Emporia Gazette,* William Allen White sent the President some advice:

> If you will just let the insurgents alone they will come home like little Bo-peep's sheep. For the most part they favor your legislative program. They are not mixed up in any return from Elba conspiracy. . . . The insurgents so far as I know them would rather see you successful for two terms as not.[41]

39. "The Insurgents and Speaker Cannon," *Current Literature* XLVIII (February, 1910), 130.
40. Joseph G. Cannon to J. W. Hill, January 25, 1910, Cannon Papers.
41. William Allen White to William Howard Taft, February 3, 1910, White Papers.

Taft remained hopeful. He thought that "circumstances" were eliminating Uncle Joe from any controversy over the Speakership for the next Congress. "The question is now getting down to one of rules, and I do not know quite where it is coming out but I sincerely hope it will not interfere with the enactment of my legislative program."[42]

In a Lincoln Day address in New York, Taft repeated his Winona assertion that the Payne-Aldrich tariff was the best ever enacted by the Republican party. But most of his remarks were on the subject of party solidarity. He asserted:

> The tendency is to resent attachment to party or party organization and to an assertion of individual opinion and purpose at the expense of discipline. The movement is toward factionalism and small groups, rather than toward large party organizations and the leaders of the party organization are subjected to the severest attacks and to the questioning of their motives without any adequate evidence to justify it.

The Democratic *New York World* noted: "The President is doing his best for Messrs. Cannon and Aldrich but is strangely neglectful of himself."[43]

Out of necessity Taft and Cannon closed ranks. The Speaker offered

> a toast to Taft: May he continue to disappoint both extremes, and, in patience and soberness, work out the policies of the great majority of the people who placed this responsibility on him, heeding neither the demands of those who would have the fire under the boilers put out. And I have confidence in his ability to do it.[44]

---

42. William Howard Taft to Horace Taft, February 1, 1910, Taft Papers.
43. "Mr. Taft on His Party's Crisis," *Literary Digest* XL (February 26, 1910), 378-9.
44. Joseph G. Cannon to J. Van Vechten Olcott, February 9, 1910, Cannon Papers.

The President, on March 5, 1910, two days after he had given a formal dinner for the Speaker, wrote to Horace Taft: "The situation in Congress is uncertain but with the assistance of my wicked partners, Cannon and Aldrich, I am hopeful that I can pull off the legislation that I have most at heart."[45] To Lucius B. Swift, an Indianapolis publisher, he explained his reasoning:

> I think Mr. Cannon represents a certain sort of control of the House that I do not agree with, and I am hopeful that he will announce his retirement from the speakership contest; but that Cannon did a great deal of work while he was Speaker goes without saying, and I cannot help attributing a great deal of the bitterness of this controversy to the counting room of the newspapers which have been affected by the failure to reduce the tariff on print paper in the tariff bill.[46]

Meanwhile, the Insurgents were biding their time, waiting for an opportunity to change the House rules. Victor Murdock reiterated their program. He wrote that the Insurgents did not propose to run the House without rules, to abolish the Rules Committee, to repeal the Reed rules for the despatch of business by orderly procedure, or to compel the Speaker to recognize a member not in order. They had only one purpose— to make the House representative in fact as well as in name as the Constitution intended it should be. They proposed that the Speaker surrender his power of monopolizing the initiation of legislation, and return to the members their rights to reflect the wishes of their constituencies. They intended to make the Speaker ineligible for the Rules Committee, to give the House the right to choose standing committees, and to restrict further the Speaker's power of recognition.[47]

---

45. William Howard Taft to Horace Taft, March 5, 1910, Taft Papers.
46. William Howard Taft to Lucius B. Swift, February 19, 1910, Taft Papers.
47. Victor Murdock, "The Insurgent Movement in Congress," *North American Review* CXCI (April, 1910), 515.

The Insurgents had displayed their strength when they caused Cannon to be overruled in the Ballinger-Pinchot committee appointments. They soon tested the Speaker again; this time for the purpose of amending the rules.

III

Adolph J. Sabath, a Democratic newcomer in the House from Chicago, was an unwitting instrument in precipitating the hectic struggle that developed between the Insurgents and the Regulars in the middle of March, 1910. Sabath, an immigrant himself from the Austro-Hungarian Empire, had introduced a bill to amend the Census Act to permit questions in the thirteenth decennial census classifying persons born abroad by their mother tongues. "Lots of people were classified as citizens of Austria-Hungary when they were Bohemians and Poles," Sabath explained. Uncle Joe was hardly interested in Sabath's bill. But he was interested in breaking down the tradition of Calendar Wednesday, a reform that the Regulars had sponsored under pressure only a year before. So he informed Edgar Crumpacker of Indiana, chairman of the Census Committee and a Regular, that he would recognize him on a day when Calendar Wednesday was in effect to take up Sabath's bill.[48]

On Calendar Wednesday, March 16, Crumpacker sought to interrupt the normal procedure with his census act amendment. He claimed that Sabath's bill was privileged under the Constitution, since that document explicitly provided for the taking of the census. The Speaker upheld Crumpacker. Later on, Uncle Joe recalled that he had felt in his bones there would be an appeal from his decision. "The House, that is the Democrats and Insurgents, was in that happy frame of mind that whenever

48. John R. Beal, "Adolph J. Sabath," in J. T. Salter, ed., *Public Men in and Out of Office,* 212.

the Speaker showed his head somebody was bound to heave a brick at him to keep everyone in good temper." [49] Cannon had really out-foxed himself. John Fitzgerald, the Tammany Democrat, raised the point of order; he claimed that Calendar Wednesday should be preserved for its original purpose of providing a day when neglected committees could report. Crumpacker, then, tried to postpone the consideration of the question so that the sanctity of "Holy Wednesday" would not be violated. But the House voted 153 to 121 against postponement–34 Insurgents voting with the majority. At that juncture, the Speaker waved aside Fitzgerald's point of order, ruling that Crumpacker's resolution was constitutionally privileged regardless of the sacredness of the day. Appeal was made from his ruling, and the Speaker was defeated by an overwhelming vote, 163 to 112. The same 34 Insurgents held together against him.[50]

Crumpacker was persistent. The next day, March 17, he again called up his census resolution. This time the House endorsed the proposition that his resolution was privileged under the Constitution and passed it. Then, Norris rose in his place and was recognized by the Speaker. He said that he desired to present a resolution made privileged by the Constitution. Cannon, unsuspecting, allowed the resolution to be read. It provided for a new fifteen man Rules Committee to be elected by the House according to geographical considerations. Nine of the members were to be chosen from the majority party, six from the minority party, and the Speaker was not to be a member of the committee. John Dalzell made a point of order at once. As the *New York Sun* reported: "The fight began at once and it will go down into the history of the House as one of the most stubborn partisan struggles ever

---

49. L. W. Busbey, *Uncle Joe Cannon*, 251-2.
50. Kenneth W. Hechler, *op. cit.*, 66. For the account by Norris, see his *Autobiography*, 111-13.

witnessed in that body."[51] Cannon recalled: "It was St. Patrick's Day. . . . The Insurgents were bent on driving the snakes out of America . . .and they were able to persuade themselves that the big snake that once coiled itself around the fabled Laocoon and his sons occupied the Speaker's chair, and had the whole government in its coils, crushing out the life and liberty of the American people."[52]

Norris had not sought to create his opportunity by connivance. He believed that it was foolish to call a census resolution privileged by the Constitution and had so voted. But when the House adjudged the Crumpacker resolution privileged, he hastened to point out that similar logic would give privileged status to his own resolution for the revision of the rules since the rules were also mentioned in the Constitution. He, therefore, took the opportunity to spring the resolution he had been carrying around in his pocket for months.[53]

Norris wrote in his *Autobiography*:

> If Speaker Cannon's emotions rose he held them well in check. Under parliamentary law he had the right to ask for debate when it became his duty to rule upon a point of order. If desired, he could call upon individual members to express their opinion and to offer arguments either for or against sustaining the order. If he ruled immediately upon the appeal a vote would follow; and if the Democratic and Insurgent members stood solidly in support of my resolution I should be sustained. In that event, the resolution would come to an immediate vote. In the uncertainty of the attitude of Democratic members, and the absence of some of his supporters, he decided to play for time in the hope of reorganizing his lines.[54]

---

51. *New York Sun* March 18, 1910.
52. L. W. Busbey, *op. cit.*, 254-5.
53. Kenneth W. Hechler, *op. cit.*, 67-8; L. W. Busbey, *op. cit.*, 254, admits that Norris was justified in introducing his resolution when he did.
54. George W. Norris, *op. cit.*, 116.

Cannon's power as Speaker definitely was at stake. The call was sent out to all absent Regulars to rush to Washington to stem the tide. As the lines of battle were drawn, the House chamber provided scenes of intense excitement. Crowds flocked into the galleries and applauded their favorites. Speeches droned on and on as the Congressmen milled about the floor. Cannon himself, outwardly calm though probably seething within, alternately wielded the gavel and consulted with his supporters on the floor. When a second motion for adjournment made by James A. Tawney was defeated about eleven o'clock in the evening, the *Chicago Record-Herald* reported that

> the Speaker actually implored the House to take a recess. He declared that it was essential that before any ruling was made the precedents, many in number, be presented so that the House as well as the Speaker could understand the situation when it comes to voting on any ruling made from the chair. But the recess lost by three votes, notwithstanding the assurances from the floor that the parliamentary status of affairs would be maintained after a period of rest.[55]

Insurgent Henry Allen Cooper, in the midst of a thoroughgoing attack on the Speaker and the rules, cited the case of Insurgent A. P. Gardner's loss of a committee chairmanship as an illustration of the Speaker's tyranny. Gardner, at Cannon's request, set his fellow Insurgent straight. He took the floor and explained that he had asked the Speaker to be relieved as a chairman so that the Insurgents would not think that he had sold out to the Regulars.[56]

"All pretense of the politeness that normally rules proceedings in the House was thrown aside in the early morning hours," the *New York Evening Post* reported. "The

55. *Chicago Record-Herald,* March 18, 1910.
56. *New York Sun,* March 18, 1910; See also, Busbey, *op. cit.,* 256-60.

atmosphere was that of a hard-fought political convention rather than of a legislative body. This is readily ascribable to the fact that the members of the House were sitting as a political convention, so far as the majority of the next Congress is concerned." Uncle Joe spent the night in his room now and then emerging into the House chamber where John Dalzell held the fort for the Regulars. About 5:30 A.M. on the 18th there was a hot debate on the possibility of selecting an assistant Sergeant-at-Arms and other officers necessary to bring in the many members who were absent. Dalzell ruled that the minority there present was powerless to appoint additional officers.[57]

Cannon recalled that most of the Regulars and some of the Insurgent-Democratic coalition had gone home and that "in some mysterious manner" the official Sergeant-at-Arms was most adept at rousing Democrats and Insurgents to return to the House. That, of course, angered their ineffectual brethren on the floor who found in the practice another instance of Cannonism.[58]

Cannon came on to the scene at 6 A.M., and keeping his temper with difficulty, engaged in an argument with Albert Sidney Burleson, the Texas Democrat. The *New York Evening Post* pictured Uncle Joe "idly toying with his gavel with the same fondness often manifested by an old hunter for a gun with which he has brought down much game. Some of his Democratic friends took advantage of the opportunity of a social visit with him and the conversation was jovial in character." Then the Speaker and many of the others went out for leisurely breakfasts. By 11 A. M. the galleries were filled as they been almost all night. The members were irritable, snappish, and disheveled. Cannon reappeared and answered Democratic cries that he rule on the point of order made almost 24 hours before by saying that he would — "in the near

57. *New York Evening Post,* March 18, 1910.

58. L. W. Busbey, *op. cit.,* 263-4.

future." The debate drifted on; Uncle Joe remained grimly determined. But at 1 P.M. announcement was made that Regulars John Dalzell, Marlin Olmsted, and Walter I. Smith of Iowa were going to meet with Insurgents George W. Norris, A. P. Gardner, Everis Hayes and Irvine L. Lenroot. Earlier in the day Norris and Champ Clark had announced that the Norris resolution would carry by 10 to 15 votes. So the House was being provided with the strange spectacle of its organization conducting a fillibuster, because the Speaker had not seen fit to announce his ruling. Finally, at 2 P.M., after having been in continuous session for 26 hours, the House ceased its dreary oratory. By a vote of 161 to 151, a two hour recess was taken to enable the demoralized Regulars and Insurgents, if possible, to work out a compromise.[59]

Just before the recess, Charles Townsend of Michigan sounded a hopeful note. He said that the rules difficulty could be settled within the GOP.

> There has been too close a corporation within the party in this House. The men who run constantly to the Speaker's room are not more possessed of high ability than those who work quietly on this floor. I am certain that if this corporation should be broken up, and 'insurgent' Republicans so called made a part of the Republican organization of the House, and consulted as are the few who have the Speaker's ear, three-fourths of them will be voting with the 'regulars' from this time henceforth.

But unless the unexpected happened and a break was made in the Insurgent-Democratic ranks, the Speaker seemed doomed to defeat.[60]

The President, enroute from Chicago to Rochester, New York, would make no comment. According to Archie Butt, he did not get excited and refused overtures from

59. *New York Evening Post,* March 18, 1910.
60. *Ibid.*

Attorney-General George Wickersham and others to return to Washington to save the Regulars from defeat.[61] But Taft was concerned. If Cannon were humiliated and removed from the Rules Committee, he did not know whether it would be possible to keep

> a Republican majority sufficiently loyal and disciplined to pass the legislation which we promised. Cannon would feel himself vindicated by a failure to do so. So you see my lot doesn't promise to be a happy one for the next two months. It would please me very much if they could effect a compromise by which the old man should not be eliminated from the Rules Committee even though they enlarge the Rules Committee and allow a number of other Representatives in the House on it.[62]

During the two hour interval when the House was recessed, the Regulars promised to back the Norris resolution on the condition that the sentence banning the Speaker from membership on the Committee be stricken out. The compromise attempts were wrecked on that issue. Reconvening at 4 P.M., the House heard the Speaker say that he was prepared to rule on the validity of Dalzell's point of order against the Norris resolution. But a motion was carried, 163 to 151, to postpone the ruling until noon the following day, Saturday, March 19th. The radical Insurgent resistance reached a low of 17 on the vote.[63]

The Speaker's closest friends were sure that he was beaten. But Cannon himself refused to accept the humiliation of being deposed from the Rules Committee. Said he: "If I agreed to get off the committee I would lose no less than I would if I should be beaten in a fight on this proposition on the floor of the House. If I must get off the committee

61. Archie Butt, *op. cit.*, I, 306.
62. William Howard Taft to Mrs. Taft, March 19, 1910, Taft Papers.
63. Kenneth W. Hechler, *op. cit.*, 71.

I prefer to fight it out."[64] With the help of James E. Watson he prepared a speech, in the library of his Vermont Avenue home, to defend his actions and beliefs in the House the next day.[65]

All was not serene in the camp of the Insurgents and the Democrats. As the chief Insurgent spokesman, Norris conferred with Democratic leaders, Champ Clark and Oscar W. Underwood, on a number of occasions during the long night of discontent. He was surprised to learn that the Democrats did not like his proposed method of selecting a fifteen man Rules Committee on a geographical as well as on a partisan basis. The Democrats threatened to withdraw their support unless Norris agreed to amend his resolution to their specifications—they wanted the geographical feature deleted.[66] Champ Clark wrote: "Norris demanded that he should offer it, and I yielded to his demand not intending to lose on a punctilio the great battle after it was virtually won." Several of his fellow Democrats, however were angered to the point of profanity, Henry D. Clayton of Alabama being disgusted about "the tail wagging the dog."[67]

On the morning of the 19th, Gardner, Hayes, Norris, and Lenroot for the Insurgents conferred with Democrats Clark and Underwood, and Regulars Dalzell, Payne, Mann, and Tawney. Their deliberations accomplished nothing. The Regulars were in an embarrassing position, because Cannon had instructed them under no circumstances to yield on the vital point of his membership on the Rules Committee. So it seemed probable that the revised Norris resolution would win. That resolution provided for a ten man Rules Committee to be selected by the House, six members from the majority party and four from minority. The Speaker was excluded from member-

64. *Chicago Tribune,* March 19, 1910.
65. James E. Watson, *As I Saw Them,* 119.
66. George W. Norris, *op. cit.,* 117-8.
67. Champ Clark, *My Quarter Century of American Politics,* II, 277.

ship, and the Committee was to elect its own chairman. The Speaker's power to appoint the other committees was left intact.[68]

The House met at noon on the 19th with galleries filled to overflowing. The day was a strenuous one both for performers and for spectators. Said the *New York Times*: "Speaker Cannon made an appealing record for himself during the day. Admiration for his gameness, never displayed to better advantage, was manifest on the floor as well as in the galleries."[69]

Spectators and members listened intently as the Speaker talked for a few minutes in matter of fact tones. He announced his ruling, upholding Dalzell's point of order made two days previously against Norris. He was overruled, 182 - 163. Then, the Norris resolution as amended was presented and voted on. It carried, 191 to 156. Insurgency had reached its highest point of influence when 42 Republicans, not all of them Insurgents, united with the Democrats to pass the revision of the rules.[70] Champ Clark later admitted that Cannon, "technically speaking," had construed the House Rules correctly in ruling on the Norris resolution.[71]

Shortly after the adoption of the Norris resolution one of the most dramatic events in the entire rules fight occurred. Norris moved to adjourn, but Uncle Joe asked for time to read a statement. As Kenneth W. Hechler has put it: "The old Speaker then brilliantly defended the principle of government by parties. After three days of fumbling and bungling, this was a most astute piece of political strategy."[72]

Reading the address which he and Watson had prepared carefully, Cannon called attention to the existence

68. Kenneth W. Hechler, *op. cit.*, 71-2.
69. *New York Times*, March 20, 1910.
70. Kenneth W. Hechler, *op. cit.*, 72.
71. Champ Clark, *op. cit.*, II, 279.
72. Keneth W. Hechler, *op. cit.*, 74-5.

of a new majority in the House composed of Democrats and Insurgents. Evidently, he as Speaker was not in harmony with that majority. Two courses were open to him. He might resign and permit the "new combination . . . to choose a Speaker in harmony with its aims and purposes," or the combination might declare "a vacancy in the office of the Speaker and proceed to the election of a new Speaker." But Uncle Joe declared he would not resign, because a contest for the Speakership might be precipitated which would tie up all legislative activities. "And Another reason is this: in the judgment of the present Speaker, a resignation is in and of itself a confession of weakness or mistake of an apology for past actions. The Speaker is not conscious of having done any political wrong." Loud and continued applause greeted that statement; Cannon went on. "The real majority," he said, "ought to have the courage of its convictions and logically meet the situation that confronts it." He had always bowed to the will of the majority and had always contended that under the Constitution, it was a question of highest privilege for an actual majority of the House at any time to choose a new Speaker." He wanted the new majority to have the "power and responsibility, of conducting the business of the House, and therefore he was ready to entertain a motion to declare the Speakership vacant. Relinquishing the chair to Sereno E. Payne, he left the floor, accompanied by applause, and retired to the Speaker's room.[73]

The House was converted into a bedlam unequalled during the preceding two days when Democrat Albert Sidney Burleson, without consulting anyone, offered the motion to declare the Speakership vacant that Cannon had invited. Neither Champ Clark nor George Norris took kindly to Burleson's resolution. Norris said that he regretted the motion, because he had not wanted to punish

73. James E. Watson, *op. cit.*, 120-22.

Joe Cannon but to relieve his office of "autocratic powers."[74]

By a vote of 192 to 155 the Burleson resolution was defeated. Only 9 of the more radical Insurgents voted for it. These were: William Cary, Henry Allen Cooper, Irvine L. Lenroot, and John Nelson of Wisconsin, Charles R. Davis and Charles A. Lindbergh of Minnesota, Miles Poindexter of Washington, Victor Murdock of Kansas, and Asle J. Gronna of North Dakota.[75]

Uncle Joe considered the result a triumph: "I was given more votes than at the beginning of Congress and when I went back to resume the Chair I received a demonstration from both sides such as the House has seldom witnessed."[76] In complete agreement with that line of thinking were other conservatives. James W. Van Cleave and John Kirby Jr. of the National Association of Manufacturers both wired him their congratulations. Van Cleave said: "Your fight was magnificent. Your victory great. We love you for the enemies you make. We honor you for your unselfish services in behalf of the whole people. May God spare you to the Nation."[77]

The *New York Sun* made the point that Cannon's very defeat on the rules proved that he had never been the tyrant his foes made him out to be. In fact, they had supplied the incident that supported "most convincingly" Cannon's oft repeated assertion that the majority always rules in the House and that the Speaker was the servant of the Representatives.[78]

The *Cincinnati Times-Star,* owned and edited by the President's brother, Charles P. Taft, thought the GOP would profit by the event and said confidently:

74. Champ Clark, *op cit.,* II, 278; George W. Norris, *op. cit.,* 118.

75. Kenneth W. Hechler, *op. cit.,* 76-77.

76. L. W. Busbey, *op. cit.,* 266

77. James W. Van Cleave to Joseph G. Cannon, March 20, 1910, and John Kirby Jr. to Cannon, March 20, 1910, Cannon Papers.

78. "The Uprising Against Cannon," *Literary Digest* XL (March 26, 1910), 573.

> The Democrats have been optimistic of carrying the next House of Representatives. They have based this hope on two things. One is that remarkable combination of things that were and things that never have been, which pervades the public mind under the label, 'Cannonism.' The other is popular dissatisfaction with the new tariff law. 'Cannonism' has now been removed as a factor in American politics; and the Payne Tariff Law, being a good law in itself, ought not to be difficult to defend under the white light of the great national campaign.[79]

The *Chicago Tribune* said: "The Republican party has weathered a great storm and has sailed into peaceful seas." The *Tribune* even took this optimistic view after Uncle Joe, speaking before the Illinois Republican Association, denounced those Insurgents as cowards who had stood by him in the final test. "May God bless and keep these men, for, as far as I am concerned, He only can bless them," proclaimed the stubborn Speaker.[80] Some Insurgents wanted to try to oust Cannon for good after that, but Champ Clark refused them his support. He wanted to keep the issue of Cannonism around for the November elections.[81]

Momentarily, at least, the Republicans did manage to achieve a fair measure of harmony. All the Insurgents except A. P. Gardner attended the party caucus on March 23 to select the GOP's six representatives on the new Rules Committee. Those selected were: John Dalzell of Pennsylvania, Walter I. Smith of Iowa, George Lawrence of Massachusetts, Jacob Fassett of New York, Sylvester Smith of California, and Henry S. Boutell of Illinois. Not an Insurgent in the lot! Dalzell and Walter Smith had been on the old Rules Committee, and all six were Cannon stalwarts. But Norris appeared to be satisfied. "It was

79. "Republican Disaffection," *Literary Digest* XL (April 2, 1910), 629.
80. *Chicago Tribune,* March 21, 1910.
81. Champ Clark, *op. cit.*, II, 280-1.

a fair, square deal. I think everybody is very well satisfied. Of course, the men selected are not the men I would have named if I had had the choosing." Joe Cannon was also present and issued a statement signifying his satisfaction with the result. He said the new committee had no more power and no less than the old one, but as Speaker he was "very glad to be relieved of service upon the committee." He had enough other duties to keep him busy, and furthermore, "The Speaker of this Congress, and of future Congresses, if he is not made a member of the committee, will be free from the false accusations that he is responsible for the action of the committee in putting up special rules for the expedition of business."[82]

As a matter of incidental interest, the English commentator, A. Maurice Low, was especially sarcastic about the enlargement of the Rules Committee. He wrote: "Instead of the Speaker and his two colleagues meeting, the six majority members meet in private and after agreeing to a rule submit it to the four minority members of the Committee. This is the triumph of reform. The rights of the minority have been won by substituting four-tenths for two-fifths! With such trumpery toys does reform distract that overgrown body, the public."[83]

On April Fool's Day, the Democrats attempted to repeal the entire Payne-Aldrich tariff in one swoop on a resolution offered by John Fitzgerald. The Speaker and Asher C. Hinds, House parliamentarian, searched the precedents while Mann and Tawney held the floor against Fitzgerald. That gentleman smiled and said: "O, I know how distasteful it will be for the other side to have to vote to retain the present tariff law, but it doesn't embarass us any, and I insist on my motion." Cannon, after

82. *Chicago Interocean,* March 24, 1910.

83. Paul DeWitt Hasbrouck, *Party Government in the House of Representatives,* 9. *LaFollette's Weekly* II (March 26, 1910), 3, represented Insurgent opinion when it declared: "The victory will strengthen the morale of the progressive organization . . . . But it will be clearly understood that little was achieved besides the temporary humiliation of an old man of bad eminence."

a diligent search, ruled it out of order. Fitzgerald, undismayed and apparently hoping for Insurgent support, appealed from the decision of the chair. "The flag of harmony waved on the Republican side, however. Congressman Tawney moved that Mr. Fitzgerald's appeal be laid on the table, and with all the insurgent Republicans voting 'straight,' the Democratic attempt at manufacturing campaign material was beaten 150 to 116."[84]

But more often the Republicans gave indication that their wounds had not healed. On April 9 President Taft and Attorney-General Wickersham delivered major addresses, the President before the National League of Republicans in Washington and Wickersham before the Hamilton Club of Chicago. Taft told his listeners: "The time has come for doing and voting and passing the measures which have been placed before this Congress. . . . Tonight we are reading nobody out of the Republican party. We want all in the ranks and all have the opportunity to establish their claims to Republicanism by what they shall do in both Houses of Congress in helping to enact the legislation before them. . . . I want everybody in the ranks, whether they may have slipt away a little or not." These sentiments received almost uniform approval in the party's press. Wickersham's did not. He admonished the Insurgents by saying "the time of running with the hares and hunting with the hounds is over." He added with emphasis: "Treason has ever consisted in giving aid and comfort to the enemy. If anyone wishes to join the Democratic party, let him do so; but let him not claim to be a Republican and work in and out of season to defeat Republican measures and to subvert the influence of the Republican President."[85]

The party soon had another case of Insurgency—a mild yet significant one. Nineteen Insurgents, including Norris,

84. *Chicago Tribune,* April 2, 1910.

85. "Are the Insurgents Traitors?", *Literary Digest* XL (April 23, 1910), 793.

Lenroot, Cooper, Nelson, Murdock, and Lindbergh, joined the Democrats to defeat Senate amendments to an appropriation bill, particularly the appropriation for the Speaker's automobile. James R. Mann accused minority leader Clark of "child's politics." Uncle Joe placed Mann in the Chair and took the floor to declare vehemently that the proposed automobile appropriation had not received his support. He gave a typical picturesque performance featuring arm waving and floor pacing. The honor and dignity of the Speakership was at stake, he said. If the country should be so unfortunate as to return the Democrats to power, he would not vote to humiliate the Democratic Speaker in such a fashion. The Insurgents and Democrats were simply acting out of personal spite.[86] Two months later the question of passing an appropriation for the Speaker's "whizz wagon" came up again and was defeated, this time without debate.[87]

Uncle Joe was still unrepentant. Theodore Roosevelt, writing to Lodge, might think that "Taft, Cannon, Aldrich and the others" had "totally misestimated" the political situation and that the party was in "a very uncomfortable position."[88] But Cannon still clung to his time tested beliefs. On April 30, he addressed the Middlesex Club of Boston on Ulysses S. Grant. Much of his speech was devoted to attacking the Liberal Republicans who had opposed Grant. He did not fail to note that history was repeating itself with the Insurgents. "While the critic has his place he does very little to help make the wheels go round. He may get into the clouds and spread a mist of hazy talk about progressive ideas, or go down in the mire throwing mud at everybody, but we need men who will keep on the level and deal with realities to work out definite plans. . . . We had better fight and fail, than to fight and

86. *Chicago Interocean,* April 12, 1910.

87. *Chicago Journal,* June 11, 1910.

88. Henry Cabot Lodge, ed., *op. cit.,* II, 379-80.

win and have the victory, like dead sea fruit, turned to ashes on our lips."[89]

President Taft himself told Theodore Roosevelt on May 26, 1910, that the Insurgent Senators had done all in their power to thwart his administration. "They have probably furnished ammunition enough to the press and the public to make a Democratic House."[90] Cannon had told the NAM in New York a week before, "Our Democratic-Populist friends have full power in both House and Senate." He had warned that if they were successful in November, a depression might result. So it was good policy for the NAM to work for a "sound, real Republican majority" in both Houses of Congress. Uncle Joe assured his audience that he was not "sore" simply because he had been "dethroned." Surely, they, as a great organization of employers, did not want to put "the uplift magazines and the college professors in command!"[91]

A second action toward liberalizing the rules was taken on June 17, 1910, shortly before the second session of the 61st Congress adjourned. This was the adoption of a rule allowing the House, on the petition of any member and by a majority vote of the entire membership, to discharge committees from further consideration of bills they had failed to report. A plea for such a rule had been made in the 60th Congress to no avail by Champ Clark. Hamilton Fish, New York Republican, had renewed the plea in March, 1910, again without success. But the new ten-man Rules Committee was more amenable to suggestion than Cannon's committee had been. The Committee considered several resolutions, accepting one drafted by Champ Clark. Chairman John Dalzell, a Regular, then reported the first discharge rule the House had ever had; it was adopted after one hour of debate without a record vote.[92]

89. 61st Congress, 2nd Session, *Senate Document* 567, 4; 15.
90. William Howard Taft to Theodore Roosevelt, May 26, 1910, Taft Papers.
91. Cannon Speech to NAM, May, 1910, Cannon Papers.
92. Paul DeWitt Hasbrouck, *op. cit.*, 9; 138-41.

Democrat Swagar Sherley of Kentucky declared in support of the amendment: "The adoption of this rule marks the greatest march forward that has ever been made during my service in the House." Insurgent Victor Murdock noted that once upon a time members had had to go to the Speaker "hat in hand" to arrange for recognition. That had been corrected and the new discharge rule, he thought, was another step on the way to taking the appointment of committees out of the Speaker's hands. Champ Clark, the author of the discharge rule, told his colleagues: "If this rule is adopted we will never have very much occasion to put it into operation, because it will be held in terrorism over the committees . . . and they will report out the bills desired by the membership of the House."[93] As events showed, Clark was right but for the wrong reason. James R. Mann, with the tenacity of a bulldog, spent the rest of his career in the House, making Clark's discharge rule and a subsequent modification of it look as ridiculous as possible.[94]

But in June, 1910, Joe Cannon was sufficiently roused to make a fighting speech. After a night's meditation, he exploded in a ten minute speech full of "seething language." Calling James R. Mann to the chair, Uncle Joe stepped into the aisle, rolled up one sleeve, shook his fists right and left, and waded in. He disputed Murdock's assertion that members ever had to go to him "hat in hand;" he berated the Regulars who had voted for the discharge rule; and he defied uplifters and demagogues to do their worst against him.[95] It was evident that Cannon, as determined and self righteous as ever, was simply warming up for the Congressional elections in November when his beliefs and even his political life were certain to be at stake.

---

93. Chang-wei Chiu, *The Speaker of the House of Representatives,* 260-62.
94. Paul DeWitt Hasbrouck, *op. cit.,* 142-7. See Chapter Seven, Section II.
95. *Chicago Tribune,* June 19, 1910.

CHAPTER SEVEN

NOVEMBER, 1910 — THE DEMOCRATS WIN AN ELECTION

> "I seek no personal vindication from anybody except from my constituents. If they vindicate me by an election, I will form a part of the majority or minority in the House, as the case may be, but I will keep the Republican faith. . . . God hates a coward, and for one I will not play that part. I will at least, come what may, retain my own self respect, for I must associate with myself during the remainder of my life."
>
> Joseph G. Cannon to Edwin Denby, October 5, 1910, Cannon Papers.

When the first session of the 61st Congress adjourned in June, 1910, many Republicans and newspapers favorable to the party viewed the November elections with optimism. In reality there were also portents of disaster in the air. Regular-Insurgent divergences had not disappeared and were not likely to despite the efforts of President Taft for harmony. Certainly the chances of the Democrats, though they had not won control of Congress since 1894, could not be discounted.

Before departing from Washington for the summer for the House on Vermilion Street in Danville, Joe Cannon issued a farewell statement:

> God willing, I'll be here next session and it will be for the Republican majority to determine who shall be Speaker. . . .

> To make a hare pie, you have got first to catch your hare. I may not be living when the next session of Congress comes around. But if I am, I will be in the hands of the grand old Republican party to do with me as they will.
>
> There are a lot of folks who think chaos would reign if I came back as speaker. They prate about czarism and all that sort of thing, but let that go.
>
> In all my life I have never seen a situation so full of promise for a Republican victory in the fall. It always happens that the Democrats win hands down at this time of year, but when the ballots are counted, they come out behind as usual.[1]

Indeed, there was something more than political hokum in Uncle Joe's words. The Congress, after getting off to a slow start, had passed the Mann-Elkins Act which bestowed more regulatory powers on the Interstate Commerce Commission; it had set up the Postal Savings system; it had approved statehood for New Mexico and Arizona. *The St. Louis Globe-Democrat* editorialized: "To say that the record has brightened Republican prospects is to state the case mildly. . . . The old divisions between Republicans and insurgents have practically disappeared" Taft, in a signed statement printed in the *Cincinnati Times-Star,* radiated optimism. The independent *New York Evening Post* paid Taft the compliment of observing that during the closing days of the session "it seemed as if the Congressional walls of Jericho were falling before his trumpet." The Republican *New York Tribune* exuded confidence when it said, "These are trying days for Democratic Representatives who have already carried the next House, elected Champ Clark Speaker, and installed themselves in desirable committee chairmanships."[2]

Complicating the Republican situation was the presence of Theodore Roosevelt just returned from hunting in

1. *Chicago Evening Post,* June 27, 1910.
2. "What Congress Did," *Literary Digest* XLI (July 2, 1910), 1.

Africa and visiting the crowned heads of Europe. T.R. was angry with Taft but wanted to do all he could to heal "the great schism in the party." Characteristically, he had not been incensed most by Taft's working with Cannon and Aldrich, but that by doing so Taft had split the party dangerously. He was proud of the fact that he had left the party in an "impregnable position." His own admiration for the GOP and "his unbounded contempt for the Democratic party" made him especially indignant. "Roosevelt," George Mowry has written, "was not condemning his successor for being a conservative, but rather for his failure as a politician." Nevertheless, at the outset of the campaign at least, the ex-President determined to strive for party unity.[3]

The Democrats, as their *Campaign Book* indicated, had some powerful arguments on their side. The *Campaign Book* devoted 170 pages to "The Tariff and the High Cost of Living," 44 pages to "Republican Extravagance," and 33 pages to "Cannon and Cannonism."[4] During the actual campaign the emphasis on Cannon was sure to be even greater. For Uncle Joe besides being a wicked old czar, was the embodiment of Republicanism in the House.

Cannon quite characteristically, stood by his guns. He invaded Insurgent Kansas before the primary elections to "Cannonize" the unfaithful. He even collapsed from the heat while making a speech at Winfield, but continued his tour against the advice of his friends.[5] The old guard might die, but it would never surrender. Scorning the terms, Regular, and Insurgent, Uncle Joe called himself "just a plain Republican." He added: "Whenever it is necessary to use an adjective to describe the Republicans, then before God, I will leave the Republican party and climb a tree or join the Democrats." He announced ag-

3. George E. Mowry, "Theodore Roosevelt and the Election of 1910," *Mississippi Valley Historical Review* XXV (March, 1939), 523-5.
4. *Democratic Campaign Book for* 1910.
5. *Chicago Tribune*, July 18, 1910.

gressively: "As long as God lets me live, the muck-raking periodicals and so-called independent or progressive Republicans shall not make me say, that I will not be a candidate for Speaker, any more than they shall make me say, if I am again elected to Congress, that I will not vote when my name is called."[6]

Victor Murdock retorted in a stump speech: "Speaker Cannon for thirty years has been opposed to locomotion in any direction." Senator Bristow remarked: "Kansas is not taking Mr. Cannon seriously." Bristow also argued that the Insurgents, not the Regulars, were the champions of "party integrity." Uncle Joe went home convinced that the "present delegation will be renominated as it ought to be." But his confidence was not shared by the party's press.[7]

The *Springfield Republican* commented: "The eminent ability of Republicans to harmonize on the eve of important elections is about to be tested." The *Milwaukee Sentinel* thought Cannon's invasion of Kansas "a fine exhibition of pluck" but the reverse of helpful. The *New York Press* said that the Speaker's bold intimation that he was still a candidate for re-election imposed on Regular Republicans

> a painful embarrassment. . . . We congratulate Uncle Joe on his frankness, albeit it does him credit more for obstinate courage than for loyalty to his party or for consideration of those who stood by him in the battle with the insurgents. It helps the voters to separate the sheep from the goats. It forces candidates out into the open and aids in exacting from them pledges to stick to Cannon or vote to turn him out. It tests the good faith of those who have professed to be with Uncle Joe for the sake of principle. They should be prepared to die for their convictions, even if they

6. "Cannon Standing By His Guns," *Literary Digest* XLI (July 30, 1910).
7. *Ibid.*

cannot hang the old warhorse for making the issue of Cannonism so acute.[8]

Six of the eight Congressmen, for whom Uncle Joe stumped the state, were Regulars; four of the six failed of renomination and were replaced by Insurgents. The two incumbent Insurgents, Edmond Madison and Victor Murdock, were renominated without opposition. The *Kansas City Journal,* fearing the state had gone Populist, was disgusted. It called the Insurgents "the plain-clothesmen of Democracy." But the *New York Evening Post* pointed out: "Kansas insurgents are now the regulars, and can point to their strong endorsement by the voter of the party as a sufficient warrant for all that they have done or intend to do." The *New York Tribune* still hoped: "The system with which Mr. Cannon has been identified has been overthrown. The voters are through with it, and it is time to forget it in the interest of party progress and harmony."[9]

But neither the Insurgents nor Cannon wanted "to forget it." William Allen White, whose *Emporia Gazette* trumpeted Insurgency, wrote to Theodore Roosevelt: "I hope you have seen how we cleaned them up in Kansas. We have nominated six out of eight progressive congressmen on a straight issue. The standpatters declared that a vote for them was a vote for Taft and that a vote for our men was a vote against Taft. We did not admit that Taft was in the fight in any way; we put up a fight for a free party—free from domination of predatory interests."[10] And White was proud that the unorganized Insurgents had won in a campaign of "Injun fighting from behind the trees and in the fence corners."[11]

8. *Ibid.,* 153-4.
9. "Insurgent Victories in Kansas and Iowa," *Literary Digest* XLI (August 13, 1910), 221-2.
10. William Allen White to Theodore Roosevelt, August 4, 1910, White Papers.
11. William Allen White to Winston Churchill of Windsor, Vermont, August 11, 1910, White Papers.

Senator Robert M. LaFollette's magazine had been fighting openly and tirelessly all summer on behalf of the Insurgents and continued to do so. Its writers left no adjectives and figures of speech unturned. One of them, Ralph Flanders, took a stand at Armageddon two years ahead of T.R. "It is a great thing to be an insurgent," he wrote.

> There is distinction in it. It takes no courage to be numbered among the soldiers of the 'god of things as they are.' And the worshippers of that god are on the losing side. Maybe not tomorrow, or next week, or next year, or for many years, will we make substantial headway against their dull and stolid phalanx. But we are cheered by the thought that again and again in the world's history have they been thrown into rout, while precious ground was gained in the fight for the kingdom of God on earth.[12]

Judson C. Welliver, also aligned himself with the forces of progress and light in defining Insurgency. "It is a national arousal of conscience," he shouted, . . . "the world-old fight of the Many for an even chance with the Few. It is a contest of classes as truly as was the fight for Magna Charta; a contest of the unprivileged against the privileged. It proves that the world moves."[13] It is against such prose, prophetic of a golden age that may be gained through political action, that conservatives of any age must contend.

Uncle Joe, who did not include *LaFollette's Weekly* among his favorite reading, was harassed but unconquered; he announced from his home in Danville: "I intend to die fighting. When the end comes no one will be able to say, 'He was a quitter!'" He issued a statement to the

---

12. Ralph Flanders, "Insurgency," *LaFollette's Weekly Magazine* II, August 6, 1910), 10.
13. Judson C. Welliver, "What is Insurgency?" *LaFollette's Weekly Magazine* II, (August 13, 1910), 1.

press to answer the question of whether he would be a candidate for re-election as Speaker:

> I know of no reason, personal or political, that would prevent my being speaker again if a majority of the House of Representatives should so desire. Under these conditions, pending a campaign, I could not say in the demand of the enemy pledge, in the event of my re-election to Congress, that I will not be a candidate for speaker without acknowledging that the record of the House of Representatives, during the past seven years is subject to just criticism and that the Republican majority with which I have cooperated in the enactment of legislation is subject to just criticism.
>
> This I will not do, because I believe that the record of the party for the past seven years should be indorsed, and not condemned.
>
> . . . I would add that no Republican Representative in the next Congress will be elected Speaker unless there is a majority of real Republicans in the House that will unite in a caucus touching the organization of the House and abide the action of the caucus in the selection of Speaker and other officers.
>
> If I am a member of the next House, I will attend a caucus of the Republican members, cheerfully abide the action of the caucus, and vote in the House to vitalize the action of the caucus.[15]

During the remaining two and one-half months of the campaign, Uncle Joe received some pledges of support from GOP Candidates. [16] There were others, among them William Humphrey of Washington, who believed discretion to be the better part of valor. Humphrey wrote to

---

15. *Chicago Interocean,* August 16, 1910.
16. C. C. Pratt to Joseph G. Cannon, August 24, 1910; Napoleon B. Thistlewood to Cannon, September 9, 1910; Charles E. Fuller to Cannon, September 10, 1910; Joseph V. Graff to Cannon, September 12, 1910; William A. Rodenberg to Cannon, September 14, 1910; Harry C. Woodyard to Cannon, September 24, 1910, Cannon Papers.

Uncle Joe: "The condition of our state is almost as wildly hysterical as it was in 1896; . . . the Republicans of the state never were in so bad a condition." Of the 52 papers in his district, 50 of them were opposed to Cannon's re-election as Speaker. "In any event, I anticipate that the House is going to be Democratic, and that in saying I will not support you I am simply saying what I would never have an opportunity to do anyway. . . . Nothing in my political life has given me as much regret."[17]

New York's GOP Congressman, Herbert Parsons, told his constituents: "I do not favor the re-election of Mr. Cannon to the speakership. The powers of that office have been materially curtailed, but they still remain sufficient to make it undesirable to have it filled by one, who in my opinion, is so little favorable at heart to a number of the party policies."[18]

The *Literary Digest* ventured an observation: "A pathetic feature of Speaker Cannon's desperate struggles to retain his grip on the gavel is the conviction felt by many Republicans and all Democrats that the oftener he says he will stick the surer he makes it that the next Speaker will be a Democrat, so that whether he stays or goes, he loses anyway."[19]

Speculation concerning the President's attitude was aroused when Representative Nicholas Longworth of Ohio, T.R.'s son-in-law, issued a statement from Beverley, Massachusetts, site of Taft's summer home. Longworth admitted having "a genuine affection" for Uncle Joe and "the highest respect for his splendid fighting qualities." But he wanted no part of Cannon as Speaker again:

> I shall oppose Mr. Cannon's election as Speaker and I shall do so in the manner that I consider proper and effective on the settlement of controver-

---

17. William Humphrey to Joseph G. Cannon, August 21, 1910, Cannon Papers.
18. Herbert Parsons Campaign Letter, October 31, 1910, Cannon Papers.
19. "Trying to Drop Cannon," *Literary Digest* XLI (September 3, 1910), 330.

> sies in my party, namely the Republican caucus. I made up my mind before the adjournment of the last session of Congress that Mr. Cannon could not be re-elected Speaker, and my opinion has been strengthened since through correspondence and talks with my colleagues. I am not referring to those who have openly opposed him in the past, but to those who, like myself, have supported him.

Longworth said in conclusion that he was "absolutely convinced, if there is a full attendance at the Republican caucus, that Mr. Cannon cannot be again elected Speaker."[20]

The Speaker replied that if the President assailed his Republicanism, there was time enough to answer. He said he would not fight "windmills fanned by breezes blown from lungs of political personal enemies and cowards." In a more formal statement, Uncle Joe reaffirmed his stand and his hope for a Republican majority without which there could be no Republican Speaker. "In the event of my re-election as a member of the House," he declared, "I shall attend and abide by the action of the Republican caucus, and, from his statement, Mr. Longworth will do the same."[21]

Newspaper comment on the Longworth-Cannon exchange was varied, of course, but the nation's press generally added fuel to the fires of partisanship already burning brightly. The *Philadelphia Ledger* observed that the country had not reached the stage "when a Congressman need shrink back in affright because Nicholas Longworth is against him." The *Indianapolis Sun* hit a little harder: "Back to the wall fights Uncle Joe, grim and defiant: . . . back of the wall the men he 'made' treacherously desert him and try to add their serpent thrusts to the honest blows of his honest enemies, the insurgents." The *Louisville Post* aimed a blast at Uncle Joe: "It would be far

20. *Ibid.*
21. *Ibid.*

more to the credit of this ill-governed old man if he had delivered his farewell from the chair when Congress adjourned," said the *Post*. The Regular *Chicago Interocean* urged harmony in the name of common sense lest the Democrats win the election. The Insurgent *Omaha Bee* tried to minimize Cannonism as an issue: "The Democrats will doubtless try to continue beating the drum on Cannon and Cannonism in the impending campaign, but it is a bogie that should scare no one. Mr. Cannon will not be Speaker after this Congress expires and Cannonism is so wrapt up in his personality that it will be quickly forgotten after the new Speaker is installed."[22]

All this sound and fury signified that Cannonism was an off-year election issue of considerable though perhaps exaggerated importance. Rumors were plentiful that Regular Republicans, despite Uncle Joe's dogged persistence in his course, were ready to overthrow him as Speaker, and make James R. Mann, a Regular who had voted against the Payne-Aldrich tariff, their candidate for the speakership in the 62nd Congress.[23] But William B. McKinley, an Illinois Congressman who headed the GOP Congressional Campaign, vigorously denied that he would oppose the re-election of Cannon as Speaker if Uncle Joe was a serious candidate for the office. McKinley stated: "I am Mr. Cannon's friend, and if he is a candidate for the speakership, I shall certainly vote for him."[24]

Meanwhile, Theodore Roosevelt's campaign for unity had been going on. About the middle of July, President Taft, "approaching the sheer heights of political fatuity," had sent a plan for compromise to T.R. at Oyster Bay through Lloyd C. Griscom. Taft, in return for Roosevelt's "unequivocal endorsement" of his administration, promised to overthrow Aldrich and Cannon as advisers and to give Roosevelt a voice in all subsequent important actions

---

22. *Ibid.*, 330-1.
23. *Chicago Record-Herald*, August 20, 1910.
24. *Chicago Evening Post*, August 20, 1910.

of the government. His move was futile. A few days later when the New York GOP chose Vice-President James S. Sherman, a Taft man, as temporary chairman of its convention instead of Roosevelt himself, the ex-President felt himself publicly humiliated. The Taft-Roosevelt break was not open, but T.R. wrote bluntly to Elihu Root in October that if he were to support the Taft administration, it would be under no illusions "but simply the best thing that conditions present."[25]

In late August T.R. went west to deliver a series of radical sounding speeches. In the judgment of George Mowry, "on the whole . . . his effusions at Denver on the American judiciary and his remarks at Osawatomie, Kansas, were probably designed to gain the confidence of western Republicans with the view of bringing them back to the party fold." But in the east "conservative Republicans became almost apoplectic over the speeches and denounced Roosevelt as the destroyer of the party."[26] The President himself was rather bitter. He felt that Roosevelt had allowed his sympathy with the views of the Insurgents to be made known and that was a "peculiar" way to support his administration. Taft conceded that Roosevelt's western tour had been "one continual ovation," but he was hardly happy about it. "I am bound to say," he wrote to Charles P. Taft, "that his speeches are fuller of the ego now than they ever were, and he allows himself to fall into style that makes one think he considers himself still the President of the United States."[27]

As September progressed, the Insurgents added one victory after another to their original primary success in Kansas. In Michigan, the venerable Julius Caesar Burrows who had been slated to succeed the retiring Aldrich as chairman of the Senate Finance Committee, was defeated by Representative Charles Townsend, an anti-Can-

25. George Mowry, *loc. cit.*, 527-30.
26. *Ibid.*, 530-1.
27. William Howard Taft to Charles P. Taft, September 10, 1910, Taft Papers.

non Insurgent.[28] In Massachusetts, Eugene Foss, a Democrat was elected to represent the 14th district; the district had never gone Democratic before. In the Rochester, New York district which had been Republican for twenty years in a row, James S. Havens, a Democrat, was elected. In both of these races the GOP had been so confident that it had put up weak candidates. Six of Cannon's committee chairmen went down to defeat in the primaries, including James A. Tawney of Minnesota, chairman of the Appropriations Committee, for whom Taft had made his unfortunate Winona speech.[29] Tawney sent a disgruntled explanation of his defeat to Uncle Joe. He said that neither the "progressives," the "African hunter," nor "the former chief forester" were responsible. My defeat is due entirely to political chicanery and debauchery, of the betrayal of my opponent for the nomination of his party into the hands of the Democrats."[30] President Taft, incidentally, agreed with Tawney's belief that the "vicious influence" of Democratic votes in the GOP primary had been responsible for his defeat.[31]

Maine experienced a "political earthquake." Frederick W. Plaisted, son of the state's last previous Democratic governor in 1880, was elected governor. Senator Eugene Hale lost out, and Democrats were elected for two of the state's four Congressional seats. "If Maine can thus be swept away, what state is safe?" asked the *New York Evening Post*. Said the *Boston Transcript*: "Maine's returns are so sensational in character as to make their interpretation impossible on any basis other than as a portent of Republican disaster."[32]

---

28. "Insurgent Victories, East and West," *Literary Digest* LXI (September 17, 1910), 428.
29. "Condition of the Republican Party," *Independent* LXIX (September 29, 1910), 711.
30. James A. Tawney to Joseph G. Cannon, October 4, 1910, Cannon Papers.
31. William Howard Taft to James A. Tawney, October 11, 1910, Taft Papers.
32. "Maine's Political Earthquake," *Literary Digest* XLI (September 24, 1910), 473.

When the primary contests were over, it was evident that the Insurgents or Progressives had administered a licking to the Old Guard. By the end of September forty-one incumbent GOP Congressmen had been defeated, and only one, Charles N. Fowler of New Jersey, could be considered as an Insurgent casualty. The majority of the others were beaten by avowed progressives.[33] The President, perhaps inadvertently, widened the party breach. Late in September the so-called Norton Letter written by the President's secretary was published. The letter stated: "The President felt it to be his duty to the party and to the country to withhold patronage from certain Senators and Congressmen who seemed to be in opposition to the Administration's efforts to carry out the party platform." (Insurgents could criticize that as "spoils doctrine.") The letter also said: "That attitude, however, ended with the primary elections and nominations which have now been held and in which the voters have had an opportunity to declare themselves." William Dudley Foulke, a Hoosier partisan of T.R.'s criticized that, too. He wrote: "The meaning of this was that the President was willing to yield when he found the votes were against him."[34]

Uncle Joe Cannon still had no intention of yielding to anyone. Edwin Denby, a rather desperate Michigan Regular, wrote him at length concerning the Speakership of the 62nd Congress. Denby said he thought Cannon would probably not be Speaker, because the Republicans would not control the House.

> Such being the case . . . I think it would be better for you and better for the party, if, recognizing the facts, you should announce that, for whatever reason you choose to give you do not care to be a candidate for Speaker again. . . . It is hard for a man pure in heart and conscious of no wrong, to yield to the as-

33. George Mowry, *loc. cit.*, 530.
34. William Dudley Foulke, *A Hoosier Autobiography*, 157.

saults of his enemies. But will there be any gain for you in not so yielding at this time? Will you not by yielding give one more splendid proof of your fidelity to the party and your anxiety to serve it always, even to your own cost? However wicked the persecution is, to which you have been subjected, yet its effects are apparent and cannot be denied. I am afraid that there are districts in which your earnest friends and supporters are suffering loss of strength, and may suffer defeat, because of their friendship for you.[35]

Uncle Joe turned a deaf ear to Denby's plea, replying, with a full statement of his views:

I have at no time, directly or indirectly, announced myself as a candidate for the Speaker in the next House. I shall not do so at this time, if ever. . . . I agree with you that there is no reasonable prospect of a Republican majority in the House of Representatives of the 62nd Congress; and, frankly, in my judgment the Senate will be as badly off in this respect as the House.

He reiterated his answer to Nicholas Longworth and went on to say:

I seek no personal vindication from anybody, except from my constituents. If they vindicate me by an election, I will form a part of the majority or minority in the House, as the case may be, but I will keep the Republican faith. This being my position, I cannot determine what course Republicans should pursue. It is for each individual to choose his own path. My own judgment is, however, that a pledge to vote against me and denunciation of me personally will not win any votes for any real Republican candidate from insurgent sources but may possibly lose votes of men like unto you and me, who are Republi-

35. Edwin Denby to Joseph G. Cannon, October 4, 1910, Cannon Papers.

cans and who would rather be defeated standing by the time honored principles and policies of real Republicanism than to win by impliedly, if not directly, repudiating the record which the Republican party has made. I shall not, therefore, pursue a course which, in my judgment, will amount to a confession that the record of the party is indefensible and which will bring weakness rather than strength to every Republican candidate who assisted in making that record.

If there is to be an attempted vicarious atonement, might it not be well that the President of the United States (who participated in making the record of the present Congress and who occupies a much more important position in the country than I do) should announce that he will not be a candidate for re-election; or if other goats are needed, might it not be well that he should sacrifice his secretary of the Interior to appease the wrath of our friends the enemy.

God hates a coward, and for one I will not play that part. I will at least, come what may, retain my own respect, for I must associate with myself during the remainder of my life.[36]

President Taft, who had under-estimated Republican strength in 1908, ventured a modest prediction on November 3rd for the 1910 contest: "If I were to guess I should think there would probably be a general Republican slump, with a majority in Congress against us of from "twenty to twenty-five."[37] He was too optimistic. The GOP won only 161 seats, a net loss of 58; the Democrats won 228, the highest total the party had secured since 1890, and took control of the House for the first time in sixteen years. The GOP lost 10 seats in the Senate, but retained control, 51 to 41.[38] Of course, a number of the victorious Republicans—between thirty and forty of them—could be considered Insurgents. So the Regulars had been trounced even more soundly than the party figures indicated.

36. Joseph G. Cannon to Edwin Denby, October 5, 1910, Cannon Papers.
37. William Howard Taft to Horace Taft, November 3, 1910, Taft Papers.
38. *Historical Statistics of the United States,* 293.

Uncle Joe Cannon won in the 18th Illinois district, though not with his usual majority. Vice-President Sherman congratulated him: "You have sat with a minority in the House of Representatives but the majority always knew you were there when you did so sit. Constancy being one of your attributes, I am convinced that our Democratic brethren will be aware of your presence in the next House."[39] Uncle Joe had no regrets. He wrote to Edwin Denby who had been defeated: "I am still of the opinion that showing of the white feather on my part would not only have degraded me personally (which would have been of little consequence to anyone but myself), but would have been an acknowledgment from one occupyiing a responsible position that the legislation and record of the present Congress was wrong."[49]

If William Allen White's letters can be taken as an indication of Insurgent sentiment, the conclusion can be formed that the Insurgents were not displeased with the election results. The editor of the *Emporia Gazette* wrote Theodore Roosevelt: "It is all right. The one big lesson of the election is that the people in the long run will not be ruled by the bosses. . . . It is a marvelous victory for the primary as a party organ . . . the people out West are with you; you need have no fear along that line."[41] Pointing with pride, White also wrote President Taft: "It may interest you to know that Kansas is the banner Republican state. We have an absolutely solid delegation in both Houses of Congress; . . . I believe that no state has shown such staunch Republicanism in this recent landslide as Kansas."[42] He told Mark Sullivan: "Our big Republican victories this year were in the radical Republican states and our big Republican losses were in the conservative

39. James S. Sherman to Joseph G. Cannon, November 10, 1910, Cannon Papers.
40. Joseph G. Cannon to Edwin Denby, November 10, 1910, Cannon Papers.
41. William Allen White to Theodore Roosevelt, November 12, 1910, White Papers.
42. William Allen White to William Howard Taft, November 22, 1910, White Papers.

Republican states where they compromised and pow-wowed and pussy-footed on the Payne-Aldrich tariff bill."[43]

Different reasons for the Democratic successes were given by conservative Republicans. Herbert S. Duffy expressed their viewpoint in his biography of Taft. He wrote: "When the people went to the polls that November of 1910, they forgot many things. They were eager to reprimand Taft for what they considered his political blunders. Failing to understand properly all the facts about the Pinchot-Ballinger controversy, the Payne-Aldrich Tariff Act, and the insurgent insurrection against Cannon, they wrongly considered these incidents as examples of Taft's deficiencies as an executive."[44] Numerous newspapers moaned that Theodore Roosevelt's appearance in the campaign had wrecked the party and his own chances for 1912.[45] On that point George Mowry has written: "In truth, Theodore Roosevelt, had, if he had done anything, driven the two wings of the party further apart and personally had been successful only in alienating himself from both factions. He had failed to see that the party split was on issues so fundamental as to make a drawing together impossible. His characteristic political approach to any problem and his inability to feel deeply on any issue had led him into the impasse of trying to reconcile the irreconciliable." Late in November, reflecting on the future, T.R. finally concluded that it would not be possible to reorganize the GOP on a compromise basis. He felt certain that whichever side captured the party, defeat in 1912 would follow.[46]

Regulars might console themselves by saying that the country was fundamentally sound, that it was Democratic but unreasonably discontented. Carefully analyzing the

43. William Allen White to Mark Sullivan, November 23, 1910, White Papers.

44. Herbert S. Duffy, *William Howard Taft,* 261.

45. "Meaning of the Republican Waterloo," *Literary Digest* XLI (November 19, 1910), 915-6.

46. George Mowry, *loc. cit.,* 532-3.

results at his Wisconsin home, Senator LaFollette, who rode with the Insurgents, was also convinced that the election was not a Democratic party victory where the Democrats had won. It was a defeat of reactionary Republicanism which condemned the Taft administration and repudiated "Aldrichism in the Senate and Cannonism in the House."[47]

Unfortunately the discontented electorate had been presented with a ready target to shoot at in the person of Joe Cannon, who had stood forth impervious to change as the embodiment of stand-pat Republicanism. Although "vindicated" by his own constituents, Uncle Joe had not gained votes for his fellow Regulars by his stubborn refusal to announce that he would be willing to retire as Speaker. Did he or the stand-pat element learn anything from their defeat in 1910? Not in the judgment of the party's historian, William Starr Myers: "They had learned nothing and forgotten nothing, and down to defeat they went." The party was not destroyed only because of the loyalty of its adherents to the name "Republican" and because of the mistakes of the Democrats in Wilson's second administration.[48] Ogden L. Mills, Secretary of the Treasury under Herbert Hoover, came to a somewhat similar conclusion in 1937 after watching the GOP absorb the most decisive defeat in its history. Mills noted gloomily that divisions in the Republican ranks which caused the party to lose its sense of direction and the electorate to lose interest in the party had first definitely appeared in 1910.[49]

II

Before the Democrats had a chance to enjoy the fruits of their victory, the lame duck session of the 61st Con-

---

47. *LaFollette's Weekly Magazine* II (November 19, 1910), 3.
48. William Starr Myers, *The Republican Party, A History,* 397.
49. Ogden L. Mills, *The Seventeen Millions,* 8-9.

gress had to be concluded. "Just contemplate for a moment the serene contentment of Uncle Joe Cannon as he looks around him on the wreck of political worlds," declared the *Portland Oregonian,* "Disaster befell stand-patter and insurgent, but he shows up smilingly at the short session of the sixty-first Congress with the approval of his constituents at the recent election, the assurance that nothing untoward will happen for the remainder of his term as Speaker and with the certainty that neither regular nor insurgent Republican will take the gavel away from him in the next Congress."[50]

Uncle Joe soon showed that he meant to wield his gavel as vigorously as he had since 1903. On December 19, 1910, with the able assistance of James R. Mann and others of the Old Guard, he gave his blessing to attempts to filibuster to a standstill the committee discharge rule adopted only six months before. When the rule was adopted, Uncle Joe had prophesied that it would only result in clogging the House machinery. He took elaborate pains to see that it did on the first day of the session when it was in order to call up motions to discharge committees from the consideration of bills they had buried and to bring them before the House for direct action.[51]

Representative Fitzgerald asked consideration to discharge the Ways and Means Committee from further deliberation on his bill to remove import duties from meat products; Representative Fuller of Illinois sought prior consideration for a pension bill of his. As the *Chicago Tribune* reported the affair: "After considerable wrangling that killed so much time that all the standpatters were put into a good humor, Mr. Mann quietly called attention to the fact that the first motion on the calendar was his proposal to discharge the post office committee from consideration of the post office reorganization bill.

50. *Portland Oregonian,* December 8, 1910.

51. *Chicago Tribune,* December 20, 1910.

> The Mann motion was given the right of way and Speaker Cannon ordered the reading of the bill. Solemnly the clerk produced a volume two inches thick and containing 50,000 words of text and began reading, not omitting the index which he rendered with impressive effect.
>
> The progressives gasped for they saw it would take a week to read the bill and their suspicions were verified by a study of Uncle Joe's happy expression. On every side the standpatters were snorting with delight.[52]

The Insurgents planned an amendment to the rules to eliminate a repetition of Mann's performance. As the discharge motions were recognized only on the first and third Mondays of each month, all similar motions would have been delayed for about two months by Mann's motion. The Insurgents proposed an amendment to the rules to require simply the reading of the title of a bill when a motion had been made for discharge. But the Regulars, having put a crimp in the Insurgent plans, were certain to fight gleefully to keep it there.[53] They soon recorded another success. The *New York Times* of January 10, 1911, said: "Speaker Cannon had his hour of triumph in the House today. Badly battered in the three days storm that swept the House last March and tore from him much of the power that had been his, the Speaker 'came back' in a way that brought a grim smile of satisfaction to his countenance."[54]

James R. Mann, who had industriously filled the calendar with 107 discharge petitions to show the impotence of the rule, started the affair. Fuller had offered a motion to amend the House rules so that discharge motions would not be given precedence over motions to suspend the rules. Mann objected that Fuller's motion was not

52. *Ibid.*
53. *Ibid.,* December 21, 1910.
54. *New York Times,* January 10, 1911.

privileged. The Speaker's decision was necessary and Cannon did not let the opportunity pass. For Fuller's parliamentary position was precisely that taken by Norris at the start of his St. Patrick's Day insurrection, and his motion could only be privileged if the House adopted the same position it had taken then.

While Cannon was preparing his decision, the House except for a few Democrats and the Insurgents, was entertained by the confessions of two Democratic leaders, Oscar W. Underwood and John Fitzgerald. Both admitted that Cannon had been right on March 19, 1910, when he had held the Norris resolution out of order and that the House by overruling him had resorted to revolutionary tactics. Regular Republicans enjoyed the proceedings, reported the *Chicago Record-Herald,* "laughing uproariously and long, as the discomfiture of the Republicans insurgents was pressed home by their former allies, the Democrats." Cannon delivered his ruling in his most impressive manner. His decision, upholding Mann's point of order, was identical in its effect with the one he had delivered on March, 19, 1910, preliminary to the revolution which deposed him from the Rules Committee. He prefaced his decision by having read into the *Record* again his remarks made on the occasion. He took the opportunity to chastise verbally Champ Clark and the Democrats for having used the Norris resolution to manufacture campaign material. Since the election was over, he expressed confidence that their judgment would now be calm and deliberate. His "confidence" was well placed. The House scrambled to his support, sustaining his ruling, much to the chagrin of the Insurgents, by the overwhelming majority of 222 to 53. Voting against him were 27 Insurgents but only 26 Democrats.[55] The Speaker could consider himself "vindicated."

In an editorial, "The House Rules," the *New York Tri-*

55. *Chicago Record-Herald,* January 10, 1911.

bune agreed that Uncle Joe was entitled to enjoy what he might consider a vindication. But the *Tribune* was careful to point out that Cannon himself had given Norris the opportunity to claim immediate consideration for his resolution reconstructing the Rules Committee by a ruling he had made permitting Crumpacker's bill to be taken up out of order as a matter of Constitutional privilege. The *Tribune* concluded:

> The arguments made by the supporters of the census bill were expropriated to excuse Mr. Norris's demand, and the House has now shown that it considers the Speaker's ruling on the Norris resolution sound and his ruling on the Crumpacker bill unsound, although last March it sustained the latter and reversed the former. Parliamentary inconsistencies of this sort weigh lightly on any legislative body, for rules have value, not in themselves but only as a means to orderly and expeditious transaction of business.[56]

Of course, in joining Cannon belatedly, the Democrats hardly could have been unmindful that, as the majority party in the 62nd Congress, they might find it expedient to have the House rules universally respected. But the Democratic *New York World* took a dim view of their vote to sustain Joe Cannon. "The Democrats did not cover themselves with glory yesterday," the *World* asserted; "If Mr. Cannon's controverted ruling last spring was wrong it was wrong again yesterday; yet only twenty-six Democrats stood out against 'despotism' with twenty-seven unterrified Republicans. Possibly after March 4 the Democrats will gain nerve with numbers. If not, the Congressional honor of some of them will be brief."[57]

---

56. *New York Tribune,* January 11, 1911.
57. *New York World,* January 10, 1911.

III

After Cannonism had been blunted by the adoption of the Norris resolution in March, 1910, speculation was widespread concerning the significance of the result. Asher C. Hinds of Maine, the House Parliamentarian, admitted that the Speaker had lost influence when a larger Rules Committee was created from which he was excluded. But Hinds said that the very essence of the Speaker's power remained—his right to appoint committees. He warned that should the Speaker be stripped of that right, the power of appointment would only be lodged elsewhere, and wherever it resided criticism would follow. The proposition that the Speakership should lose its qualities of leadership inherent since pre-Revolutionary days, Hinds believed, emanated from a cult favoring Presidential supremacy. The Norris amendment, by dividing responsibility in the House, had aided those who wanted to rely on the President to express the popular will.[58]

But Champ Clark, in the summer of 1910, had expressed the hope that the selection of committees could be taken away from the Speaker. Victor Murdock was of like opinion. According to him, the House had lost and the executive branch had gained public esteem, because the House could not acquire popular support for its personally dominated "committees in waiting." He argued: "The thing now to consider is that Cannonism does not necessarily pass with the retirement of Cannon. The one certain way to see that it does pass is to take away from the Speakership the power, concurrent with the office, to appoint committees."[59]

The Democrats, victorious in the 1910 elections, were presented with the opportunity of modifying the Speaker's

58. Asher C. Hinds, "The Speaker and the House," *McClure's* XXXV (June, 1910), 196-202.

59. Victor Murdock, "After Cannonism—What?" *Independent* LXIX (September 22, 1910), 624, 622.

appointment powers which had existed since George Washington's day. Not all of them desired further changes in the rules. Edward W. Pou, a Louisiana Democrat, wrote to a party colleague:

> My own idea is that we will make a mistake if we take the power to name the Committees away from the Speaker. . . . I have made some investigation of the sentiment of the members from the South and I think I can show you that the above is true. The country does not demand the election of a Committee on Committees, but it does demand that legislation shall not be stifled. In my judgment we will all regret the day we permit such a radical departure from the time honored custom. . . . A Committee on Committees has all the objectionable elements of appointment by the Speaker with not one of the beneficial reasons to sustain it. The power is taken from the House and the responsibility is divided. No single man can be held responsible to the country.[60]

Behind the scenes, four Democratic Congressmen worked to devise a plan for choosing committees that would meet the approval of the Democratic membership. The four were: Dorsey Shackleford of Missouri, James Hay of Virginia, William Hughes of New Jersey, and Cordell Hull of Tennessee. They proposed that the power to appoint committees be taken from the Speaker and placed in the hands of the Ways and Means Committee which would be appointed by the party caucus. This committee would select the membership of all the other committees subject to the formality of approval by the entire House. This procedure became established and still lasts. One result of it, incidentally, was the privilege given the minority party to select the minority members of the committees.[61]

---

60. Edward W. Pou to Francis Burton Harrison, December 23, 1910, Harrison Papers.

61. Cordell Hull, *The Memoirs of Cordell Hull* I, 62-3; The new rule vested the right of appointment in the House itself, but Democratic policy has been to

The new Democratic House, in adopting its rules in April, 1911, to a great extent repeated the rules of former Congresses. Calendar Wednesday and the Unanimous Consent Calendar were continued. So were the so-called Reed rules. The main innovation was the adoption of the revolutionary rule depriving the Speaker of his power to appoint standing committees and providing for their election by the House. Cannon and Mann presented caustic arguments against the new rule, Mann contending that he could see no difference between the Democratic floor leader offering a resolution for the appointment of committees and the Speaker simply announcing their appointment when in both instances the memberships had been previously arranged.[62] The House took two hours to elect its own committees. Cannon taunted the Democrats for having approved as Republican representatives on the various committees practically the same men he had chosen in the previous Congress. In reality, the GOP selections had been prepared by Mann at the direction of the party's caucus. Once again Uncle Joe became the party's ranking member on the Appropriations Committee. But the Insurgents were not neglected. Edmond Madison and Irvine L. Lenroot were placed on the Rules Committee. Gilbert Haugen was made the ranking minority member on the Agriculture Committee, and Norris was appointed to the Judiciary Committee.[63]

The *Chicago Tribune* was satisfied that the Insurgents had received "fair treatment." Any other course would have been "highly impolitic as well as unjust." The *Tribune* also had a word for Cannon: "He has been made the ranking Republican member of the committee on appropriations. It will now be his pleasing task to guard the

allow the Ways and Means Committee Democrats to choose a party list; the GOP relies on a Committee on Committees—George B. Galloway, *Congress at the Crossroads*, 107.

62. *Chicago Interocean*, April 6, 1911.

63. *Chicago Tribune*, April 12, 1911.

treasury against Democratic extravagance. And to that he might devote himself, leaving to Mr. Mann the work of generally badgering and taunting the Democrats."[64]

It later developed that depriving the Speaker of his power to appoint committees brought no light to thousands of bills imprisoned in "dim dungeons" of the committees. For no legislative device was formulated to check the flood of private bills, thereby facilitating committee work and lessening the opportunity for a few powerful House leaders to control legislation.[65] And Chang-wei Chiu concluded: "The removal of the power of the Speaker over committee appointments has not in effect rescued the House from the control of a few of the powerful and important leaders. Nor has it removed the many defects which have impeded the progress of the work of the committees."[66] Indeed, George Norris was not satisfied with that part of the Insurgent-Democratic revolution. He complained that, "It left appointment of standing committees largely to the partisan machines."[67] And we have the word of the Democratic Speaker, Sam Rayburn of Texas, to the effect that Speakers since 1911 have not been without influence on the committees. Said he in 1950: "The rules were liberalized in 1911, when the Democrats took Congress in the middle of Taft's administration. But I would think that the average Speaker still has a good deal of influence in naming committees. Of course, he has the responsibility of naming all the special committees and I don't think there's been a Speaker up there for quite a while that hasn't had quite a bit of influence on Committees.[68]

Cannon was called a czar when he asked, "For what purpose does the gentleman rise?" But Champ Clark and

---

64. *Ibid.*, April 13, 1911.
65. Chang-wei Chiu, *The Speaker of the House of Representatives Since* 1896, 91-2.
66. *Ibid.*, 107.
67. George W. Norris, *op. cit.*, 119.
68. Sam Rayburn, "What Influences Congress," *U. S. News & World Report* XXIX (October 13, 1950), 30.

succeeding Speakers found the practice desirable for the good of the House.[69] In fact practical politicians on the Democratic side were never hampered by their one time adherence to the idealistic notions promulgated by the Insurgents. As Henry T. Rainey of Illinois expressed it late in 1911, Champ Clark as Speaker, "on questions of fundamental Democratic belief" had the right "not only to suggest, but to lead and I expect to see him do it."[70]

In February, 1912, a Democratic House even rescinded partially the rules reform of 1910, when an amendment to the rules was adopted which provided that motions to suspend the rules would thereafter have precedence over discharge motions. James R. Mann had repeatedly shown the discharge rule to be unworkable, and the Democratic majority was also thinking of its own interests. Insurgent Norris was peeved. Regular Republican John Dalzell orated: "Gentlemen of the majority you are on the back track. Your reforms are all shams and fraud. You have taken the power away from the speaker, but you put it all in the chairman of the ways and means committee. Instead of Cannonism and Reedism and Crispism, you have today Underwoodism, and," Dalzell found that "the gentleman from Alabama wears his crown and scepter like one to the manor born."[71] The *Chicago Tribune* crowed:

> No doubt Mr. Mann retains his innocence of aspect, but the traces of jam and satisfaction are not obliterated. . . . Speaker Clark and his House organization have been obliged to revise procedure in such a way that the discharge rule now is reported virtually nonexistent. Clark, the jubilant old crowd Republicans say, is as autocratic as Cannon ever dared to be. The exasperated Mr. Clark had to have the fires built in

69. Chang-wei Chiu, *op. cit.*, 194.

70. Henry T. Rainey to H. N. Wheeler, December 6, 1911, Rainey Papers.

71. *Detroit News*, February 3, 1912.

the old steam roller to get over impediments thrown in the way.[72]

Evidently, the overthrow of Cannon by the Democrat-Insurgent combination had not resulted in the abolition of partisan politics. Nor had it lessened the desire of the majority party to control legislation through its chieftains.

---

72. *Chicago Tribune,* February 11, 1912.

CHAPTER EIGHT

CANNONISM BECOMES HISTORY

> "I congratulate myself that I have seen a greater advancement in civilization than did all the men from the days of Moses to the days of Washington. . . . I am thankful that my life has been cast in pleasant places, and that men have been constantly striving to reach higher ideals. For that reason it seems a crime to me to wail about our future, to accept the absurd ideas of a few malicious theorists and to have the doubts about the present and future of our country."
>
> Joseph G. Cannon in L. W. Busbey's *Uncle Joe Cannon,* 353-5.

When Uncle Joe left the Speakership in March, 1911, he was not on any better terms with Taft than he had been with Roosevelt in 1909. In his view, Taft never was enough of a partisan. When Edward Douglass White, a Catholic and a Democrat from Louisiana, first appointed to the Supreme Court by Cleveland, was elevated by Taft to the position of Chief Justice, the Sage of Danville was not pleased. He expostulated: "The trouble with Taft is that if he were Pope he would think it necessary to appoint a few Protestant Cardinals."[1] The President had given him yeoman support against his better judgment of

1. Herbert S. Duffy, *William Howard Taft,* 328.

many occasions, but it is doubtful whether Joe Cannon was ever grateful.

Uncle Joe had fought for his views until the end of his term of office. Speaking before the Woolen Manufacturer's Association in the Willard Hotel on February 1, 1911, he had advised caution in the consideration of President Taft's reciprocity treaty with Canada, declaring: "If there is a weakness among the friends of protection and in the protective policy, it is that we are trimming our sails to satisfy the dissatisfied and if you satisfy them today, you will find them doubly dissatisfied tomorrow."[2]

Taft thought Cannon's opposition "the lowest politics I have ever seen in Congress," but he gave the "old scoundrel" his annual formal dinner anyway.[3] The *New York Tribune,* thankful for "better days in the House," was glad that the enlarged Rules Committee permitted favorable action on a bill enabling the President to make reciprocal tariff reductions with Canada by treaty. The *Tribune* believed that since the Ways and Means Committee was no longer under the iron hand of the Speaker, it also had been able to act freely. Under a special rule the reciprocity bill passed the House easily.[4]

When Cannon retired as Speaker with the close of the 61st Congress in March, 1911, he declined to serve the party as minority leader. He moved his belongings out of the Speaker's Room and into the new House Office Building, becoming an ordinary member again.[5] Uncle Joe announced his decision in a written statement. No other

---

2. *Washington Evening Star,* February 2, 1911.
3. Archie Butt, *Taft and Roosevelt: The Intimate Letters of Archie Butt,* II, 594-99.
4. *New York Tribune,* February 15, 1911. The session closed March 4 without action on the reciprocity bill in the Senate. President Taft then called a special session of the new Congress in April, 1911, which passed the legislation he desired. The whole reciprocity scheme unexpectedly broke down on the Canadian side. House Democrats continued to make life miserable for Taft and political capital for themselves by sending him three separate tariff reduction measures to be vetoed. F. A. Ogg, *National Progress,* 1907-1917, 177-82.
5. *Chicago Daily News,* March 29, 1911.

Speaker, he said, had served continuously for so long and he was "deeply appreciative" of that "singular favor" from his Republican associates. But he had no intention of serving as Speaker again and wanted to avoid "even a remote appearance of such intention."[6] The party caucus then met in a spirit of harmony and chose, on Cannon's motion, James R. Mann for its leader.[7]

Although renowned as a Watchdog of the Treasury, Uncle Joe changed his role with the Democrats in power. He wanted to increase appropriations planned by the majority for the enforcement of anti-trust laws by 100%.[8] He pestered Fitzgerald of the Ways and Means Committee to spend more money for the upkeep of government buildings, arguing that Congress could not bargain with the Weather Bureau to keep the rain from coming through leaky roofs. Fitzgerald, in reply, said that he did not like to assume that Congress had been so derelict during the previous eight years when Cannon was Speaker that the public buildings were in an advanced state of dilapidation.[9]

Since Canada had not agreed to a reciprocal tariff arrangement, an ineffectual move was made in the House in 1912 to repeal the Canadian Reciprocity Law. Cannon was all for repeal. He argued that any reciprocity arrangement would harm the great American farmer, and

> to give Canada the opportunity through the coming years to agree to validate this treaty at her sweet will, or to continue to reject it, is giving Canada an advantage that I am not willing to give her, because I believe the agreement is vicious.[10]

---

6. *Chicago Tribune,* April 1, 1911. Rather than become "a part of a barnstorming aggregation," Uncle Joe declined a handsome offer to go on the Chautauqua circuit. Busbey, *op. cit.,* 351.
7 *Ibid.,* April 4, 1911.
8. *Congressional Record,* 62-2, 8788-9.
9. *Ibid.,* 62-2, 8125-8.
10. *Ibid.,* 62-2, 8391-2.

In February, 1912, Cannon was noticeably disappointed when an anti-third term resolution authored by James Slayden, a Texas Democrat, was not considered by the House. Obviously aimed at Theodore Roosevelt, Slayden's resolution had sought to express as "the opinion of the House" that the example of Washington's retirement after two terms had by universal concurrence become time honored custom, a violation of which "would be fraught with peril to free institutions." Thetus Sims of Tennessee and other Democrats convinced their fellows that the adoption of such a resolution would be accepted by the country as evidence that they feared Roosevelt. Only four Republicans voted for the immediate consideration of the resolution. They were Henry Bingham of Pennsylvania, Edwin Higgins of Connecticut, Samuel W. McCall of Massachusetts, and Joe Cannon. Uncle Joe, noted the *Washington Evening Star,* looked particularly sad and dejected when the resolution was shoved to one side.[11]

With the national conventions approaching, Uncle Joe reluctantly worked for Taft's renomination. Explained the *Chicago Tribune*: "Cannon dislikes Taft, whom he caustically criticized in his speech opposing reciprocity, but he hates Roosevelt so cordially that he tries to be actually in favor of the president."[12] The rise of the Bull Moose movement for T.R. caused the *Tribune* to print a scathing editorial on the quality of the Illinois delegation in Congress:

> Illinois ought to avail itself of the opportunity to get rid of its ancient, in idea, and honorable, by courtesy, delegation to Congress. If the state were judged by its congressmen the observer would be warranted in concluding that Illinois was about as wide awake as Rhode Island. The delegation includes a few efficient men like Mann, . . . but in mass and lump it

11. *Washington Evening Star,* February 6, 1912.
12. *Chicago Tribune,* April 1, 1912.

is an inert body of nonentities associated in a fellowship of incompetence.[13]

As the paper had considered Joe Cannon beyond reform for some time,[14] it is fair to assume that he was included in the blanket denunciation.

Uncle Joe continued to keep "the Republican faith" as he understood it. He favored the two term tradition, urging the voters of his district at Kankakee not to "despoil" their votes for the Bull Moose ticket and thereby assist a Democratic administration into power.

> No man has a greater admiration for Theodore Roosevelt personally than I have but when he says the Republican and Democratic parties have outlived their usefulness, and makes a platform as big as a newspaper, and advocates a doctrine for the recall of judges and presidents, I do not agree with him. If such a principle had been in force Lincoln would have been recalled in 1862 and the union never would have been preserved.[15]

In Cannon's district in 1912, the 18th Illinois, the victorious Democratic candidate, Frank T. O'Hair, received 19,485 votes, 2000 fewer than the party's losing candidate in 1908 had received. The Socialist and Prohibitionist candidates drew 2411 votes between them, about their usual total. But the Progressive candidate, Royse, secured 9511 votes and accounted for Uncle Joe's second involuntary vacation from Congress. He had secured only 18,707

13. *Ibid.*, August 2, 1912.

14. *Ibid.*, April 6, 1912.

15. *Kankakee Republican*, October 16, 1912. Roosevelt had said at Denver that he favored the recall of presidents, although it was not part of the progressive platform—*Chicago Tribune*, September 20, 1912. It is reasonable to assume that Cannon's personal feelings were stronger than he let on in public. His papers contain a number of clippings of editorial opinion which are invariably unfavorable to T. R. and his third party, e.g. *New York Sun, Chicago Interocean,* and the *Washington Evening Star*.

votes, his lowest total since 1890 when his career had been interrupted the first time. He had plenty of company for GOP strength in the House fell to an all time low in 1912 as Woodrow Wilson went to the White House.

Uncle Joe received condolence from John Ireland, Archbishop of St. Paul, who wrote:

> Allow me to tell you how deeply I regret your defeat at yesterday's polls. I could not have expected before hand that such an occurrence was at all possible. Your splendid services to the nation, during so many long years, should have put far beyond the perils of an electoral campaign. But a wave of restlessness and revolution is passing over the country—and even the pillars of truest patriotism are made to bend towards the ground. Let us hope, and still work, that the fatal wave shall soon have spent its fury, and that calm common sense again reigning, the country may arise into a safe atmosphere.[16]

An old antagonist, John Sharp Williams, sent his sympathy: "Of course, I wanted a Democrat elected to Congress from every district in the United States, but I confess that in spite of that I am sorry to see you go out of public life."[17]

The Democratic *New York World* was moved to editorialize about Joe Cannon as "The Greatest of Living Republicans." The *World* proclaimed its respect for "his courage and his freedom from cant and humbug." It regretted that the country was to be deprived of his services in Congress. "Whether his party is in a majority or a minority, he belongs in the House of Representatives and should be there as long as he lives."[18] The *Washington Post,* predicting that Uncle Joe would return, stated:

---

16. John Ireland to Joseph G. Cannon, November 6, 1912, Cannon Papers.
17. John Sharp Williams to Joseph G. Cannon, November 11, 1912, Cannon Papers.
18. *New York World,* February 10, 1913.

> The intolerant spirit in politics that drove the Illinois statesman from the chair has been tempered in the rough school of experience. Nobody on the ground where history is being made under the methods which supplanted those of 'Cannonism' is today satisfied with the new machinery. Depriving the Speaker of his power and distributing the responsibility among the numerous chairmen of committees has made the House top heavy and incapable of keeping out of its own way.

What was needed, said the *Post* was a revival of the practical methods of Cannonism.[19]

The *Post* was correct in predicting Uncle Joe's return. He was re-elected four more times, finishing his forty-six year career in the House in 1923. As the years passed, the bitterness of the days of Insurgency was all but forgotten.

II

On May 7, 1916, the House of Representatives took time to commemorate Uncle Joe's eightieth birthday. Speech-making was the order of the day, good fellowship the prevailing atmosphere. An Illinois Republican, William A. Rodenberg, was equal to the occasion with remarks about Cannon's sterling qualities which had made him one of "the ablest and most courageous statesmen of his day and generation." He had made mistakes, of course, but no man had ever seen him "lower his colors and hoist the white flag of surrender."[20] Frederick L. Gillette, a Republican from Massachusetts, chimed in that Cannon, bearing his eighty years lightly, was "a sort of perpetual statesman emeritus" and "an honor and a blessing to the American Congress."[21]

19. *Washington Post,* February 17, 1913.
20. *Congressional Record,* 64-1, 7524.
21. *Ibid.,* 64-1, 7526.

During the rules fight, Cannon's performance in a losing cause had been courageous. Now that both youth and democracy had been served, the House deemed it fitting to pay tribute to the old man who had managed to survive political storms for decades and who remained on the Washington scene as a rather picturesque relic. He had played the game of politics for all it was worth, and the Democrats were not far behind their GOP brethen in paying him compliments. Claude Kitchin of North Carolina, recalling the fight over the rules, pictured Cannon as the complete master of that situation who had not lost his temper for one moment. He pointed out that the system of "Cannonism" had largely been inherited from preceding Congresses, and that only a weak man would have used the rules differently than Cannon had. "Before the eyes of friend and foe alike he always stood for the embodiment of courage, of directness, of integrity."[22]

These words must have been heartwarming to the old gentleman who lingered on the national scene, unrepentant about his conduct of the Speakership and distrustful of the Wilson administration. After absorbing his second defeat in 1912, Cannon had been restored to Congress in 1914. He spent eight years more there "in the subdued role of a mere member."[23] As the *Kansas City Journal* pointed out, he had not really staged a "comeback." The voters of his district had simply returned to their traditional allegiance. Uncle Joe had not changed a bit; he was the same kind of Republican he had been for half a century.[24] As Champ Clark, the Democratic veteran from Missouri, explained to the House, Cannon had remained in Congress for so long because except for "two short seasons of mental aberration," his district had always shown faith in him.[25]

22. *Ibid.*, 64-1, 7526-7.
23. *Time* VIII (November 23, 1926), 11.
24. *Kansas City Journal,* April 24, 1915.
25. *Congressional Record,* 66-3, 794.

Cannon was always ready to tell those who would listen about the follies of Insurgents and Wilsonians. In his opinion these twin evils were really two facets of the same one — government dominated by the executive without sufficient recourse to the party counsels in Congress. The Democrats in the House had boasted of a revolution when a new Rules Committee was established with the Speaker excluded from membership. But, said Uncle Joe, always the champion of the collective wisdom of Congress and certainly mindful of the success of Wilson's New Freedom in 1913-14, the Democrats had surrendered the independence of the legislative branch and bowed as suppliants to the will of the President. Their revolution had continued to work until it had made the Democratic party "the abject slave of the executive not only to do his bidding, but to do it without having the satisfaction of being told why they should do it."[26] Of course, such a turn of affairs was not surprising to Cannon. The rules revolt in 1910, he said, had left the House a "headless organization incapable of working without a boss." Wilson supplied the boss in his own person and became the master of the House as completely as Richard Croker or Charles F. Murphy ever were in Tammany. He was the Democratic party and the state; the Congress was afraid to beg "the poor privilege of knowing why they are to do a thing or if they will have to undo it as soon as it is done."[27] Such bitter oratory was an example of the old-fashioned partisanship in which Cannon always delighted and excelled.

For the Insurgents of old who had once plagued him, Uncle Joe also had faint praise. While he had been the "humble Speaker of the House of Representatives," they and their Democratic allies had done him honor by calling him a "Czar," when "a majority of the House any hour of any day under the Constitution could have removed me."

---

26. 1916 Speech, Cannon Papers.
27. *Ibid.*

The Democrats, in their 1908 platform, proclaimed that the wicked old czar was wrecking the Republic, but in reality, Cannon still maintained, he had had little power as Speaker and could have done nothing without the support of a majority in the House. Cannon took great satisfaction in the fact that the resolution of Democrat Albert S. Burleson to declare the Speakership vacant during that 1910 fight had been defeated by a larger majority than he had received when elected Speaker. As far as Cannon was concerned, the result was a vindication of his conduct in the Speaker's chair.[28]

Not so active in affairs as he had once been and, if possible, more inflexible in his judgments, Cannon was still a power to be reckoned with in Republican ranks. For example, when the Republicans regained control of Congress in the 1918 elections, the *New York Times* reported that Uncle Joe dictated the selection of the GOP Steering Committee and floor leaders in the House.[29] As the party's eldest statesman he had the pleasure of riding to Harding's inauguration in an open car carrying the President-elect, Woodrow Wilson, and Philander C. Knox.

Plain language and a ready wit were, as ever, his stock in trade. One picturesque speech employing both was delivered to the House in 1916 against the restriction of immigration by a literacy test. Uncle Joe questioned the complaints of "native Americans" who favored building fences between themselves and those of alien blood. In his view, immigration had resulted in the United States being peopled by a new and virile type of men. And who could deny that anyone else's name was not American?[30]

Applying his impression of American superiority to the then rambunctious Mexicans—as he once had to the Spanish in 1898—he called for plain words and plain action. Villa, Carranza, Zapata and company, he said, were no-

---

28. July 29, 1916, Speech, Cannon Papers.
29. *New York Times*, March 12, 1919.
30. "Native American," *Outlook* CXII (April 5, 1916), 787-8.

thing but bandits. The United States should establish, by force if necessary, a government strong enough to keep law and order until the Mexicans were capable of conducting their own affairs. Only God knew how long that would be. "I mean I would go in there for the benefit of civilization," said Uncle Joe, "for the benefit of the whole world, for the benefit of the people of the United States and for our peace and comfort."[31]

The *New Republic* of December 11, 1915 noted that a number of Democratic papers were praising Cannon for saying: "I didn't vote for Mr. Wilson in 1912 and I won't vote for him in 1916, but I will not criticize his attitude in the European matter. It is not a time for partisanship." The periodical took a dim view of this praise and could not resist asking what the proper time for partisanship was. It concluded that Cannon had thrown "a rather severe illumination on American political sincerity." In effect, the *New Republic* thought he had said:

> I realize this and know how to keep quiet in an international crisis. But that is about as far as my patriotic modesty goes. When nothing but the prosperity and civilization of ordinary people are at stake, I am quite ready to utter my opinions, to play for every political advantage, to upset the Democratic apple-cart. My opinions on domestic affairs are of course ninety-nine percent campaign buncombe, but this is a government of parties, and a man must live.[32]

In the spring of 1917, Cannon cast his vote in favor of United States participation in World War I with great reluctance—he sympathized more with Russia than the other allies,[33] In vain he urged Jeannette Rankin of Montana, the first woman elected to Congress, to go on record

31. Joseph G. Cannon, "We are at War with Mexico," *Independent* LXXXVII (July 10, 1916), 55.
32. *New Republic* V (December 11, 1915), 131-2.
33. *Congressional Record,* 65-1, 343-4, 412-3. *New York Times,* April 15, 1917.

for the women of America in favor of the war resolution.[34] Generally in favor of a volunteer army, the successful precedent for which he found in the Civil War, Cannon also spoke kindly of Theodore Roosevelt's idea (which never received Wilson's approval) of acting in the Rough-rider tradition to raise a division or more of volunteers.[35] He had an anwer for "volunteer swivel-chair warriors" wearing uniforms complete with spurs. They wore spurs, he said, "in order that their heels might not slip off the desks so easily."[36] Although he was not over-critical of the way the administration handled the war effort, Uncle Joe had no use for the government's publicity chief, George Creel, and of course he assailed President Wilson's plea for the election of a Democratic Congress in 1918. Uncle Joe had only ridicule and scorn for Wilson's peace aims, and for the League of Nations in particular.[37] Other Washington lawmakers might not have been too perturbed whether the multi-billion dollar loans to the allied governments were ever repaid; Senator Cummins was for outright gifts lest the allies emerge bankrupt and cause general financial hardship. Old House Regulars like Mann talked about fighting in a common cause and America's duty to aid its allies whatever the cost. But Joe Cannon wanted it understood that the war loans were not gifts and had to be repaid like any other loan.[38]

As always Uncle Joe was more interested in domestic affairs. He stubbornly continued to defend what he considered to be the prerogatives of Congress against encroachment by the executive after the war. The plan for creating a Budget Bureau in the Treasury Department

34. Walter Millis, *Road to War: America,* 1914-1917, 455-6.
35. *Congressional Record,* 65-1, 2214-5.
36. Frederic L. Paxson, *American Democracy and the World War,* II, 292.
37. William MacDonald, "Joseph Gurney Cannon," *Dictionary of American Biography,* III, 477; *New York Times,* January 9, 1918, May 15, 1918 and October 26, 1918.
38. Denna Frank Fleming, *The United States and World Organization,* 1920-1933, 119-20.

which, through the President would present estimates for each fiscal year to the Congress on the subjects of appropriations, receipts, and government indebtedness, drew Uncle Joe's fire. It reminded him of a bit of newspaper verse:

> I'm thankful that the sun and moon
> Are both hung up so high
> That no pretentious hand can stretch
> And pull them from the sky.
>
> If they were not, I have no doubt
> but some reforming ass
> Would recommend to take them down
> And light the world by gas.

Although President Taft had been the first to suggest the new budget system, Cannon thought that its advocates were "unconscious revolutionists" who wanted "to strike out the 'government of the people and the government by the people' from Lincoln's celebrated phrase and retain only a 'government for the people.'" Cannon fretted:

> When Congress consents to the executive making the budget it will have surrendered the most important part of representative government, and put the country back where it was when the shot at Lexington was 'heard round the world.' Taxation without representation brought this nation into being, and I think we had better stick pretty close to the Constitution with its division of powers well defined and the taxing power close to the people.[39]

The House of Representatives, of course, was closest to the people, and it was the branch of government held responsible for taxation as well as expenditures under the Constitution. Cannon believed that the House Committee on Appropriations should continue as the main finan-

39. Joseph Gurney Cannon, "The National Budget," *Harper's* CXXXIX (October, 1919), 625, 628.

cial watchdog.[40] But his opposition was futile. On June 10, 1921, President Harding signed into law a bill creating a Budget Bureau. The first director of the Budget was a good friend of Uncle Joe's, Charles G. Dawes, a Chicago banker who became Vice-President under Calvin Coolidge.[41]

Finally, in 1923, Uncle Joe voluntarily retired from the political arena to his home in Danville where muckraking journalists and Insurgent Republicans by all their efforts had never been able to send him. By the time of his retirement, no Republican under 71 years of age in the 18th Congressional district had ever been able to vote for any other champion of Republican principles for the United States Congress.[42]

From the vantage point of his 87 years, and perhaps reassured by the restoration of the GOP to power in the Harding sweep, the old Speaker was optimistic. In an interview for the *New York Times,* he declared:

> When I am inclined to grow pessimistic after reading some of the wailings and criticisms of the latter-day economists and reformers, I take down a map of the United States and a volume of the census reports, and I find there the realization of the finest dreams of the greatest optimists who ever lived.

Had the war and threats of socialism harmed American institutions? Uncle Joe thought not.

> America today is resting on solid ground. Sometimes the best ideals are drowned in the clamor and shouting of the mob, but ever in critical times we return to our first principles. I have little patience

40. *Ibid.*, 628.
41. A. H. McDonald, "American National Budget," *Encyclopedia Americana* IV, 678-9, 1936 edition.
42. *Congressional Record,* 67-4, 5714. Busbey, *op. cit.*, 323 says "as an advocate of the national budget, I was one of those who recommended Dawes to President Harding as director of that new economic machine."

with those who prate about the decadence of the spirit of liberty in this country and howl for socialism and a pure democracy. In saying good-by to public life, I think I can honestly say that the nation is the strongest in the world, and the people are growing better and better every day.[43]

The last few years he had been "lagging superfluously on the stage on which he had once played a great role." Yet Cannon was still a wise old man in the eyes of Cyrenus Cole, an Iowa editor recently arrived in the House, though it was pitiful to see him limping off the stage when he ought to have been reclining in an easy chair. To Cole he explained the best way for a new Congressman to get his name in headlines across the country. His plan involved simply the introduction of a resolution calling for the investigation of the White House with reference to the presence of whiskey in the mansion. The new statesman was doubtful of the propriety of such an act, but his elderly adviser was not. "If you are never going to do anything impertinent or absurd you will never illuminate the headlines of the country," Uncle Joe opined. "The boys up there in the press gallery begin to stretch their necks and to strain their ears only when someone on the floor begins to make a fool of himself."[44] As a youngster

43. "Uncle Joe Quits with Optimism and a Smile," *Literary Digest* LXXVI (March 17, 1923), 47-8. Perhaps holding the Speakership is conducive to optimism—Sam Rayburn could declare in 1952: "In spite of everything the professional croakers are saying the country is prosperous. Yes, I know that the country is said to be going to ruin. According to some people in every generation it is always ruined . . .

"Well, the country hasn't been ruined yet, and I don't see any prospect of it being ruined. There is little, indeed, that Americans can't do, if they can only imagine themselves wanting to do it. The potentials of our resources, material and spiritual, have never been tapped to the utmost. We still do not know the limits of our strength. This is the greatest country on earth. Let those beware, therefore, who think they will find us easy prey. . . .

"We have a nation without precedent in the history of man, made up of members of all racial stocks of the world; people of different religious and political faiths. Our political and economic system has given more people more happiness and prosperity over a wider area and for a longer period of time than any system ever created by men in their long history." *Congressional Record*, 82-2, A 1479.

44. Cyrenus Cole, *I Remember, I Remember*, 388-9.

in Congress Cannon had used a similar technique to get himself dubbed as "The Illinois Hayseed."

President Warren G. Harding, a Congressional alumnus in the White House more to Uncle Joe's liking than the Princeton professor had ever been, echoed what he called "a very widespread regret" over Cannon's retirement. He said that it was a delight to record that through 50 years of public service Cannon had not only commanded the respect of the American people but had won from them a reverent personal regard.[45]

The home folks in Danville marked their leading citizen's 87th birthday on May 7, 1923, with a gala celebration. The *Commercial-News* brought out a special edition with double headlines in red ink to salute the occasion. According to the paper, some 50,000 participated in the various events, including such distinguished Republican visitors as Governor Len Small, Senator James E. Watson of Indiana, once Cannon's right hand man in the House, and the Secretary of Labor, James J. Davis. Davis made the principal speech. In paying high tribute to Uncle Joe, the Secretary brought in an extravagant comparison to Lincoln:

> The greatest monument to the American public man lies in the hearts of the people. And in the hearts of the American people, that same reverence that claimed Lincoln as 'Honest Abe' has made Joseph Gurney Cannon, 'Uncle Joe,' to America and all the world.

Uncle Joe, the object of "The Greatest Birthday Celebration Ever Held in the History of the Nation," was so choked by emotion that he was unable to deliver his prepared remarks to the throng assembled. He he done so they would have heard a homely farewell address in the Lincoln tradition, which Cannon had adopted so long

45. Warren G. Harding to Joseph G. Cannon, May 5, 1923, Cannon Papers.

ago that it had become his own. For the American people, he had a simple, optimistic creed:

> Have faith in the government of your fathers.
> Show your faith by works to support that government.
> Have faith that right will prevail.[46]

On November 12, 1926, in the middle of the good, sound Republican administration of Calvin Coolidge, Uncle Joe Cannon died of old age. Still the personification of standpat politics, "dimmed to an ember by the weight of ninety years," he died peacefully in his home on North Vermilion Street.[47] An unusually sturdy man even at the last, he had been confined to his bed for only two weeks before his death. His physicians announced simply that the body machinery had worn out.[48]

Apparently, Uncle Joe's sins were forgiven, the bitterness over Cannonism all but gone. Newspapers, magazines, and politicians who had been his sworn opponents gracefully found something complimentary to say.

The *Outlook,* once a haven for Insurgents, doubted that Cannon had ever been a czar or that the method of running the House which succeeded him was an improvement. It readily admitted that "on the political railway Mr. Cannon all his life was not an engineer but a brakeman."[49] The ever-liberal *Nation* acknowledged the time–worn Lincoln analogies, accounting for Uncle Joe's electoral success by saying that no Congressman could have been more typical of his community for "Joe Cannon was rural Illinois in Washington." A rare, rugged personality who recognized but one master, the Republican party,

46. *Danville Commercial-News,* May 7, 1923.
47. Frederic L. Paxson, *Recent History of the United States,* 1865-1927, 651.
48. C. C. Burford, "Vermilion County in Illinois History," *Journal of the Illinois State Historical Society* XXXIV (December, 1941), 477.
49. "Uncle Joe Cannon," *Outlook* CXLIV (November 24, 1926), 393.

Cannon was enamored of its every principle and especially high protective tariffs. The span of his own political life which had begun during the Civil War, recalled *The Nation,* measured the rise of the party and its transformation from a home for idealists into "a sordid organization" which had become the tool of big business. As a Simon Legree wielding the party whip, Cannon:

> helped to enthrone the swollen capitalism of today in the seats of the mighty in Washington. . . . Like his party, he became entirely cynical; unlike it he was not corrupt. Dethroned as Speaker he could take defeat philosophically and live to see a greater triumph for party control of the House and for the crass materialism of the hour than he had ever dared to hope.[50]

The *Chicago Tribune,* solidly Republican but often at odds with Cannon, featured a sentimental cartoon by John T. McCutcheon on its front page along with plenty of space in its news columns by way of obituary. Friend and foe alike in national politics united in expressing their sorrow at Uncle Joe's passing. Senator George W. Norris of Nebraska, whose resolution had stirred up the hornet's nest in 1910 and stripped the Speakership of some of its power, was deeply affected. He took the opportunity of reiterating that the Insurgents had never had anything personal against Speaker Cannon who had always conducted his office according to his beliefs. Senator Carter Glass, the Virginia Democrat, pointed out that Cannon had been the most diligent member of Congress he had ever encountered.[51] Even before his death, Cannon's friends had placed a bust of the former Speaker in the rotunda of the House Office Building.[52] On December 7,

50. "Joseph Cannon," *Nation* CXXIII (November 24, 1926), 521.
51. *Chicago Tribune,* November 13, 1926.
52. *Congressional Record,* 66-3, 758.

1926, Representative Martin B. Madden of Illinois sponsored a resolution of tribute which was agreed to unanimously as the House adjourned its new session out of respect for an old member.[53] Senator Claude Swanson of Virginia summed up his feelings neatly when he described the departed politician as "an American not afraid of power or opportunity."[54] Brief but apt was that description of a life that had begun in pioneer surroundings almost a century before.

II.

When it celebrated the fiftieth anniversary of Czar Reed's quorum count in 1939, the House also directed some tribute to Uncle Joe. "When I used to look upon Mr. Cannon in this House," said Sam Rayburn, "a man who in many ways was like Speaker Reed, I always thought that I looked upon a man with iron in his backbone and brains in his head." Edward T. Taylor, a Colorado Democrat who had joined in the vote against Cannon in 1910, recalled: "He and Speaker Reed had many traits in common. Both were vehemently denounced and vilified. But history will record them as two of the greatest Speakers this House has ever had, and that this House and our country are better off for their courageous public careers." Speaker William Bankhead, looking backward, somewhat nostalgically, upon the methods of Reed and Cannon in wielding their party's strength in the House, concluded: "We must necessarily admire the grip they had on their parties and their firm determination to rule this House in large measure according to their view of their public and party duties."[55]

Under the impact of public clamor for more and more democracy everywhere, the House of Representatives has

53. *Ibid.*, 69-2, 68-9.

54. *Chicago Tribune*, November 13, 1926.

55. *Congressional Record*, 76-2, 570-2.

never restored the discredited system called "Cannonism," however much its members might believe in party hierarchies, party responsibility, the seniority principle for committee appointments, and the multi-volume set of precedents on, the rules. Uncle Joe Cannon eventually left the House as a picturesque relic. But as long as the House carries out its functions under the Constitution, his name will be remembered as a symbol of courageous partisanship. And his system called "Cannonism" will be debated over and over as the House by revising its rules endeavors to solve the perennial problem of providing for efficient party responsibility without unreasonably depriving the minority of its right to object.

It seems appropriate, by way of conclusion, to consider the opinion of a half-dozen historians and political scientists whose views are relevant to Cannonism and the forms of procedure in the House.

According to Kenneth W. Hechler, the Insurgent victory over Cannon

> gave the entire progressive movement an impetus that can never be measured by a studious analysis of legislative procedure within the House of Representatives. Cannonism was a great symbol of reactionary tyranny, and when the blasts of Norris' trumpet felled its walls the Insurgents were spurred to press foward with the balance of their legislative program.[56]

That is all very well, but the subsequent developments in the "legislative procedure within the House of Representatives" cannot be dismissed so easily.

As Robert Luce wrote in 1922:

> The reformers believed they had put an end to dictatorship. Yet that some few men continued to guide is not to be questioned. What was really accom-

56. Kenneth W. Hechler, *Insurgency,* 82.

plished was to lessen the public knowledge of who those men were. Congressmen might know, but since 1910 the public generally has not known who should be rewarded or punished. Irresponsibility has been increased. Perhaps the party caucus has had more chance to commend or scold the men who pull the strings. Perhaps a potential insurgent has had more opportunity to air his views. The Committee on Rules is no longer the organ of the Speaker. But the benefits of the change have not been conspicuous enough to impress anybody as important.[57]

In other words, "when the acrimony was all over, the great reform was found to be a gold brick."[58]

Writing in 1926, Lindsay Rogers concluded that the "voluntary submission by the House to the role of a rubber stamp" had become more noticeable since the dethronement of the Speaker.[59] This tendency became especially pronounced with the advent of the New Deal. For despite the creation of a "steering committee . . . to satisfy the Democratic Congressmen, the real leader in legislation was President Roosevelt."[60]

As expressed by Roland Young:

> The movement to break down the power of the Speaker was a part of a belief then current that the correct answer to political questions could be evolved if power was widely enough dispersed. . . . It was a peculiar thesis that one could break down the institutions of power and the policy would develop from the people with no institutions to make the policy effective.[61]

---

57. Robert Luce, *Legislative Procedure,* 483.
58. Richard Bartholdt, *From Steerage to Congress,* 130.
59. Lindsay Rogers, *The American Senate,* 118.
60. Wilfred E. Binkley, *President and Congress,* 241-2.
61. Roland Young, *This is Congress,* 90-1.

Yet even today as Floyd M. Riddick has indicated:

> The Speaker of the House does more than just preside; he still has sufficent prerogatives to make himself powerful if he so desires and has the capacity. Some of the more recent Speakers have displayed or wielded a strong hand over the House at times, each developing his own method of control.[62]

So despite the formal reduction in his power, the Speaker remains "the second most powerful national officer."[63]

But the power and prestige of the President has been so exalted that "the second most powerful national officer" holds an office much less consequential than it was in 1910. Of course, the increased entanglement of the United States in world affairs as well as the pressure of greater demands on the national government have aided the Presidents in accentuating the inherent powers of the executive office. As far as their relations with the Congress have been concerned, the fragmentation of power in the House, which was the chief result of the overthrow of Joe Cannon and "Cannonism," has been of material assistance to the Presidents in augmenting ther own influence.

According to Lewis Deschler, who became House Parliamentarian in 1928, the rules are

> perhaps the most finely adusted, scientifically balanced, and highly technical rules of any parliamentary body in the world. Under them a majority may work its will at all times in the face of the most determined and vigorous opposition of a minority.[64]

But the powerful post-Cannon Rules Committee, in the view of James MacGregor Burns

62. Floyd M. Riddick, *The United States Congress: Organization and Procedure*, 64.
63. Wilfred E. Binkley and Malcolm C. Moos, *A Grammar of American Politics*, 438.
64. George B. Galloway, *Congress at the Crossroads*, 13.

has little responsibility to the House or to the majority party. Until 1910 the Speaker was its chairman and helmsman and he was able to use it as an instrument of the party controlling the House. With his dethronement the committee lost its only formal link with the majority, and was left adrift on the seas of sectionalism and socialism. Under the present system the members stay on the committee as long as they remain in Congress; they need only answer to the voters back home. They can defy the President, the House leadership, and public opinion with impunity, and have often done so.[65]

Apparently the ghost of Joe Cannon still haunts the House of Representatives. It was a rather live ghost during the 81st Congress when a new restriction on the jurisdiction of the Rules Committee for the benefit of the Speaker was added to the rules against vigorous opposition.[66] The debates on the new rule proved at least one thing—Cannonism is still a diabolical symbol of tyranny. Proponents and antagonists of the rules change (which prevented the Rules Committee from blocking a bill for more than 21 days if the chairman of the committee sponsoring it wished to report the bill to the floor and could get recognition for doing so from the Speaker) used the ugly term against each other. Adolph J. Sabath of Illinois, the octogenarian Rules chairman and the only man left in the House who had voted against Cannon in 1910, provided a spectacle unique in Congressional annals; since he could not control the committee, he asked the House to reduce its powers, for he intimated that too many members of the committee were the spiritual brethren of Joe Cannon in their political outlook. Opponents of the Sabath rule, on the other hand, gazing upon the benevolent countenance of Speaker Sam Rayburn, thought

65. James MacGregor Burns, *Congress on Trial*, 56.

66. *Congressional Record*, 81-1, 10-11; 81-2, 732-46, 749. *New York Times*, January 2, 3, 4, 9, 1949 and January 17, 24, 1950.

they saw him sprouting the whiskers of "Cannonism." The opponents, Republicans and Southern Democrats, had their way in the 82nd Congress.[67] The Sabath rule was revoked, and again the rafters rang with cries of "Cannonism." It appears that the issue of who is going to manage or to boss the activities of the House has not yet perished from the earth. And Joe Cannon has achieved a dubious kind of immortality, for his name is taken in vain whenever the subject is considered.

67. *Congressional Record,* 82-1, 9-18.

APPENDIX

Illinois Election Results – Joseph G. Cannon for Congress

Election Year	*District*	*Candidates and Votes*
1872	XIV	Cannon –11,244; Pickrell (D) – 10,603.
1874	XIV	Cannon – 15,162; Nelson (D) – 11,405.
1876	XIV	Cannon – 17,796; Black (D) – 16,404.
1878	XIV	Cannon – 13,687; Jones (D) – 11,527; Harper (NG) – 4,449.
1880	XIV	Cannon – 19,710; Scott (D) – 17,734.
1882	XV	Cannon – 15,868; Hunter (D) – 14,651; Barnes (Pro) – 536.
1884	XV	Cannon – 17,852; Black (D) – 17,360; Thornton (Pro) – 334.
1886	XV	Cannon – 16,739; Lindsay (D) – 15,314; Easton (Pro) – 810.
1888	XV	Cannon – 19,897; McKinley (D) – 17,204; Barton (UL) – 189; Sheldon (Pro)–1095.
1890	XV	Cannon – 18,428; Busey (D) – 19,908; Sargeant (Pro) – 652; Harper (FA)–160.
1892	XV	Cannon – 20,596; Busey (D) – 19,908; Buckner (Pro)–1248; Varner (P) – 560.

1894	XII	Cannon – 21,122; Donovan (D) – 11,925; Hays (Pro)–993;Leavitt (Pop) – 1575.
1896	XII	Cannon – 28,566; Vance (D) – 18,613; Hales (Pro) – 478.
1898	XII	Cannon – 21,484; Thompson (D)–14,178; Jones (Pro) 682.
1900	XII	Cannon – 30,633; Briggs (D) – 19,226; Gaiser (Pro) – 1039.
1902	XVIII	Cannon – 22,941; Bell (D) – 15,254; Wright (Pro) – 1166.
1904	XVIII	Cannon–30,520; McClenathan (D)–15,168; Jones (Pro) –2456; Rogers (Soc)–1099.
1906	XVIII	Cannon – 22,804; Taylor (D) – 12,777; Shouse (Pro)–1897; Walker (Soc)–1551.
1908	XVIII	Cannon – 29,170; Bell (D) – 21,795; Winter (Pro)1727; Walls (Soc) – 490.
1910	XVIII	Cannon – 20,943; Cundiff (D) – 16,186; Woolsey (Pro) –1664; Brooks (Soc)–725.
1912	XVIII	Cannon – 18,707; O'Hair (D) – 19,485; Royse (Prog)–9511; Gaumer (Pro)–1279; Walker (Soc) – 1132.
1914	XVIII	Cannon – 22,035; O'Hair (D) – 19,485; Kay (Prog) – 4112; Meyers (Soc) – 591.
1916	XVIII	Cannon – 29,378; Smith (D) – 23,688; Dunn (Prog) – 280; Mehe (Soc) 465.
1918	XVIII	Cannon – 22,427; Crangle (D) – 14,402; Christensen (Soc) – 371.

1920 XVIII Cannon – 53,772; Smith (D) –27,295; Christensen (FL) –2147; Balloh (Soc)–678.

District XIV included the following counties: Champaign, Coles, Douglas, Macon, Piatt, Vermilion.

District XV included the following counties: Champaign, Coles, Douglas, Edgar, Vermilion.

District XII included the following counties: Iroquois, Kankakee, Vermilion, Will.

District XVIII included the following counties: Clark, Cumberland, Edgar, Iroquois, Kankakee, Vermilion.

Abbreviations: (D)–Democrat. (FA)–Farmer's Alliance. (FL)–Farmer Labor. (NG)–National Greenback. (P)–People's. (Pop)–Populist. (Pro)–Prohibition. (Prog)–Progressive. (UL)–United Labor. (Soc)–Socialist.

Sources: *New York Tribune Almanac* (1876) for 1872 and 1874, *American Almanac* (1879) for 1876 and 1878; (1883) for 1882; *World Almanac* (1888) for 1886; (1890) for 1888; (1891) for 1890; (1893) for 1892; (1895) for 1894; (1897) for 1896; (1901) for 1900; (1903) for 1902; (1906) for 1904; (1907) for 1906; (1909) for 1908; (1911) for 1910; (1913) for 1912; (1915) for 1914; *Chicago Daily News Almanac* (1900) for 1898; (1917) for 1916; (1919) for 1918; (1921) for 1920.
Illinois State Library for 1880 and 1884.

BIBLIOGRAPHY

Manuscripts—

Joseph G. Cannon Papers, Illinois State Historical Library, Springfield, Illinois. Twenty-five scrapbooks of newspaper clippings and approximately five thousand pieces of manucript material, the bulk of which covers the years of Insurgency in bloom, 1908-1910.

Francis Burton Harrison Papers, Library of Congress. A few letters on the tariff and on the rules from the Democratic viewpoint.

James R. Mann Papers, Library of Congress. A few letters and some very useful scrapbooks of newspaper material on the tariff, pure food and railroad legislation, and the rules of the House and Cannonism.

George W. Norris Papers, Library of Congress. Some correspondence with Cannon, 1902-1906, showing that Norris was not a born Insurgent. (Courtesy of Richard M. Lowitt).

Henry T. Rainey Papers, Library of Congress. A few insights into the Democratic participation in the fight against Cannon.

Theodore Roosevelt Papers, Library of Congress. Valuable for a thorough coverage of T.R.'s administration and in particular for the Roosevelt-Cannon and Roosevelt-Taft correspondence.

William Howard Taft Papers, Library of Congress. Voluminous and detailed on every issue including the tariff, the rules, patronage, Cannonism, and the Insurgents.

William Allen White Papers, Library of Congress. No letters written to White before 1910 are saved but there are considerable on the views of the Kansas editor toward Cannon and the Insurgents, Roosevelt and Taft.

U.S. Government Publications—

Annals of Congress, 1st Congress, 2nd Session.

Biographical Directory of the American Congress, 1774-1927, Government Printing Office, 1928.

Congressional Record, 1873-1923, 1939-41, 1949-51.

Hinds, Asher C. *Precedents of the House of Representatives,* Government Printing Office 1907, 8 volumes.

Historical Statistics of the United States, United States Department of Commerce, Bureau of the Census, 1949.

House Report 591, 59th Congress, 2nd Session. The Hepburn Bill.

Senate Document 163, 61st Congress, 2nd Session. Cannon's defense of the Payne-Aldrich tariff.

Senate Document 567, 61st Congress, 2nd Session. Cannon on the Insurgents.

Senate Document 719, 61st Congress, 3rd Session. The Ballinger-Pinchot investigation.

Books (Biographies, Memoirs, Histories)

Adams, Henry, *The Education of Henry Adams,* New York: Random House (Modern Library Edition), 1931.

Alexander, De Alva Stanwood, *History and Procedure of the House of Representatives.* Boston and New York: Houghton Mifflin, 1916. Alexander was a GOP Congressman from western New York during the Cannon regime as Speaker.

Allen, Frederick Lewis, *The Big Change: America Transforms Itself* 1900-1950. New York: Harper and Brothers, 1952.

Atkinson, Charles R. and Charles A. Beard, *The Committee on Rules and the Overthrow of Speaker Cannon.* New York: Columbia University Press, 1911.

Baker, Ray Stannard and William E. Dodd, ed., *The Public Papers of Woodrow Wilson.* New York and London: Harper and Brothers, 1925, Volume I.

Baker, Richard Cleveland, *The Tariff Under Roosevelt and Taft.* Hastings, Nebraska: Democrat Printing Company, 1941. An excellent account of the personal and political factors involved in the issue.

Barnes, James A., *John G. Carlisle, Financial Statesman,* New York: Dodd, Mead and Company, 1931. Carlisle was one of Uncle Joe's predecessors in the Speaker's chair.

Bartholdt, Richard, *From Steerage to Congress.* Philadelphia: Dorrance and Company, 1930. The autobiography of a GOP Regular from Missouri.

Bates, Ernest Sutherland, *The Story of Congress,* 1879-1935. New York: Harper and Brothers, 1936.

Binkley, Wilfred E., *President and Congress.* New York: Alfred A. Knopf, 1947.

Binkley, Wilfred E. and Malcolm C. Moos, *A Grammar of American Politics,* New York: Alfred A. Knopf, 1949.

Blum, John Morton, *The Republican Roosevelt.* Cambridge: Harvard University Press, 1954. Blum was the principal aid to Elting E. Morison in compiling the 8 volume correspondence of T. R.

Bogart, Ernest Ludlow and Charles Manfred Thompson, *The Industrial State,* 1870-1893. Springfield, Illinois: Illinois Centennial Commission, 1920. (Volume IV of the five volume centennial history of Illinois).

Bolles, Blair, *Tyrant from Illinois, Uncle Joe Cannon's Experiment with Personal Power.* New York: W. W. Norton and Company, 1951. Based on manuscript sources and dealing mainly with the period of the Speakership, this book presents a novel theme.

Bowers, Claude G., *Beveridge and the Progressive Era.* Boston: Houghton Mifflin Company, 1932.

Briggs, John Ely, *William Peters Hepburn.* Iowa City: The State Historical Society of Iowa, 1919. An old-fashioned biography of the influential Iowa Republican who was one of the first Insurgents.

Brown, George Rothwell, *The Leadership of Congress.* Indianapolis: Bobbs Merrill, 1922.

Bryan, William Jennings, *The Commoner Condensed.* Lincoln, Nebraska: The Woodruff-Collins Printing Co., 1905-6. Volumes IV and V. Volume IV, 237-9, "Cannon's Complacent Philosophy;" 386-7, "Independence Not a 'Scuttle' Policy," Volume V, 366-9, "'Uncle Joe' Cannon's Straw Man."

Bryce, James, *The American Commonwealth,* New York and London: The Macmillan Company, 1897 (3rd edition) 2 volumes.

Burns, James MacGregor, *Congress on Trial.* New York: Harper and Brothers, 1949.

Busbey, L. W., *Uncle Joe Cannon.* New York: Henry Holt and Company, 1927. Written in informal autobiographical style by Cannon's private secretary, good natured reminiscence for the most part.

Butler, Nicholas Murray, *Across the Busy Years.* New York: Charles Scribner's Sons, 1939, 2 volumes. Volume I.

Butt, Archie, *Taft and Roosevelt: The Intimate Letters of Archie Butt.* Garden City, New York: Doubleday, Doran and Company, 1930, 2 volumes. Archie Butt was military aide of both Presidents.

Carlson, Oliver and Ernest Sutherland Bates, *Hearst, Lord of San Simeon.* New York: The Viking Press, 1936.

Chamberlain, Lawrence, *The President, Congress, and Legislation,* New York: Columbia University Press, 1946. Useful on railroad and tariff laws.

Chiu, Chang-wei, *The Speaker of the House of Representatives Since* 1896. New York: Columbia University Press, 1928. A continuation of Follett's work.

Church, Charles A., *History of the Republican Party in Illinois.* Rockford Illinois: Wilson Brothers Company, 1912.

Clark, Champ, *My Quarter Century of American Politics.* New York: Harper and Brothers, 1920. 2 Volumes. The autobiography of the Democratic floor leader at the time of the Insurgent revolt is indispensable to a study of Cannonism.

Cole, Cyrenus, *I Remember, I Remember*. Iowa City: The State Historical Society of Iowa, 1936.

Cox, James M., *Journey Through My Years,* New York: Simon and Schuster, 1946. Another Democratic view.

Cullom, Shelby M., *Fifty Years of Public Service*. Chicago: A. C. McClurg and Company, 1911.

Davenport, Walter, *Power and Glory, The Life of Boies Penrose,* New York: G. P. Putnam's Sons, 1931.

Dawes, Charles G., *A Journal of the McKinley Years*. Chicago: The Lakeside Press, 1950.

Democratic Campaign Book (1906, 1908, 1910).

Dewey, David Rich, *National Problems,* 1885-1897. New York: Harper and Brothers, 1907.

Dictionary of American Biography. New York: Charles Scribner's Sons, 1928-1944. 22 Volumes.

Dreier, Thomas, *Heroes of Insurgency*. Boston: Human Life, 1910.

Drury, John, *Old Illinois Houses*. Springfield: Illinois State Historical Society, 1948.

Duffy, Herbert S., *William Howard Taft*. New York: Minton Balch and Company, 1930. A defense of Taft's conduct of the Presidency on almost every point.

Dunn, Arthur Wallace. *From Harrison to Harding*. New York and London: G. P. Putnam's Sons. 1922. 2 Volumes.

Dunn, Arthur Wallace, *Gridiron Nights,* New York: Frederick A. Stokes, 1915.

Fleming, Denna Frank. *The United States and World Organization,* 1920-1933. New York: Columbia University Press, 1938

Follett, M.P., *The Speaker of the House of Representatives.* New York: Longmans Green and Company. 1896. A classic in its field.

Foraker, Joseph Benson, *Notes of a Busy Life*. Cincinnati: Stewart and Kidd Company, 1916, 2 Volumes.

Ford, Worthington Chauncey ed.: *Letters of Henry Adams,* 1858-1918. Boston and New York: Houghton Mifflin, 1938. 2 Volumes. Volume II.

Foulke, William Dudley. *A Hoosier Autobiography,* New York: Oxford University Press, 1922. Foulke was a civil service commissioner under T.R.

Fuller, Hubert Bruce. *The Speakers of the House*. Boston: Little, Brown and Company, 1909. A helpful historical survey.

Galloway, George B., *Congress at the Crossroads,* New York: Thomas Y. Crowell Company, 1946.

Gardner, Constance Gardner, ed., *Some Letters of Augustus Peabody Gardner*. Boston and New York: Houghton Mifflin, 1920. Gardner, a son-in-law of Henry Cabot Lodge, was a leading Insurgent.

Gompers, Samuel, *Seventy Years of Life and Labor.* New York: E. P. Dutton, 1925, 2 Volumes. The patriarch of the A. F. of L. makes clear his opposition to Cannon.

Gwynn, Stephen, ed., *The Letters and Friendships of Cecil Spring Rice.* Boston and New York: Houghton Mifflin, 1929. 2 Volumes.

Haines, Lynn and Dora B., *The Lindberghs.* New York: The Vanguard Press, 1931.

Hammond, John Hays, *The Autobiography of John Hays Hammond.* New York: Farrar and Rinehart, 1935, 2 Volumes, Volume II. The world famous engineer was a Taft partisan.

Harvey, Rowland Hill, *Samuel Gompers, Champion of the Toiling Masses.* Stanford University Press, 1935. Adds nothing to the Gompers autobiography with regard to Cannon.

Hasbrouck, Paul Dewitt, *Party Government in the House of Representatives.* New York: Macmillan, 1927. An important work on the House!

Hechler, Kenneth W., *Insurgency, Personalities and Politics of the Taft Era.* New York: Columbia University Press, 1940. An outstanding piece of work dealing with all phases of Insurgency.

Hibben, Paxton, *The Peerless Leader, William Jennings Bryan.* New York: Farrar and Rinehart, 1929.

Hinton, Harold B., *Cordell Hull.* New York: Doubleday, Doran and Company, 1942.

Hoover, Irwin Hood 'Ike', *42 Years of the White House.* Boston, and New York: Houghton Mifflin, 1934

Howe, M.A. DeWolfe, *George von Lengerke Meyer, His Life and Public Services.* New York: Dodd, Mead and Company, 1920. Meyer was a loyal Taft Cabinet member.

Howland, Harold Jacobs, *Theodore Roosevelt and His Times.* New Haven: Yale University Press, 1921.

Hull, Cordell, *The Memoirs of Cordell Hull.* New York: Macmillan Company, 1948, 2 volumes, Volume I. Contains an account of the adoption of the Democratic method for selecting committees in 1911.

Ise, John, *The United States Forest Policy.* New Haven: Yale University Press, 1921.

Jessup, Philip C., *Elihu Root.* New York: Dodd, Mead and Company, 1938, 2 volumes.

Johnson, Gerald W., *American Heroes and Hero Worship.* New York: Harper and Brothers, 1943.

Johnson, Walter., *Selected Letters of William Allen White.* New York: Henry Holt and Company, 1947.

Johnson, Walter, *William Allen White's America*. New York: Henry Holt and Company, 1947.

Josephson, Matthew, *The Politicos.* New York: Harcourt, Brace and Company, 1940.

Josephson, Matthew. *The President Makers,* 1896-1919. New York: Harcourt, Brace and Company, 1940.

Konesberg, Henry, ed., *Addresses at the Republican National Convention* 1904. New York: Isaac H. Blanchard Company, 1904.

Kinsley, Philip, *The Chicago Tribune: Its First Hundred Years.* New York: Alfred A. Knopf, 1946, Volume III.

Koch, Adrienne and William Peden, ed., *The Life and Selected Writings of Thomas Jefferson.* New York: Random House (Modern Library Edition), 1944. Jefferson to Francis Hopkinson on parties and factions.

Krock, Arthur, *The Editorials of Henry Watterson.* New York: George H. Doran Company, 1923.

LaFollette, Belle Case and Fola, *Robert M. LaFollette.* New York: Macmillan, 1953, 2 volumes.

LaFollette, Robert M., *Autobiography.* Madison, Wisconsin: The Robert M. LaFollette Company, 1913. The leading Senate Insurgent sets forth his views in forceful fashion.

LaGuardia, Fiorello, *The Making of an Insurgent: An Autobiography,* 1882-1919. Philadelphia and New York: J. B. Lippincott, 1948.

Laski, Harold J., *The American Presidency, An Interpretation.* New York and London: Harper and Brothers, 1940.

Latane, J. H., *America as a World Power.* New York and London: Harper and Brothers, 1907.

Lodge, Henry Cabot, *Selections From the Correspondence of Theodore Roosevelt and Henry Cabot Lodge,* 1884-1918. New York: Charles Scribner's Sons, 1925, 2 volumes. A valuable compilation.

Luce, Robert, *Congress: An Explanation,* Cambridge: Harvard University Press, 1926. A Regular Republican view of the results of Insurgency.

Luce, Robert, *Legislative Procedure.* Boston and New York: Houghton Mifflin, 1922.

McCall, Samuel W., *The Business of Congress.* New York: Columbia University Press, 1911. Another Regular interpretation.

McCall, Samuel W., *The Life of Thomas Brackett Reed.* New York: Houghton Mifflin, 1914. A sympathetic portrait of the first czar.

McCutcheon, John T., *Drawn from Memory.* Indianapolis: Bobbs-Merrill, 1950.

Mason, Alpheus, Thomas, *Bureaucracy Convicts Itself: The Ballinger-Pinchot Controversy of* 1910. New York: The Viking Press, 1941.

Mayhill, George R., *Speaker Cannon Under the Roosevelt Administration.* 1903-1907. University of Illinois, 1942.

Miller, Marion Mills, ed., *Great Debates in American History.* New York: Current Literature Publishing Company, 1913, 14 volumes. Volumes III, IX, XII, XIV.

Millis, Walter, *The Martial Spirit.* Cambridge: The Literary Guild, 1931.

Millis, Walter, *The Road to War: America,* 1914-1917. Boston and New York: Houghton Mifflin, 1935.

Mills, Ogden L., *The Seventeen Million.* New York: Macmillan, 1937.

Moore, J. Hampton, *Roosevelt and the Old Guard.* Philadelphia: McRae Smith Company, 1925. Moore was an Old Guard Congressman himself.

Mowry, George E., *Theodore Roosevelt and the Progressive Movement*. Madison: University of Wisconsin Press, 1946. A pro-Rooseveltian interpretation of the Taft period.

Myers, William Starr, *The Republican Party, a History*. New York: Century, 1928. A pedestrian account.

National Cyclopedia of American Biography. New York: James T. White, 1891-1946, 47 volumes.

Neuberger, Richard L. and Stephen B. Kahn, *Integrity, the Life of George W. Norris*. New York: The Vanguard Press, 1937. As the title suggests, a laudatory biography of Mr. Insurgent.

Norris, George W., *Fighting Liberal — The Autobiography of George W. Norris*. New York: Macmillan, 1945. His early triumphs in Congress are a necessary part of the Cannon story.

Nye, Russel B., *Midwestern Progressive Politics*. East Lansing, Michigan: Michigan State College Press, 1951. A fine study of the origins and development of Liberal political movements in the midwest, 1870-1950.

Olcott, Charles S., *The Life of William McKinley*. Boston and New York: Houghton Mifflin, 1916, 2 volumes.

Ogg, F. A., *National Progress, 1907-1917*. New York and London: Harper and Brothers, 1918.

Orcutt, William Dana, *Burrows of Michigan and the Republican Party*. New York: Longmans Green and Company, 1917, 2 volumes.

Osborn, George Coleman, *John Sharp Williams, Planter-Statesman of the Deep South.* Baton Rouge: Louisiana State University Press, 1943. An important biography of one of Cannon's more intrepid opponents.

Palmer, James E., *Carter Glass, Unreconstructed Rebel.* Roanoke: The Institute of American Biography, 1938.

Patterson, C. Perry, *Presidential Government in the United States.* Chapel Hill: The University of North Carolina Press, 1946.

Paxson, Fredric L. *American Democracy and the World War.* Boston: Houghton Mifflin, 1936-39, 2 volumes; Berkeley and Los Angeles: University of California Press, 1948, volume 2.

Paxson, Frederic L., *Recent History of the United States, 1865-1927.* Boston and New York: Houghton Mifflin, 1928.

Peck, Harry Thurston, *Twenty Years of the Republic, 1885-1905.* New York: Dodd, Mead and Company, 1906.

Pinchot, Gifford, *Breaking New Ground.* New York: Harcourt, Brace and Company, 1947. The Chief Forester's vigorous autobiography.

Pringle, Henry F., *The Life and Times of William Howard Taft.* New York: Farrar and Rinehart, 1939, 2 volumes. A detailed, well written, and sympathetic study which utilized the Taft Papers as the principal source.

Pringle, Henry F., *Theodore Roosevelt.* New York: Harcourt, Brace and Company, 1931. A deft interpretation of the Rough Rider — undoubtedly the best of many biographies on Roosevelt.

Regier, C. C., *The Era of the Muckrakers*. Chapel Hill: The University of North Carolina Press, 1932.

Republican Campaign Book (1908, 1910) Philadelphia: The Dunlap Printing Company, (1908, 1910).

Rhodes, James Ford, *History of the United States from the Compromise of 1850 to the End of the Roosevelt Administration*. New York: MacMillan, 1892-1922, 9 volumes, Volumes VII, VIII IX.

Richardson, James D., *Messages and Papers of the Presidents of the United States*, 1789-1909. Washington, D. C.: Bureau of National Literature and Art, 1909, 11 volumes; Volumes X and XI.

Riddick, Floyd M., *The United States Congress Organization and Procedure*. Manassas, Virginia: National Capitol Publishers, 1949.

Robinson, William A., *Thomas B. Reed, Parliamentarian*. New York: Dodd, Mead and Company, 1930. An adequate biography of the great Speaker.

Rogers, Lindsay, *The American Senate*. New York: Alfred A. Knopf, 1926.

Roosevelt, Theodore, *An Autobiography*. New York: Charles Scribner's Sons, 1913. T.R.'s own inimitable version of his policies.

Rosewater, Victor, *Backstage in 1912*. Philadelphia: Dorrance and Company, 1932.

Russell, John Andrew, *Joseph Warren Fordney, An American Legislator*. Boston: Stratford, 1928.

Salter, J. T., ed., *Public Men In and Out of Office*. Chapel Hill: University of North Carolina Press, 1946.

Schriftgiesser, Karl, *The Gentleman from Massachusetts: Henry Cabot Lodge*. Boston: Little, Brown and Company, 1944.

Simkins, Francis Butler, *Pitchfork Ben Tillman, South Carolinian.* Baton Rouge: Louisiana State University Press, 1944.

Smith, James Allen, *The Spirit of American Government.* New York: Macmillan, 1915 edition. A political classic of the progressive movement.

Sparks, Edwin Erle, *National Development,* 1877-1885. New York and London: Harper and Brothers, 1907.

Stahl, Rose Mildred, *The Ballinger-Pinchot Controversy.* Northhampton, Massachusetts: Department of History of Smith College, 1926.

Stealey, O. O., *Twenty Years in the Press Gallery.* New York: Publishers Printing Company, 1906.

Stephenson, N. W., *Nelson W. Aldrich.* New York: Charles Scribner's Sons, 1930. A masterful treatment of Cannon's conservative sidekick in the Senate.

Stoddard, Henry L., *As I Knew Them, President and Politics From Grant to Coolidge.* New York and London: Harper and Brothers, 1927.

Stoddard, Henry L., *It Costs to Be President.* New York and London: Harper and Brothers, 1938.

Stone Candace, *Dana and the Sun.* New York: Dodd, Mead and Company, 1938.

Sullivan, Mark, *The Education of An American.* New York: Doubleday, Doran and Company, 1938. Includes a detailed account of the author's journalistic war against Cannonism.

Sullivan, Mark, *Our Times.* New York: Charles Scribner's Son, 1926-1935, 6 volumes. Volumes I, II, III, and IV are of particular interest for the Roosevelt and Taft administrations.

Taft, Horace Dutton, *Memories and Opinions.* New York: Macmillan, 1942.

Taft, William Howard, *Our Chief Magistrate and His Powers.* New York: Columbia University Press, 1916.

Thayer, William Roscoe, *Theodore Roosevelt.* Boston: Houghton Mifflin, 1919.

Thompson, Charles Willis, *Party Leaders of the Time.* New York: G. W. Dillingham Company, 1906. A collection of informative character sketches.

Underwood, Oscar Wilder. *Drifting Sands of Party Politics.* New York: Century 1931. Helpful on the currency question.

Villard, Oswald Garrison. *Fighting Years, Memoirs of a Liberal Editor.* New York: Harcourt, Brace and Company, 1939.

Walters, Everett, *Joseph Benson Foraker, An Uncompromising Republican.* Columbus: The Ohio State Archaeological and Historical Society, 1948.

Washburn, Charles G., *The Life of John W. Weeks.* Boston and New York: Houghton Mifflin, 1928. Weeks was a Regular from Massachusetts with a good word for Uncle Joe.

Washburn, Charles G., *Theodore Roosevelt — The Logic of His Career.* Boston and New York: Houghton Mifflin, 1916.

Watson, James E., *As I Knew Them.* Indianapolis and New York: Bobbs Merrill 1936. As one of Uncle Joe's cronies Watson presents an intimate view of the Speaker and a sympathetic account of his czarism.

Wecter, Dixon, *The Hero in America.* New York: Charles Scribner's Sons, 1941.

Wendt, Lloyd and Herman Kogan, *Big Bill of Chicago.* Indianapolis: Bobbs Merrill, 1953.

White, William Allen, *The Autobiography of William Allen White.* New York: Macmillan, 1946.

White, William Allen, *Masks in a Pageant.* New York: Macmillan, 1928.

Wiley, Harvey W., *An Autobiography.* Indianapolis: Bobbs Merrill, 1930. Disputes the belief that T.R. was a real friend of pure food.

Willoughby, William F., *Principles of Legislative Organization and Administration.* Washington: The Brookings Institution, 1934.

Wilson, Woodrow, *Congressional Government.* Boston: Houghton Mifflin, 1885.

Wilson, Woodrow, *Constitutional Government in the United States.* New York: Columbia University Press, 1908.

Young, Roland, *This Is Congress.* New York: Alfred A. Knopf, 1943.

Articles—

Abbott, Ernest Hamlin, "The Liberation of the House," *Outlook* XCIV (April 2, 1910), 750-754.

"Advance of the Insurgents," *Literary Digest* XLI (October 15, 1910), 629-630. The *Digest* is an invaluable source for nationwide newspaper opinion.

Alexander, DeAlva Stanwood, "The Speaker, Committees and the House," *Outlook* LXXXIX (May 16, 1908), 129-30.

Andrew, A. P. "Currency Legislation of 1908," *Quarterly Journal of Economics* XXII (August, 1908), 666-67.

"Are the Insurgents Traitors?" *Literary Digest* XL (April 23, 1910), 793-4.

"Attack on Cannonism," *Outlook* XCIV (March 26, 1910), 639-40.

"The Autocratic House of Representatives," *Outlook* XCI (April 10, 1909), 807-9.

Barclay, Thomas S., "Speaker of the House of Representatives," *Dictionary of American History* V, 142-3.

Beal, John R., "Adolph J. Sabath," in J. T. Salter, ed. *Public Men In and Out of Office*. Chapel Hill: University of North Carolina Press, 1946.

Benton, Glenn H., "Ballinger-Pinchot Controversy," *Dictionary of American History*, I, 148.

Brooks, Sydney, "Presidential Possibilities," *Living Age* CCLVII (June 6, 1908), 579-589.

Bryce, James, "A Word as to the Speakership," *North American Review* CLI (October, 1890), 385-398. One of a number of important articles in the *Review* on the Speakership occasioned by Czar Reed's activity.

Boutell, H. S., "Speaker Cannon and the Presidency," *Independent* LXIV (April 23, 1908), 894-99. An Illinois Regular presents his case for Cannon in the White House.

Boutell, H. S., "Joseph Gurney Cannon," *North American Review* CLXXXVII (May, 1908), 641-47.

Burford, C. C., "Vermilion County in Illinois History," *Journal of the Illinois State Historical Society* XXXIV (December, 1941), 472-81.

Cannon, Joseph G., "Dramatic Scenes in My Career," *Harpers* CXL (December, 1919 and March, 1920), 39-48; 433-441.

Cannon, Joseph G., "The National Budget," *Harpers* CXXXIX (October, 1919), 617-628.

Cannon, Joseph G., "The Power of the Speaker," *Century* LXXVIII (June, 1909), 306-312. Uncle Joe's views during a lull in the storm.

Cannon Joseph G., "We Are at War with Mexico," *Independent* LXXXVII (July 10, 1916), 55.

"Cannonism," *Time* VIII (November 23, 1926), 11.

"Cannon's Revenge," *LaFollette's Weekly Magazine* I (August 14, 1909), 4.

"Cannon Standing By His Guns," *Literary Digest* XLI (July 30, 1910). 153-55.

"Cannon Viewed By His Own Party," *Literary Digest* XL (January 29, 1910), 169-70.

Carlisle, John G., "The Limitations of the Speakership," *North American Review* CL (March, 1890), 390-99.

Carlisle, John G., "The Recent Election," *North American Review* CLI (December, 1890), 641-49.

Carmichael, Otto, "Uncle Joe Cannon as Speaker," *World's Work* VII (December, 1903), 4195-4199.

Cockrell, Ewing, "The Place and the Man: The Speaker of the House of Representatives," *Arena* XXII (December, 1899), 653-666.

Coffin, John A., "The Senatorial Career of Albert J. Beveridge," *Indiana Magazine of History* XXIV (December, 1928), 242-294.

"Condition of the Republican Party ," *Independent* LXIX (September 29, 1910) 711-713.

"Congress on Roosevelt's Hands," *Nation* LXXXII (January 18, 1906), 46.

Dalzell, John, "The Rules of the House of Representatives" *Independent* LXIV (March 12, 1908), 577-82. One of Cannon's henchmen on the Rules Committee defends the status quo.

"Effect of the Revolt in the House," *Independent* LXVIII (March 31, 1910) 667-8.

Fitch, George, "A Survey and Diagnosis of Uncle Joe," *American Magazine* LXV (December, 1907), 185-92. A witty character sketch: cartoons by John T. McCutcheon.

Flanders, Ralph, "Insurgency," *LaFollette's Weekly Magazine* II (August 6, 1910), 10.

"Flatfooted Mr. Cannon," *Nation* LXXXIII (August 23, 1906), 156.

"Forty Years of Uncle Joe," *Literary Digest* LII (May 20, 1916), 1492-98.

Ganoe, John F., "Origin of a National Reclamation Policy," *Mississippi Valley Historical* Review (June, 1931), 34-52.

Gardner, Augustus, P., "The Rules of the House of Representatives" *North American Review* CLXXXIX, (February 1909). 233-41. An Insurgent argument.

Gates, Paul W., "Cattle Kings in the Prairies," *Mississippi Valley Historical Review* XXXV (December, 1948), 379-412.

"Government by Oligarchy," *Outlook* LXXXIX (May 2, 1908), 12-4.

"Groping for a Budget," *Nation* XCVII (July 3, 1913), 4.

Hale, William Bayard, "The Speaker or the People?" *World's Work* XIX (April, 1910), 12805-12812. One of many such journalistic attacks on Cannon.

Hart, Albert Bushnell, "Speaker of the House," *Cyclopedia of American Government*. New York and London: D. Appleton and Company, 1914, III, 369-371.

Hinds, Asher C. "The Speaker of the House of Representatives," *American Political Science Review* III (May, 1909), 155-166. Hinds, a friend of Czar Reed's was House Parliamentarian under Cannon.

Hinds, Asher C., "The Speaker and the House," *McClure's* XXXV (June, 1910), 195-202. Doubt is expressed that the March Revolution will be of lasting benefit.

House, Albert V., "The Contributions of Samuel J. Randall to the Rules of the National House of Representatives," *American Political Science Review* XXIX (October, 1935), 837-41.

"How Not to Legislate," *Nation* LXXXII (February 15, 1906), 130.

Ickes, Harold L., "Not Guilty! Richard Ballinger, an American Dreyfus," *Saturday Evening Post* CCXII (May 25, 1940), 9-11; 123-98.

"The Insurgents and Speaker Cannon," *Current Literature* XLVIII (February, 1910), 127-131.

"The Insurgent Problem," *Independent* LXVIII (April 14, 1910), 782.

"Insurgent Victories, East and West." *Literary Digest* XLI (September 17, 1910), 428-9.

"Insurgent Victories in Kansas and Iowa," *Literary Digest* XLI (August 13, 1910), 221-3.

"Joseph Gurney Cannon," *National Cyclopedia of American Biography* XXII, 4-5.

"Joseph Cannon," *Nation* CXXIII (November 24, 1926). 521.

Judex, "The Speaker and His Critics," *North American Review* CLI (August, 1890), 237-50.

"A Legislative Grimace," *Nation* LXXX (February 16, 1905), 127.

Leupp, Francis E., "The New Speaker," *Outlook* LXXV (November 21, 1903), 684-88.

Lewis, Alfred Henry, "Some Presidential Candidates — Speaker Joseph Gurney Cannon," *Human Life* (April, 1910), 9-10.

Lucas, William Dennis, "A Study of the Speaking and Debating of Joseph Gurney Cannon," *Summaries of Doctoral Dissertations, Northwestern University* XVI. 114-119, (1948).

McCall, Samuel W., "How the Speaker Looks to the Regulars," *Saturday Evening Post* CLXXXII (January 15, 1910), 3-4; 24-5.

McClellan, George Brinton, "Leadership in the House of Representatives," *Scribner's Monthly* XLIX (May, 1911), 594-99. A Democratic view not unfavorable to Cannon.

McComb, Walter Jay, "The Insurgent Movement in the Republican Party during the Roosevelt and Taft Administration," *Summaries of Ph. D. Theses, University of Minnesota* II, 260-4, (1943). Fighting Bob LaFollette might have written this thesis.

McDonald, William, "Joseph Gurney Cannon," *Dictionary of American Biography* III, 476-7.

McPherson, William L., "The Next Speaker," *Munsey's* XXVIII (February, 1903), 649-51.

"Maine's Political Earthquake," *Literary Digest* XLI (September 24, 1910), 473-5.

Maxey, Edwin, "The Power of the Speaker," XLI *Forum* (April, 1909), 344-50.

"Meaning of the Republican Waterloo," *Literary Digest* XLI (November, 1910). 915-8.

Messenger, North Overton. "The Speaker Prospective of the Next House," *Independent* LV (February 5, 1903), 306-11.

Montgomery, Kirt Earl, "The Speaking of Thomas Brackett Reed," *Summaries of Doctoral Dissertations, Northwestern University,* XVI, 130-34, (1948).

Mowry, George E., "Theodore Roosevelt and the Election of 1910," *Mississippi Valley Historical Review* XXV (March, 1939), 523-34. An excellent article.

"Mr. Taft and His Party's Crisis," *Literary Digest* XL (February 26, 1910), 377-9.

"The Muck Rake Congress," *Nation* LXXXIII (July 5, 1906), 4.

"Murdock, the Red Insurgent," *Current Literature* XLVIII (February, 1910), 149-50.

Murdock, Victor, "After Cannonism — What?" *Independent* LXXIX (September 22, 1910), 622-25.

Murdock, Victor, "The Insurgent Movement in Congress," *North American Review.* CXCI (April, 1910), 510-6.

"Native American," *Outlook* CXII (April 5, 1916), 787-8.

Needham, Henry Beach, "Insurgents vs. Aldrich, Cannon et al," *Everybody's* XXII (January, 1910), 102-9.

Nelson, John M., "The American Frankenstein," *LaFollette's Weekly Magazine* I (January 23, 1909), 6: 14-5. As the title suggests Insurgent Nelson did not like Joseph Cannon.

Norris, George W., "The Secret of His Power," *LaFollette's Weekly Magazine* II (January 8, 1910), 7-9.

"Opposition to Speaker Cannon", *Independent* LXIX (August 25, 1910), 384-5.

Osborn, George Coleman, "Joseph G. Cannon and John Sharp Williams," *Indiana Magazine of History* XXXV (June, 1939), 283-94.

Payne, Will, "A Plutocrat in Homespun," *Saturday Evening Post* (July 28, 1906), 10-12.

"The Pending Step in Railroad Legislation," *Nation* LXXX (February 9, 1905), 108.

"The President's Programme," *Nation* LXXXIV (June 13, 1907), 534.

"The Programme," *Nation* LXXX (January 12, 1905) 24.

Rayburn, Sam, "What Influences Congress," *U.S. News & World Report* XXIX (October 13, 1950), 28-31.

Reed, Thomas B., "The Limitations of the Speakership," *North American Review* CL (March, 1890), 382-90.

Reed, Thomas B., "Reforms Needed in the House," *North American Review* CL (May, 1890), 537-46.

Reed, Thomas B., "A Reply to X.M.C.," *North American Review* CLI (August, 1890), 228-36.

Reed, Thomas B., "The Rules of the House of Representatives," *Century* XXXVII (March, 1889), 792-5.

"Re-Enter the Rough Rider," *Nation* LXXIX (September 15, 1904). 210.

"Republican Disaffection." *Literary Digest* XL (April 2, 1910), 627-30.

"Republican Press on the Party Rift," *Literary Digest* XL (January 22, 1910), 125-7.

"Revolt Against Speaker Cannon," *Independent* LXVIII (March 24, 1910), 599-600.

Robinson, William A., "Thomas B. Reed," *Dictionary of American Biography* XV, 456-9.

Roosevelt, Theodore, "Thomas Brackett Reed and the 51st Congress," *Forum* XX (December, 1895), 410-8.

"The Skirmish in the House," *Lafollette's Weekly Magazine* II (March 26, 1910), 3.

"The Speaker and His Power," *Independent* LXVIII (March 24, 1910), 653-4.

"Speaker Cannon and the Destruction of Popular Rule in the House of Representatives," *Arena* XL (July, 1908), 89-91.

"Speaker Cannon and His Foes," *Current Literature* XLVIII (January, 1910), 9-12.

"Speaker Cannon: A Character Sketch," *Review of Reviews* XXVIII (December, 1903), 673-6.

"Speaker Cannon as the Friend of the Privileged Interests," *Arena* XXXVI (September, 1906), 307-8.

"Speaker Cannon's Contentment With Present Foods," *Literary Digest* XXXII (June 16, 1906), 894-5.

"Speaker Cannon's Reply to His Critics," *Literary Digest* XXXII (June 30, 1906), 960.

Stevens, Frederick, "The Rules of the House of Representatives: A Criticism," *Review of Reviews* XXXIX (April, 1909), 470-74. The ideas of a Minnesota Regular.

Swanson, Claude, "The Rules of the House of Representative: A Criticism," *Review of Review* XXXIX (April,, 1909), 465-70. The ideas of a Virginia Democrat.

"Taking the Patronage Club to the Insurgent," *Literary Digest* XL (January 15, 1910), 86-7.

"Taps for Uncle Joe, Old Fashioned American," *Literary Digest* XCI (December 4, 1926), 36-42.

"Trying to Drop Cannon," *Literary Digest* XLI (September 3, 1910), 330-1.

"Uncle Joe Cannon," *Outlook* CXLIV (November 24, 1926), 393.

"Uncle Joe Quits With Optimism and a Smile," *Literary Digest* LXXVI (March 17, 1923), 47-8.

"The Uprising Against Cannon." *Literary Digest* XL March 26, 1910), 573-4.

Welliver, Judson. "The End of Cannonism," *Success Magazine* XIII (January, 1910), 7-8, 57-8.

Welliver, Judson, "What Is Insurgency?" *LaFollette's Weekly Magazine* II (August 13, 1910), 1.

West, Henry Litchfield, "American Politics," XXXII to XLI *Forum* (1901-1909).

"What Congress Did," *Literary Digest* XLI (July 2, 1910), 1-3.

Willis, H. Parker, "The Tariff of 1909," *Journal of Political Economy* XVII (November, 1909), 589-619; XVIII (January, 1910), 1-35.

Wilson, Woodrow, "The Tariff Make-Believe," *North American Review* CLXL (October, 1909), 535-56.

X.M.C. "Speaker Reed's Error." *North American Review* CLI (July, 1890), 90-111.

"The Year of the Food Laws," *Nation* LXXXII (June 28, 1906), 522-3.

Newspapers — (With a few exceptions the newspaper material used in this thesis was deiived from the Cannon and Mann Papers.

Boston Evening Transcript, 1908.

Chicago Chronicle, 1905.

Chicago Daily News, 1911.

Chicago Evening Post, 1906-1910.

Chicago Examiner, 1908-1909.

Chicago Interocean, 1906-1912.

Chicago Journal, 1910.

Chicago Record-Herald, 1908-1911.

Chicago Tribune, 1903-1912; 1926.

Danville Commercial News, 1908-1910; 1923.

Danville Democrat, 1908.

Detroit News, 1912.

Illinois Issue, 1908.

Kankakee Republican, 1912.

Kansas City Journal, 1915.

Kansas City Star, 1908.

LaFollette's Weekly, 1909-1910.

Milwaukee News, 1907

New York Evening Post, 1906-1910.

New York Herald, 1906-1908.

New York Sun, 1904-1912.

New York Times, 1903-1910; 1917-1918; 1927; 1949-1950.

New York Tribune, 1906-1911.

New York World, 1906; 1911-1913.

Norfolk (Nebraska) *Daily News,* 1908.

Northwestern Christian Advocate, 1908.

Philadelphia Ledger, 1910.

Portland Oregonian, 1910.

Racine Times, 1906.

St. Louis Globe-Democrat, 1908.

Spokane Spokesman-Review, 1909.

Topeka State Journal, 1909.

Washington Evening Star, 1896-1912.

Washington Herald, 1907.

Washington Post, 1906-1907; 1913.

INDEX